# THE emerging
## CHRISTIAN WAY

# THE
# emerging
## CHRISTIAN WAY

Thoughts,

Stories, and

Wisdom for

a Faith of

Transformation

CopperHouse

Editor: Michael Schwartzentruber
Cover and interior design: Margaret Kyle
Proofreader: Dianne Greenslade

**Permissions**
"Consider the Lilies of the Field: How Should Christians Love Nature?" from *Super, Natural Christians: How we should love nature*, by Sallie McFague, copyright © 1997 Augsburg Fortress (www.fortresspress.com). Used by permission.

"On Being a Postdenominational Priest in a Postdenominational Era," was adapted from "A Postdenominational Priest Standing Outside the Rusty Gate," from *Confessions: The Making of a Postdenominational Priest*, by Matthew Fox, copyright © 1996 by Matthew Fox, published by HarperCollins. Used by permission.

"Paying Homage: Being Christian in a World of Many Faiths," from *Summoning the Whirlwind: Unconventional Sermons for a Relevant Christian Faith*, by Bruce Sanguin, copyright © 2005 by Bruce Sanguin. Published by Canadian Memorial Press. Used by permission.

"The Great Work," from *The Great Work: Our Way into the Future*, by Thomas Berry, copyright © 1999 by Thomas Berry. Used by permission of Bell Tower, a division of Random House, Inc.

COPPERHOUSE is an imprint of WOOD LAKE BOOKS, INC. Wood Lake Books acknowledges the financial support of the Government of Canada, through the Book Publishing Industry Development Program (BPIDP) for its publishing activities.

At Wood Lake Books, we practice what we publish, being guided by a concern for fairness, justice, and equal opportunity in all of our relationships with employees and customers. WOOD LAKE BOOKS is an employee-owned company, committed to caring for the environment and all creation. Wood Lake Books recycles, reuses, and encourages readers to do the same. Resources are printed on recycled paper and more environmentally friendly groundwood papers (newsprint), whenever possible. A percentage of all profit is donated to charitable organizations.

**Library and Archives Canada Cataloguing in Publication**
The emerging Christian way: thoughts, stories, and wisdom for a faith of transformation.
Edited by Michael Schwartzentruber.
Includes bibliographical references.
1. Theology, Doctrinal–Popular works. I. Schwartzentruber, Michael, 1960- II. Title.
BT10.E45 2006    230    C2006-900234-7

Published by CopperHouse
an imprint of Wood Lake Books, Inc.
9590 Jim Bailey Road, Kelowna, BC, Canada, V4V 1R2
www.copperhousepress.com and www.woodlakebooks.com
250.766.2778

Printing 10 9 8 7 6 5 4 3 2 1
Printed in Canada by
Houghton Boston

# table of contents

## Part One – **the emerging Christian way**

CHAPTER ONE    An Emerging Christian Way    9
*Marcus Borg*

CHAPTER TWO    Experience: The Heart of Transformation  33
*Tim Scorer*

## Part Two – **key perspectives**

CHAPTER THREE    New Creeds    51
*Tom Harpur*

CHAPTER FOUR    The Great Work    65
*Thomas Berry*

CHAPTER FIVE    Consider the Lilies of the Field:
How Should Christians Love Nature?    77
*Sallie McFague*

CHAPTER SIX    On Being a Postdenominational Priest in
a Postdenominatinal Era    101
*Matthew Fox*

CHAPTER SEVEN    Paying Homage: Being Christian in
a World of Many Faiths              137
*Bruce Sanguin*

CHAPTER EIGHT    Radical Inclusion                   143
*Anne Squire*

CHAPTER NINE    Social Justice and a Spirituality of
Transformation                      155
*Bill Phipps*

# Part Three – **emerging forms**

CHAPTER TEN    Worship: Pilgrims in the Faith       171
*Mark MacLean*

CHAPTER ELEVEN    To Sing or Not to Sing:
That Is the Question                189
*Bruce Harding*

CHAPTER TWELVE    Christian Education and the
Imaginative Spirit                  201
*Susan Burt*

CHAPTER THIRTEEN    Pastoral Care for the 21st Century   219
*Donald Grayston*

CHAPTER FOURTEEN    Spiritual Discernment               233
*Nancy Reeves*

CONCLUSION    Inclusion in the Midst of Evolution   245
*Michael Schwartzentruber*

ENDNOTES                                            249

Part One

# the emerging Christian way

# one

# An Emerging Christian Way

## *Marcus Borg*

A new way of being Christian is emerging in the churches of North America in our time. It is most visible in mainline denominations, now sometimes called the "old" mainline. These include Anglicans (Episcopalians in the United States), United Church of Canada, Presbyterians, Methodists, United Church of Christ (Congregationalists), the largest Lutheran denomination, the Christian Church (Disciples of Christ), and a small minority of Baptists. It is also found among Roman Catholics, and is a minority voice in evangelical circles, where it is commonly known as "the emergent church." There its most prominent proponent, Brian McLaren, speaks of "a new kind of Christian."

This "new kind of Christian," this emerging vision, exists side by side with an earlier vision of being Christian that has been the most common form of Western Christianity for the past 300 to 400 years. The two visions are so different from each other that I sometimes speak of the story of the church in North America today as a tale of two Christianities. To echo the opening sentence of Charles Dickens' *A Tale of Two Cities*, it is the best of times and the worst of times in the church. Perhaps "best" and "worst" are a bit hyperbolic. But it is a time of exciting Christian renewal and deep Christian division.

The division is not only deep, but often acrimonious. Followers of the earlier vision (fundamentalists, many conservative-evangelicals, and some mainline Christians) see the new way of being Christian as a watering down or even abandonment of Christianity. From their point of view, it makes too many concessions to modern thought, producing an anemic, politically correct, and vaguely theistic humanism. On the other side of the divide, emerging Christians often see the more rigid forms of the earlier vision as anti-intellectual, literalistic, judgmental, self-righteous, and uncritically committed to right-wing politics.

The division is so great that it virtually produces two different religions, both using the same Bible and the same language. It is most publicly visible around specific controversies that make headlines, such as creation versus evolution, and the status of gays and lesbians in the church. But beneath specific issues is a larger conflict between two very different visions of Christianity and what it means to be Christian.

To reduce the manifold forms of Christianity in our time to two is a grand simplification, of course. But sometimes such simplifications are illuminating. Albert Einstein once said that it's important to be as simple as possible – and then he cautioned: but no simpler. And I think he also said that anything that can be put in a nutshell probably belongs there. Nevertheless, I will take the risk and speak of two primary visions of Christianity in North America today, in deep conflict with each other.

## A Paradigm Conflict

The conflict is a paradigm conflict. Because this term is central for understanding what is happening in the church today, I concisely define it with three simple synonymous phrases: a paradigm is a way of seeing a whole; it is a comprehensive way of seeing; it is a large framework that affects the way particulars are seen. We see *with* paradigms, see *through* paradigms; they function as lenses.

To illustrate briefly from the history of astronomy: both the Ptolemaic and Copernican ways of seeing the earth in relation to the sun were lenses, paradigms. The former was geocentric; it saw the earth as the stationary center of the universe and understood the motions of the sun, moon, planets and stars accordingly. It worked quite well. Eclipses of the sun and moon could even be accurately predicted within it. Then, in the 16th and 17th centuries, largely through the work of Copernicus and Galileo, it began to be replaced by a heliocentric paradigm that placed the sun at the center of what was now a solar system, and that understood the movements of the planets (including the earth) accordingly.

This change illustrates the difference that paradigms make. Both the Ptolemaic and Copernican paradigms are ways of seeing a whole. But the whole is seen differently because of the shift in paradigms. Importantly, the same data are being seen – the motions of the heavenly bodies – but the data look different because of the change in paradigms.

This is what is happening in the churches of North America today. Two very different Christian paradigms, two very different ways of seeing Christianity and the Christian life as a whole, are in conflict with each other. Importantly, both are ways of seeing the same particulars, the same "data" – namely, the Bible, Christian theology, and Christian tradition – but they look different because of the different paradigms.

## Naming the Paradigms

In my book *The Heart of Christianity*, I call these two ways of seeing *an earlier Christian paradigm* and *an emerging Christian paradigm*. I chose these phrases because I was seeking relatively neutral language that also suggested a chronological transition. I could perhaps have used the terms "conservative" and "liberal," but decided not to for more than one reason. There is, as we shall see, much about the earlier paradigm that is innovative and not conservative; and the emerging paradigm is conservative in the sense that it conserves what is most central to Christianity. Moreover, the term "liberal" has acquired such negative connotations in the last few decades that it may be a half century or more before it can again be used as a descriptive (and not negative) term.

As just mentioned, "earlier" and "emerging" paradigms are chronological terms. I continue to use them in this chapter, and I also now name them in a way that suggests not only chronology, but content. The earlier paradigm is *a belief-centered paradigm* and it generates belief-centered Christianity: Christians are people who believe in the central claims of the Bible and of Christianity. The emerging paradigm is *a transformation-centered paradigm* and it generates transformation-centered Christianity: Christians are people committed to a way, a path of transformation, as known especially in Jesus.

Before I turn to describing these paradigms more fully, it is important to realize that both are the product of the last three to four centuries. Though both have roots in antiquity, neither is simply a continuation of traditional Christianity. Rather, both are modern; they are different Christian responses to the encounter of Christianity with the Enlightenment, the birth of modern science and scientific ways of knowing in the 1600s that revolutionized Western culture. The perspectives represented by the Enlightenment have become, in the centuries since, the dominant mindset of modern Western culture. As we shall see, the belief-centered paradigm is a defensive (and sometimes aggressive) rejection of the Enlightenment, whereas the transformation-centered paradigm involves an appreciative and discerning integration of the Enlightenment.

## THE BELIEF-CENTERED PARADIGM

As I describe the earlier belief-centered paradigm, I intend that my description will make it familiar rather than a caricature. It has been the most common form of Western Christianity for the past three to four centuries. Most of us over age 40 grew up with it, as have many under 40. The majority of Christians in North America, with varying degrees of confidence, think that being Christian means affirming this vision of Christianity. And many who are not Christian think this is what it means to be Christian.

### The uniqueness of Christianity

For the belief-centered paradigm, the Bible, Jesus, and Christianity are unique. Their uniqueness is understood to mean that only here has God truly become known: the Bible and Jesus are the exclusive revelation of God. From this it follows that Christianity is the only way of salvation.

### Salvation as afterlife

Salvation is seen as being primarily about the next world. "Are you saved?" means, "Are you confident you will go to heaven when you die?" Salvation and the afterlife are virtually identified. So central was this identification in the Christianity I learned growing up that if you had been able to convince me at age ten or 12 that there was no afterlife, I would have had no idea why I should be Christian. Heaven was what it was all about.

### Requirements and rewards

For this vision, Christianity is a religion of requirements and rewards. This is true even though the language of grace is commonly emphasized. The reward, of course, is heaven. The requirement is what you need to believe and/or do to get there. This flows directly from the emphasis on the afterlife; if there is a blessed afterlife, it doesn't seem fair that everybody gets one, so there must be something that differentiates those who do from those who don't. Unless we think that God arbitrarily decides who will be saved, that "something" must be something we believe or do. Thus, this vision sees Christianity as a religion of requirements. There are those who meet them and those who don't, those who will be saved and those who won't, those who will be taken to be with Jesus and those who will be left behind.

### Sin, guilt, and forgiveness

The emphasis on requirements leads to an emphasis on sin, guilt, and forgiveness as the central dynamic of the Christian life. We fall short again and again of measuring up to God's requirements of belief and behavior, and thus need forgiveness. This understanding of our predicament shapes its way of seeing the significance of Jesus: his primary purpose was to die for the sins of the world so that we can be forgiven. Because Mel Gibson's movie *The Passion of the Christ* so graphically portrayed the huge cost of our redemption, it was enthusiastically received by many earlier paradigm Christians.

### The Bible

At the center of this vision is a way of seeing the Bible. Indeed, conflict about the Bible – its authority and interpretation – is the most divisive issue separating the two paradigms.

#### Biblical authority

For the earlier paradigm, the Bible's authority is grounded in its origin: it comes from God as no other book does. For these Christians, affirming that the Bible is "inspired by God" and "the Word of God" means that it is a divine product. This is the basis of the Bible's truth: because its ultimate author is God, it has a divine guarantee to be true.

This understanding has harder and softer forms. The hard form, fundamentalism, affirms the inerrancy and infallibility of the Bible. The softer form does not insist that the Bible is inerrant in every detail, but understands "inspired by God" to mean that the Holy Spirit guided the writers of the Bible so that they did not make any serious errors – nothing that would interfere with our salvation. Thus the softer form also sees the Bible's authority as grounded in a divine guarantee tied to its divine origin.

#### Biblical interpretation

The earlier paradigm affirms that the Bible is to be interpreted literally, factually, and absolutely. If the Bible says something happened, it happened. In the hard form, biblical literalism leads to opposition to evolution; biblical factualism leads to a vigorous defense of stories of the spectacular;

and biblical absolutism leads to sharp moral boundaries. If the Bible says something is wrong, it's wrong.

The softer form is willing to grant that biblical language is sometimes symbolic (and thus it does not need to oppose evolution), but affirms that the really important events happened more or less as the Bible reports them: that the sea really *did* divide in two at the time of the exodus; that Jesus really *was* born of a virgin; really did walk on water; and so forth. The softer form is also willing to grant that some of the Bible's teaching about behavior was meant for the ancient world, not for all time. But the burden of proof lies with those who want to say that a particular biblical teaching is not absolute.

### Faith as believing

Finally, the earlier paradigm understands the primary meaning of "faith" as "belief" or "believing." This follows directly from its way of seeing the Bible and Christianity as a whole. The central claims of its way of seeing have become questionable in the modern world and that's why "faith" is required to believe them. To be Christian means believing that the Bible and the central claims of Christianity are (in harder or softer forms) literally, factually, and absolutely true.

As mentioned earlier, this paradigm – especially its view of the Bible and its understanding of faith – is not ancient, but the product of Christianity's encounter with the Enlightenment, which called many conventional Christian understandings into question, including the literal factuality of the Bible.

- The notion of biblical inerrancy is first mentioned in a book of theology published in the second half of the 1600s. It took two more centuries (the second half of the 1800s) before the notion became relatively common in some Protestant circles (about the same time that papal infallibilty was affirmed by the Roman Catholic Church in 1870). Fundamentalism, with its emphasis on biblical inerrancy, is even more recent, born in the early years of the 20th century.

- An emphasis on the literal factuality of the Bible is also modern. Prior to the Enlightenment, the more-than-literal meaning of biblical texts – what I will later call the metaphorical meaning – was most important. The literal-factual meaning was seldom emphasized.

- An understanding of the word "faith" as meaning primarily *believing* biblical and doctrinal statements to be true is also modern. Prior to about the year 1600, Christian faith did not mean believing statements, "propositions," to be true. Rather, faith meant *trusting* in God and *loyalty* – giving one's allegiance – to God. But when the Enlightenment raised questions about the truth of central Christian claims, the response of some Christians was to say, "This is why you need faith"; faith is what you need when modern knowledge calls Christian beliefs into question.

To say the obvious, this is the reason for the name "a belief-centered paradigm." Being Christian is about believing: believing that God exists; believing that the Bible is the Word of God; believing that Jesus is the Son of God, that he was born of a virgin, that he died for our sins, that he was raised physically from the dead, that he will come again, and so forth. Of course, for these Christians, the Christian life is about *more* than believing. It is also about prayer, worship, good behavior, and deeds of kindness. It (like the emerging paradigm) is about transformation. But this vision frontloads Christian transformation with a set of beliefs to be believed. Belief is foundational: believe in Christianity *now*, for the sake of eternal salvation *later*. It is the only way.

This paradigm has serious problems and they have grown more acute in recent times as more and more people have become aware of them. The issue is not that belief-centered Christianity does not work. For the last few centuries, millions of Christians have lived within it, including my parents and perhaps your parents. The Spirit of God worked through it and touched their lives.

The issue is that the belief-centered paradigm has become an intellectual and moral stumbling block for millions of people in our time, inside the church and outside of it. On the level of what many people think of as "common sense," the problems include the following.

- Biblical literalism is very hard to believe. It generates conflicts with what we have come to know through science and history.

- The claim that biblical teachings about behavior are the absolute will of God is also difficult to believe, to the point of impossible, for many people. Texts in the Bible accept slavery and regulate it, affirm the subordination of women, specify capital punishment for a wide range of actions (including adultery and cursing one's parents), and order the slaughter of men, women, children, and infants. Were these ever the will of God? Moreover, some (many?) laws in the Bible seem too trivial to be of concern to God. Does God really care about whether we wear garments made of two kinds of cloth (blends), or plant two kinds of seed in the same field?

- Its claim that Christianity is the only way of salvation is also impossible for many people to believe. Does it make sense to think that the creator of the whole universe has chosen to be known in only one religious tradition; namely, our own?

- The emphasis on "believing the right things" as the way to be saved seems strange. Is "correct belief" what God most wants from us? Does "correct belief" mean "using the right words"? And believing them? Is this what will save us, transform us?

Indeed, the belief-centered paradigm is the single biggest reason for the decline of mainline denominations over the past 40 years. Why have so many people left mainline churches? Most did not join more conservative churches, but either dropped out or turned to alternative spiritualities.

So why did they leave? For the most part, because the Christianity they grew up with – belief-centered Christianity – ceased to make sense to them, ceased to be persuasive and compelling. And for most people outside of the church, the belief-centered paradigm has made Christianity unattractive, easy to dismiss, indeed incredible.

## THE TRANSFORMATION-CENTERED PARADIGM

Thus it is good news – gospel for our time – that there is an emerging Christian paradigm. In a sentence, it sees the Christian life as a relationship with God as known in Jesus that changes us, that transforms us – and hence the name *a transformation-centered paradigm*. The Christian life is not very much about believing a set of claims to be true, but about a path, a way of transformation that leads to God and to participation in the passion of God. It resolves the intellectual obstacles generated by the belief-centered paradigm, and it does so without watering down Christianity. Rather, it robustly affirms the central elements of Christianity, but sees them differently.

Like the earlier paradigm, the transformation-centered paradigm is a Christian response to the Enlightenment. But instead of rejecting modern knowledge when it conflicts with the Bible, it involves an *appreciative* and *discerning* integration of what we have learned in the last several centuries about nature, history, culture, religions, and ourselves. Importantly, the integration needs to be *discerning*, or it risks reducing Christianity to what can be affirmed within the confines of modern thought. Reductionism is the perennial temptation of modernity.

But much of what we have learned from the Enlightenment can be integrated with a robust Christianity. This includes what we have learned from science, which has led to an understanding of the universe and ourselves much different from what our pre-modern ancestors thought. To illustrate with what was once controversial but is now commonplace: the earth is not at the center of the universe; the universe is huge; it and the earth are billions of years old; human beings have been around for millions of years. Among the vast majority of people today, these are not questionable claims, but true. If we take them seriously, the biblical portrait of a "young earth" – the earth and the universe as created in more or less their present form a relatively short time ago – cannot be understood as a literally and factually correct account of origins.

The Enlightenment also generated a historical approach to the study of the Bible. We became aware that the biblical documents have a history. This approach was first applied to the Jewish Bible in the second half of the 1600s. The Dutch Jewish scholar Spinoza and the French Catholic scholar Richard Simon argued that "the five books of Moses" are actually a combination of a number of sources written several centuries after the time of Moses. They thus tell us how ancient Israel told her story at different points in her history, and they reflect *that* history, not primarily the past history that they purport to report. In the 1700s, this approach began to be applied to the New Testament, including the gospels. Instead of seeing the Bible as a divine product, the Bible was now seen as the historical product of ancient communities. In the 1800s and 1900s, this approach began to be taught in most mainline seminaries and divinity schools. All of today's mainline clergy have encountered it.

The centuries since the Enlightenment have also generated a deeper understanding of how culture shapes consciousness and knowledge itself. We – including the way we think and what we consider to be knowledge – are very much shaped by our location in time and space, our place in the historical and cultural process. There is no vantage point completely outside this process. Of course, we are not completely confined to our time and place; the study of history and other cultures enables us to some extent to transcend time and place, but we nevertheless see from where we are. Thus there is no "absolute" knowledge. All knowledge (even scientific knowledge) is historically conditioned and relative. This does not mean that all claims to knowledge are equally valid; some understandings clearly work better than others. But it does mean that no expression of knowledge, whether religious or scientific, is absolute truth for all time. We always have the treasure of knowledge in earthen vessels.

The Enlightenment has also brought a transformation in our understanding of religions. Some of this is the result of the academic study of religion, and even more so in the last half century through increasing contact with other religions. To many people, it now seems clear that all religions (including Christianity) are shaped by the cultures in which they emerged. Rather than one religion being the unique and only adequate revelation of God, all are seen as cultural products. For some, this means that all religions are of little value. But for many religious people, including emerging Christians, this means that the religions of the world that have endured, that have stood the test of time, are different cultural responses to the experience of the sacred.

## The Bible

We turn now to how these understandings have shaped the emerging Christian paradigm, and we begin with the Bible. The emerging Christian paradigm sees the Bible as the human product of a historical and cultural process, not as a divine product. The Jewish Bible (the Christian Old Testament) is the product of ancient Israel, and the New Testament is the product of the early Christian movement. Seeing the Bible this way does not deny the reality of God or of revelation, but it sees the Bible as the response of these two communities to their experience of God, and as their understanding of what life with God involves.

### The Bible's authority

The emerging paradigm sees the Bible's authority as grounded not in its origin in God, but in decisions made by our spiritual ancestors in these ancient communities; they declared this collection of documents to be sacred, to be authoritative, to be the most important documents they knew. The Bible is thus sacred in its status and function – and this is its authority. To be Christian means to be in a continuing conversation with the Bible as our foundation document, identity document, and wisdom tradition. Its vision of life is to shape our sense of who God is, who we are, and our perception of God's intention for the whole of creation.

*The Bible's interpretation*

The emerging paradigm interprets the Bible historically and metaphorically, rather than as the literal-factual-absolute revelation of God. The historical-metaphorical way of seeing the Bible is crucial for seeing the difference between the two paradigms. So, while still seeking to be concise, I describe and illustrate it at somewhat greater length.

*Historical interpretation*: Here, "historical" does not mean "factual." Indeed, this way of interpreting the Bible is not very much concerned with the issue of how much of what the Bible reports really happened. That question is seldom of great importance. Rather, a historical approach emphasizes the illuminating power of setting these ancient texts in their ancient contexts – in their ancient literary and historical contexts.

For example, the language of the second half of Isaiah comes alive when we realize that it was addressed to a small community of Jews in exile in Babylon, in the sixth century BCE. Forcibly removed from their homeland about 50 years earlier, they were impoverished, oppressed, and disheartened. In this setting, the language of Isaiah 40, familiar to many people from Handel's *Messiah*, has extraordinary power. "'Comfort my people,' says your God, 'Speak tenderly to Jerusalem, and cry to her that her time of suffering is over.'"

The passage continues: "A voice cries out, 'In the wilderness prepare the way of the Lord, make straight in the desert a highway for our God.'" A way of return, of going home, is being prepared. The image of a way continues: "Every valley shall be lifted up, and every mountain and hill be made low; the uneven ground shall become level, and the rough places a plain." A superhighway, an interstate, an autobahn, is being built (metaphorically, of course) through the wilderness separating the place of exile from the homeland. The chapter concludes: "God gives power to the faint, and strengthens the powerless. They shall run and not be weary, they shall walk and not grow faint." We hear these ancient words best when we hear them initially in their ancient context: they announce and encourage the return from exile.

A historical approach also applies to the laws and ethical teachings of the Bible. To illustrate with one of the hot issues in the church today, the laws of Leviticus clearly prohibit homosexual behavior: "You shall not lie with a male as with a woman; it is an abomination" (Lev. 18:22). Two chapters later, in Leviticus 20:13, the penalty is specified: death. But what is the book of Leviticus? If one reads the Bible as the literal-factual-absolute revelation of God, as the earlier paradigm does, these are God's laws and thus absolute. But a historical approach – text in ancient context – understands this as one of the laws of ancient Israel (as are the Bible's laws regulating slavery, forbidding wearing garments made of two kinds of cloth, and mandating the forgiveness of all debts every seventh year). The historical approach does not assume that the laws and teachings of ancient Israel and early Christianity were meant for all time. They are relative. In some circles, "relative" is a dismissive term: if something is *only* relative, it doesn't need to be taken seriously. Here I use "relative" in its positive sense: related to. Thus to be relative is to be relevant – related to (and therefore relevant to) a particular time and place.

Thus it is up to subsequent Christian generations to make discerning judgments about which of these laws and teachings still apply. In the 19th century, most Christians became convinced that the Bible's laws about slavery did not mean that slavery is okay. In the 20th century, most Christians became convinced that the prohibition of re-marriage after divorce found in the gospels does not need to be understood as absolute teaching for all time. In our time, this approach is being extended by most emerging Christians to what the Bible says about homosexuality, even though to do so seems to earlier-paradigm Christians to be an abandonment of God's laws.

*Metaphorical interpretation:* A metaphorical approach to the Bible emphasizes the *more-than-literal* meaning of biblical stories. I use the phrase *more-than-literal* in order to counter the widespread modern notion (in both Christian and secular circles) that metaphorical meaning is *less* than literal-factual meaning, inferior to the language of factuality. So I emphasize that metaphorical meaning is the *more*-than-literal meaning. It is also the *more*-than-historical meaning. To return for a moment to the language of Isaiah cited above, the historical meaning is its meaning in its ancient context. The more-than-historical meaning, its metaphorical meaning, is its power to move us to this day; this language expresses our deep yearning to return from our life in exile to life with God – to "come home" to God by embarking on a journey of return.

Importantly, metaphorical meaning is not dependent on factuality. Stories that are "made up" (like the parables of Jesus) can be truth-filled and truthful. Metaphorical truth and factual truth are very different. This does not mean that there is no factuality behind the biblical stories. Some of them contain historical memory even as their primary purpose is metaphorical. But it does mean that the truth of the stories is not dependent on their preserving factually exact memory. For example, ancient Israel most likely came into existence through the liberation of a group of slaves from imperial Egypt. But as metaphor, the story of the exodus is true because it expresses so powerfully the human predicament as bondage and the yearning for liberation from the Pharaohs, spiritual and cultural, who enslave us.

When the Bible is interpreted metaphorically, the conflicts between the Bible and the Enlightenment simply disappear. The truth of the Genesis stories of creation is not dependent upon their being a literally factual account of the world's origins. It doesn't matter whether there ever was an Adam and Eve. The meanings of the stories of the great flood in the time of Noah and of the story of the tower of Babel do not depend upon their reporting events that happened. These stories, to echo Thomas Mann, are about the way things never were but always are.

A metaphorical approach, a more-than-literal reading, applies not only to individual stories, but also to the "macro-stories" of the Bible. These are the "large" stories that shape the Bible as a whole, and are found in the more particular stories. They image the human predicament and the remedy, the problem and the solution. These macro-stories, these large metaphors, are stories that image human life in relationship to God.

They include

- Stories of a journey. Abraham and Sarah, the father and mother of Israel, set out on a journey from the familiarity of the land they grew up in, to "a land they knew not." After the exodus from Egypt, Moses and the Israelites journey for 40 years to the Promised Land. In order to return from Exile, the Jewish people journeyed through the wilderness. Following Jesus – discipleship – is to journey with him from Galilee to Jerusalem, the place of confrontation with the authorities and the place of death and resurrection.

- Stories of exile and return. The story of Adam and Eve ends with their living "east of Eden." The Jewish people lived in exile and yearned for their homeland. The prodigal son found himself "in a far country" and began a journey home. So also are our lives: we fall into exile and we yearn for home. The Christian life is a journey of return.

- Stories of bondage and liberation. This is the central theme of the exodus story, and it continues into the New Testament. We are paralyzed and cannot walk; bent over and cannot stand upright; in bondage to the principalities and powers; possessed by alien spirits. The solution is being freed, being liberated. In Paul's words, "For freedom Christ has set us free. Stand firm, therefore, and do not submit again to a yoke of slavery" (Galatians 5:1).

- Stories of blindness and seeing. This macro-metaphor also includes the imagery of darkness and light, night and day, sleeping and being awake. We do not see very well and need to have our sight restored; we live in the darkness of night and need the light of dawn; we are commonly asleep and need to be awake, alert, to watch.

- Stories of sickness and healing. We are not well. We are sick, wounded, and need healing.

- Stories of sin, guilt, forgiveness, and new beginnings. Debts are forgiven, sins are forgiven, and we can begin again. We are accepted as we are. This is the meaning of biblical language about Jesus as the sacrifice for sin: God has taken care of whatever we think separates us from God. All that is needed is for us to see this and to live into it.

One final comment about a metaphorical approach: metaphors are not to be believed in. What would it mean to believe in a metaphor? Rather, metaphors are about meaning. Thus a historical-metaphorical approach leads from a belief-centered relationship to the Bible to a meaning-centered relationship to the Bible.

### CHRISTIANITY AND TRANSFORMATION

This way of interpreting the Bible connects directly to the emerging paradigm's emphasis upon transformation as the central dynamic of the Christian life. All of the "macro-stories" are stories of transformation. The transformation is twofold: of the self and of the world. It concerns our lives as individuals and our relation to the world.

Personal transformation is one of the most central themes of the New Testament. To cite some well-known passages that express this:

- Being Christian is about following "the Way." According to Acts 9:1, the earliest name of the movement that gathered around Jesus was "the Way." John's gospel speaks about Jesus as "the Way," as the incarnation of the path of transformation in a human life.

- It is about dying and rising with Christ – dying to an old way of being and entering into a new way of being. Paul says in Galatians 2:20, "I have been crucified with Christ; it is no longer I who live, but Christ who lives in me." In the gospels, following Jesus means following him on the path of death and resurrection. As he journeys to Jerusalem, he says, "If any would come after me, let them take up their cross and follow me" (Mark 8:34, with parallels in Matthew and Luke).

- It is about new creation. As Paul puts it in 2 Corinthians 5:17, "If anyone is in Christ, he or she is a new creation; everything old has passed away; see everything has become new."

- It is about transformation into the likeness of Christ. Paul again, this time in 2 Corinthians 3:18: "And we all, with unveiled faces, beholding the glory of the Lord, are being transformed into the likeness of Christ." So also in 1 John 3:2: "We are God's children now; what we will be has not yet been revealed. What we do know is this: when it is revealed, we will be like him."

- It is about being born again. We all need this transformation, for we are born of the flesh and need to be born of the Spirit, into a life centered in the Spirit of God (John 3).

Thus the biblical path of transformation is personal, but not *only* personal. It also means caring for the world. The Bible is personal, but never private. The path of transformation means participating more and more in God's passion *for the world*. As perhaps the best-known passage in the New Testament puts it, "God so loved *the world*."

"The world" refers to the world of nature as well as to the human world. We are to care for the earth, for the earth is the Lord's, and not ours. We are to be stewards of the earth – and stewards do not own what they care for, but do so on behalf of another. We are to care for the earth as a shepherd cares for the flock. To say the obvious, the earth includes the non-human animal world as well as the environment.

And we are to care for humans. Of course, this means caring for individuals, for "the neighbor" whom we are to love as we love ourselves. But the biblical vision also means caring about the systems within which humans live. Together, these systems are "culture" – the humanly created world of political systems, legal systems, economic systems, values systems, systems of conventional attitudes, and so forth. These can be more or less just, more or less humane, and are very frequently radically unjust.

Much of the Bible protests the injustice of political and economic systems. Indeed, perhaps half of the biblical message is political in this sense. Moses, the prophets, Jesus, Paul, and the book of Revelation all protest against human systems of domination and advocate a very different vision of life under God. They are passionately against injustice and war, the two great scourges of the ancient world, and passionately for justice and peace. In this, they participate in God's passion, for God is passionate about justice and peace. Indeed, this is what the Kingdom of God is about – it is for the earth. It is what life would be like on earth if God were king and the rulers of this world were not.

Participating in God's passion for the world also means enjoying the world. The world is a place of extraordinary beauty. It is the creation of God, and the earth is filled with the glory, the radiant presence, of God. This is true even when it is also a place of great suffering, as it often is. To be unable to see this, or to be able to see it only infrequently, is a kind of blindness. And thus we often need a transformation of perception. This does not mean that "Everything is okay." Everything is not okay; there is much that is radically wrong. But the world remains a place of beauty and we are meant to enjoy it as God enjoys it, even as we seek to transform it as God would have it transformed. As the Latin translation of John 3:16, translated into English puts it, "For God so delighted in the world."

Thus transformation-centered Christianity is political as well as personal. Emerging paradigm Christians are most often politically critical of the way things are – of economic systems that favor the wealthy and powerful, of military systems that seek to control the world through violence, of systems of conventional attitudes that degrade people. The God of the Bible wills our well-being – and the single greatest source of unnecessary misery is unjust and oppressive systems.

### Salvation
This vision leads to a different understanding of salvation.

Salvation is not about going to heaven, but is this process of transformation, a process that begins this side of death. To be saved is to be "in Christ," to be born again, to be a new creation, in the here and now — to be in the process of being transformed into the likeness of Christ. Emerging Christianity does not deny an afterlife, but recognizes that life after death is a relatively minor theme in the Bible. Rather, it represents a shift in emphasis and a willingness to leave the afterlife up to God. As Martin Luther is reported to have said, heaven is God's business — I don't have to worry about that.

## *Faith*

This vision also leads to a different understanding of faith, one that is much older than the "faith is believing" emphasis of the belief-centered paradigm. In Christianity prior to the Enlightenment, the two central meanings of faith were *trust* and *loyalty* (in Latin, *fiducia* and *fidelitas*). As trust, faith means letting go of our anxiety and fear and trusting in God. Jesus asks his followers, "Why are you anxious, O you of little faith?" Faith as trust means trusting in the buoyancy of God. Metaphorically, this is faith as being able to walk on water. In the gospel of Matthew, Peter is able to do this until he begins to become afraid — and then he sinks. As loyalty, faith means faithfulness to God, allegiance to God, commitment to God. We can see this meaning of faith by considering what it means to be faithful to a human relationship: it means to be loyal to it, to pay attention to it, to spend time in it. So faith as faithfulness, *fidelitas*, means paying attention to our relationship with God and centering in it, above all else. Indeed, faith as both trust and loyalty is about a deeper and deeper centering in God. Such centering *is* faith. And faith as centering in God has transformative power in a way that faith as belief does not.

## WHAT THIS MEANS FOR CHURCHES

What does this transformation-centered vision of Christianity mean for churches in our time? If a denomination or a congregation were to take this vision seriously, what would it do? Some research has been done on this topic. In the United States, Diana Butler Bass is engaged in a major study of mainline congregations that have embraced this vision. A preliminary report is contained in her recent book *The Practicing Congregation,* and her complete study will be published late in 2006.

As I describe a church of the emerging paradigm, I emphasize the following characteristics.

### Adult theological re-education

First, it would be a community of adult theological re-education. This is a major need in our time, simply because so many of us learned a vision of Christianity that stopped making persuasive and compelling sense to us. The re-education needs to be about the "big" topics: God, the Bible, Jesus, faith, prayer, and so forth. This can be done through adult education classes, of course. But it can also be done through reading groups in which participants commit themselves to read and discuss relevant books together. Such groups do not require expert theological leadership, but simply somebody who knows how to facilitate a group well.

### Christian practices

Second, it would be a community that teaches Christian practices. Practices are how we pay attention to our relationship with God. Practice is the means whereby Christianity moves from being about beliefs to being a way of transformation. Practice changes us. The single most important personal practice is prayer in both of its classic forms: verbal prayer and the prayer of internal silence (commonly called contemplative prayer). Also very helpful is a daily discipline, typically involving prayer and some reading, whether of a small portion of the Bible or of a devotional work.

The single most important corporate practice is worship. Though worship is *of God,* it is *for us.* Its purpose is to nourish us by drawing us out of ourselves, opening us up, forming and informing us. Taking the emerging vision seriously would shape the design of the worship service: the music we choose, the way scripture texts are read, the use of silence, the purpose of the sermon. We need to remember that worship is subversive: it proclaims that God is Lord, and the lords of this world are not. In the words of the Doxology, "Praise God from whom *all* blessings flow."

### Compassion and a passion for justice

Third, it would be a community whose ethical imperatives are compassion and a passion for justice. These are the central ethical themes of the Bible and they are related. Justice is the social form of compassion and compassion is the soul of justice. Thus it would be a community that moves toward inclusion, practices charity, and advocates justice and peace.

### Political consciousness

Fourth, it would take political consciousness-raising seriously. For centuries, most forms of Christianity have been politically domesticated, either politically indifferent or supportive of the status quo. Christian political consciousness-raising involves seeing the Bible's passion for justice and peace, and seeing the way systems impact people's lives. North American culture, with its emphasis upon individualism, is often blind to this. Such consciousness-raising would move the church beyond its captivity to convention and imperial consciousness.

### Living deeply into the Bible and the Christian tradition

Fifth, it would be a community living more deeply into the Bible and the Christian tradition. For quite a few people today, tradition is not a positive word. It suggests the dead, outmoded, and constricting voice of the past. But tradition also includes the wisdom, beauty, and goodness of the past. Of course, it contains less attractive elements as well, and they need to be rejected. Tradition needs to be discerningly received. But without tradition, we lose the riches of the past. Without tradition, we live only in the present and easily fall under the tyranny of the present and its lords. Tradition is about identity, and being Christian is about living within the Christian cultural-linguistic tradition. Indeed, being Christian means being resocialized into a Christian world. For most of us, our primary socialization was into modern Western culture with its way of seeing, its values, and its identities. The path of Christian transformation thus includes resocialization into a way of seeing, set of values, and identity very different from our primary socialization.

### Commitment and intentionality

Sixth, and finally, it follows that a church of the emerging paradigm would be a community of commitment and intentionality. The intentionality is a desire for a transforming relationship with God as known in Jesus. The commitment is to the path of transformation.

This path seems enormously attractive to me. It answers our deepest yearnings. I think we all yearn for a fuller connection to "what is," to God. Most of us would say that the best moments of our lives have been moments when we have experienced such a connection. And I think we all yearn that the world be a better place – for our sake, for the sake of our children and our children's children, and the world itself. And these two yearnings correspond to the two transformations at the center of the Christian life: loving God, and loving and caring for the world. The Christian message invites us to live in God and to participate in God's love for the world.

## CONCLUSION: RETURNING TO BELIEVING

I conclude by returning to the two paradigms and to the different meanings they assign to the words "faith" and "believe." Both paradigms agree that Christian faith means believing in God as known especially in Jesus. "As known especially in Jesus" is what makes faith Christian (and not Muslim faith or Jewish faith or Hindu faith, and so forth). But what does it mean to believe in God as known in Jesus? For the earlier paradigm, it most often means *believing in a set of beliefs* about God, the Bible, and Jesus. This is faith as belief, as *believing that* a set of claims is true.

The emerging paradigm recovers the pre-modern Christian understanding of believing. For it, the question, "Do you believe in God as known in Jesus?" has two primary meanings. "Do you *trust* in God as known in Jesus?" And, "Are you *loyal* to God as known in Jesus? Do you *give your allegiance* to God as known in Jesus?" It is trust and loyalty that transform us. Beliefs may precede them or follow them or remain quite unconnected to them. But beliefs do not save us, do not transform us. Trust and loyalty do.

This combination of trust and loyalty is the *centering* in God that I spoke of earlier as the primary meaning of faith. This centering is the purpose of the Christian life: centering in God, and centering in God's passion for the world. This is the vision at the heart of transformation-centered Christianity. Indeed, it is the heart of Christianity.

---

### ABOUT THE AUTHOR

**Marcus Borg** is Hundere Distinguished Professor of Religion and Culture at Oregon State University and the author of the bestselling books *The Heart of Christianity: Rediscovering a Life of Faith*; *Meeting Jesus Again for the First Time*; *Reading the Bible Again for the First Time*; and *The God We Never Knew*. He is in great demand as a speaker throughout the United States and Canada and he increasingly focuses on the topic of how to be a true Christian in the contemporary world.

# two

# Experience: The Heart of Transformation

## *Tim Scorer*

As I begin this exploration, I want to take seriously the full import of this word *experience*. In shaping language, our ancestors found that we needed a word to represent our capacity to try things out, to test them, and then to notice what we had done. And so, in English anyway, the word *experience* came to stand for that.

*Experience* has a significant connection to our innate tendency to be reflective. It's not in us to just "do." We also have to *notice* our doing, to stop doing it, to think about what we've done, to imagine what else we might have done, to notice the impact on us and on others of our doing, and to make notes to ourselves about how we will do it the same or differently in future. The notion of "trying and testing" only makes sense in the context of this human quality of reflectiveness.

I could continue writing on this matter of *experience* and its relationship to transformation, but I would more fully honor the spirit of the word and its significance in our lives if I invited you into the domain of *experience* and allowed you to "experience" the critical place it has in our lives of faith, and especially in *your* life of faith. So that is my intention. You may not want to enter the domain of active reflection right now. If that's the case, then you can leave this chapter, skip to the next one, set the book aside and go for a coffee, or do any one of a number of other things that are part of your way of being and doing. Whatever you choose, it will be impossible for you not to notice yourself doing it – not to notice having the experience.

★ ★ ★

If you are still reading, it is because you have chosen to go on to the next stage of this experiential journey. Welcome. In the course of the next few pages of this book, I am going to offer you a simple process of action and reflection that will, I hope, advance the intention of this chapter and of this book. All you need in addition to this book is a single sheet of writing paper and something with which to write.

Have you ever mastered the skill of drawing a five-sided star without taking your pen off the paper? If you have, you can go ahead and draw a star on the paper in such a way that the five points are not quite at the edge of the paper. (I will give you a word to write at each point.) If you've never learned how to do this simple drawing exercise, then put pen to paper and follow the arrows in the diagram that is given here.

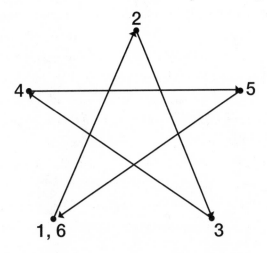

You may want to practice a few times on some scrap paper before committing your final star to your pristine work sheet! Let go of any judgment about the quality of your star; the only criterion is that it has five points.

As you look at your star, you will notice that at the heart of it is a pentagon – a space delineated by five sides. Chances are that it's not a pentagon of five equal sides, but that doesn't matter; the instructions didn't call for that. The reality is that no other pentagon drawn by any other reader of this chapter will be precisely like yours. In this unique, five-sided figure you will write something that is unique to your own life journey. I'll tell you exactly what that is and then you can take as much time as you need to choose what you will write, but first, a word about context.

One of the most helpful aspects of Marcus Borg's teaching is his emphasis on seeing our Christ-centered journey with God as a way of transformation that invites each of us to move from an identified dilemma to resolution, from a human predicament to a solution. This approach has, in itself, been transformative for many people whom I have accompanied, either in small groups or as a spiritual companion. It has provided a powerful way of moving beyond an attachment to the belief-centered emphasis on sin and salvation, on requirement and reward. I have observed people, again and again, being both liberated and empowered through this approach.

In the past weeks, four men sought me out, entirely independently, with the same human dilemma. There was a lawyer, in his early 40s, who knows that he has the personal resources and the breadth of experience to be able to make the kind of difference in the world that he really wants to make, but who is paralyzed by fear. There was a construction worker in his early 50s, with a history of violence that has alienated him from his two sons and led him to time in jail, who knows that he needs to find resolution with his father, from whom he learned the way of violence so well, but who is paralyzed by fear. There was a 60-year-old vineyard owner, who has cheated several times on his wife and who now lives a kind of façade that leaves him grieving for the man he wants to be, but who is paralyzed by fear. There was a retired schoolteacher with time on his hands, a pack full of life experience and a daily dose of antidepressant medication, who is desperate to live into his passion for life, but who is paralyzed by fear. All of these four men are in some way captive to fear, as well as to things like family dysfunction and family history, frozen relationship, depression, and repeated failure.

In each of these four situations, I met men who not only had a dilemma, but who also had a profound desire to change, to be transformed. They were each, in their own way, genuinely ready for a journey of transformation. In various ways, I introduced each of them to the journey of transformation and to the spirit of expectancy and hope that could lift them out of their bondage and into a new place in their lives. If I had asked each of these men to draw a five-pointed star and to put words in the pentagon at the center of it, they would each have written some variation on the theme of bondage.

Now it's your turn. In the pentagon, write words for the dilemma that is most pressing in your own life. Perhaps there's a way you, too, feel imprisoned, paralyzed, unable to move ahead. Or your dilemma might be named as one of exile – finding yourself in some kind of foreign land, away from home, absent from yourself and, perhaps, from God. You might be experiencing yourself as unable to see, blind, in a fog, lacking vision. Another man I met recently spoke of his condition as if he were buried under the weight of his compassionate concern for the world. I think of that as another kind of prison. Your task right now is to find a simple way of naming a pressing dilemma in your life, and then to write that in the pentagon shape.

Now it's time to move from the center of the star to begin your experience of transformation.

To begin, imagine a tree by the side of a road or a path. It's the kind of tree that has spreading branches and enough foliage to create a place of shade. Perhaps sometime in your life you've known a tree like this one: a tree that you've climbed and sat in as you watched people going by, a tree that you've lain under and looked up to the canopy of branches and foliage overhead. This particular tree that I'm telling you about lived and grew 2000 years ago by the side of a busy road in a town called Jericho. Jericho was on the way to Jerusalem – people were often passing through, seeking refreshment and shade from the hardships of the road.

Among these travelers not only were there merchants, priests, artisans, Roman soldiers, and pilgrims, there were also wandering mystics and healers – preachers calling people to mend their ways and to turn away from their destructive behaviors. And there was one healer and spirit man in particular who, in all the land from Galilee to Jerusalem, was attracting huge crowds, so much so that word went ahead of him and people gathered in anticipation of his arrival in their community. So, too, in Jericho. The day came when word went around that the one they called Joshua, or Jesus, was heading with his friends for Jerusalem and would be in Jericho by the middle of the day.

Now, in that society, there was one type of citizen who was disliked more than any other. And that was the tax collector. If you happened to be the Chief Tax Collector, people held you in even greater contempt, because you had the power to deal directly with the Romans and with the Temple authorities. As long as you gave them more than they were entitled to, you could take as much as you dared risk taking. And the great thing was that the people in power protected you. Zacchaeus was such a one. He was the Chief Tax Collector in Jericho and he was very wealthy. You could well imagine how hated he was.

Wherever he went, people turned away from him; they gathered in groups, expressed their disgust, and shared their stories of how they had been cheated by him.

I told you how word got out in Jericho about Jesus coming down the road. Well, Zacchaeus heard about Jesus' imminent arrival in the town. Now you might think that news of the presence of a holy man would be unwelcome to one who spent most of his time fleecing his neighbors. But that was not the case. In fact, no news was more welcome to Zacchaeus than the news that Jesus was about to be in his town. Frankly, Zacchaeus was desperate to see Jesus.

*Stop here for a moment. In the process of reflection on your experience, step into the shoes of Zacchaeus and answer this question for him: "Zacchaeus, why is it so important for you to see this man called Jesus?"*

And so Zacchaeus headed off to the main road to see Jesus who was passing through Jericho on the way to Jerusalem. Now, before I go any further, it's only fair to tell you that not only was Zacchaeus one of the wealthiest men if not *the* wealthiest man in Jericho, he was also the shortest. And when he got to the road he found that hundreds were there ahead of him. He had come late as usual and there was no way he was going to get a view. Imagine what that might be like. You know that Zacchaeus had set his heart on seeing Jesus and the only thing between him and the achievement of this desire was this mass of citizens, the very ones who were so essential to his livelihood and to his status in the community.

There was a tree by the side of the Jericho road that was well-known to Zacchaeus. As a child and a youth, he had spent many hours in its branches. (Perhaps you know of such a tree in your own life.) He suddenly remembered the tree and realized that if he could get to it and climb it he would be able to see Jesus pass by and that would be enough. The indignity of climbing the tree would hardly be noticed in the press of the crowd, who were only interested in the man coming down the road. And so he ran and climbed.

So there he was in his special tree. Thanks to his own ingenuity, Zacchaeus had the best seat at the parade! Suddenly, in the distance, there was a movement in the crowd. From his vantage point, Zacchaeus could see that the man they had all been waiting for was indeed coming down the road. As Jesus drew closer, Zacchaeus could see how purposeful his movement was. This was not someone who had plans to stop; he was definitely passing through, on his way to something else. Closer and closer he came – the people reached out, they cried out. Like a wave of energy moving through water, he came on. Before Zacchaeus realized it, he was right in front of his tree. Zacchaeus had seen Jesus!

*What was all this like for you, Jesus? You wanted to get to Jerusalem. You had no plans to stop in Jericho. "Just pass through," is what you said when your friends asked about the day's plans. Was there a moment as you forced your way through the clamoring crowd, when you saw a small man in a big sycamore tree and everything changed? How come you suddenly stopped under that tree and said to that man, "Zacchaeus, hurry down. Today is my day to be a guest in your home."*

Imagine that you are Jesus. What was it that made you so quickly change your mind?

It took Zacchaeus several moments to realize that Jesus was indeed talking to him. But when the truth hit him, he scrambled down the tree. He couldn't believe his good luck. He was delighted to take Jesus home with him. But first there was the crowd to contend with. Everyone who was there was indignant. They grumbled, "What business does he have getting cozy with this crook?"

Zacchaeus just stood there, a little stunned. He stammered apologetically, "Master, I will give away half my income to the poor – and if I'm caught cheating, I will pay four times the damages."

It's reported that Jesus replied with words to this effect: "Today is salvation day in this home! Here he is: Zacchaeus, a son of Abraham! For the Son of Man came to find and restore the lost." And the two of them went away to Zacchaeus' house, where Jesus dined with him.

We are not privy to the conversation that took place during that meal; nowhere is it recorded what each man said to the other. But in our imaginations we might hear Zacchaeus speaking with surprising clarity about why it was so critical for him to see Jesus that day. At the heart of his life was a dilemma that kept him from being the kind of man he truly wanted to be; a dilemma that, to this point, he had not been able to name to himself, let alone to anyone else.

*You are sharing a meal with Jesus and you, too, have an opportunity to speak to this man, who listens to you with a compassionate awareness such as you have never experienced before. You speak to him of the dilemma that is at the heart of your life just now. You experience his presence as you speak and, perhaps, his words of response. You allow yourself ample time to be present to this experience.*

Only read further when you feel that you have truly honored this time with Jesus.

As you step back from the story of Zacchaeus and the tree, turn to the page on which you have drawn the star. At the tip of one of the five points, write the word "Jesus." The star will act as a record of the experiential process in which you already find yourself. By the end of this chapter, you will have visited each of the other four points on the star, which together represent five aspects of the journey of transformation.

But before we leave the name "Jesus," it is important for us to ask some questions that will bring closure to our reflection on the place of Jesus in our own transformational journey. These are the kind of questions I would ask in the spirit of the emerging paradigm:

- As you sat with Jesus at supper and spoke about the dilemma that is on your heart and mind, what response did Jesus make? What do you want to be sure to remember from that conversation?
- Was there a particular quality in Jesus that so affected you that you could say, "From now on I want that quality to be part of my way of being"?
- How will you remember, beyond this experience, the imperative of Jesus: "Hurry down. Today is my day to be a guest in your home"?

Jesus' primary concern was to open people to a vision of a new kind of relationship with God. So it was with Zacchaeus, and so it is with us. As we live within our tradition, the Christ of our faith calls us to be transformed in our hearts, in our minds, and in our living. But what does that look like in terms of the practicality of our day-to-day living?

On several occasions now, I have heard Marcus Borg talk about the nature of the human heart and the choice we have to live with an open heart or a closed heart. As I've accompanied people on their path of healing and transformation, time and again I have been struck by the power of inviting them to think more deeply about the choice of living with an open heart or a closed heart. Attention to the condition of the human heart has become very significant in my practice of spiritual accompaniment and pastoral care and, indeed, in my own orientation to the world.

In case this notion of the open and closed heart is new to you, let me introduce it briefly by saying that Marcus Borg speaks of the closed heart as one that is turned away from God. He says that when our hearts are closed we have a darkened mind; we lack compassion and are out of touch with the suffering of others. You know you have it when you stand in a supermarket checkout line and all the people look kind of ugly! On the other hand, when our hearts are open, we are alive to wonder; we live with a spirit of gratitude and we are compassionate as God is compassionate. The open heart is the one that is turned toward God, living with grace and a spontaneous appreciation of the miracles of creation.

We can consciously turn toward God by opening our hearts. However, we can also experience God's presence when our closed hearts are opened without our initiating the process. One way of thinking about the transformation of Zacchaeus is to see that his heart was opened both through his initiative in climbing the tree and coming to Jesus, as well as through the power of Jesus' open-hearted response to him.

Now, write the word "God" at any one of the other points of the star. After you have done that, once again bring to your awareness the dilemma that you have brought to this transforming process and that is worded in some way in the pentagon at the center of your star. As you go on from this moment, I want you to do so with an intention to bring an open heart to this dilemma, whatever it is, knowing that through your initiative God will respond in some way to the condition in your life that you want to have transformed. Take a moment now to say the mantra, below.

Breathe in and say, "I open my heart to your presence."
Breathe out and say, "You are light of my path, breath of my being."
Breathe in and say, "I open my life to your shaping."
Breathe out and say, "You are source of my hope, grace of my healing."

Only read on when you feel ready to do so.

About five years ago, I was riding on the Toronto subway, lightly noticing the coming and going of people as I rode through several zones of Toronto's cultural diversity. At that time, a community of poets had posted contemporary poems in the advertising panels above the doors and windows of the subway cars. Every time I entered the train, I did so with a spirit of anticipation and open-heartedness to see what poems were waiting for me and what their impact might be on my life at the moment I read them. On the occasion I'm thinking about, the spirit of transformation met me with a poem by the Toronto poet, Roo Borson. Here it is:

The Trees

Their lives are longer, slower than ours.
They drink more deeply, slowly,
are warmed, do not shiver at dusk.
The heart unwinding makes a small noise.
Who would hear it?
Yet the trees attend,
perhaps to us, perhaps to nothing,
fragrance maybe, not of
flowering, but leaves and bark.

Trees. Dusk. Hand-coloured photographs
of the world before we were born.
Not sweet, but as water is,
sweet to a mouth long closed on itself.
Befriend them.

As I read it once again, it's hard to imagine another person not being touched as I was by the beauty of Roo Borson's words and by her thought. However, I know that it is as true of poetry as it is of change that we can only be moved by it when it is time for it to enter our lives. These were the words and this was the right moment, and so I stayed on the train long enough to write out the poem, going one stop past my station in the process!

Earlier, when I asked you to think of a special tree that you had known, did you do that? Recall that tree now and read the poem thinking of that tree. You might find yourself wanting to read the poem several times as you absorb all the layers of it and encounter its little surprises.

I bring the gift of this poem to you now because it came to me as part of my own practice of open-heartedness and because the Spirit of life, the holy presence in all creation, spoke to me through it and called me into a deeper attention to the world, particularly to the world of all living, non-human things.

- Imagine a tree actually listening to the unwinding, slow opening, of your heart! Are you willing to trust the intimacy of your opening heart to the long memory of this elder?

- This tree that you are touching, embracing, leaning into, climbing – what does it know of the world before you were born? What can it tell you of this land before your time? Will you take time to see its collection of hand-colored photographs?

- Are you ready for the awesome responsibility of befriending such a being?

Do you notice how your heart calls you into the world when you let it? The God we know through our open hearts and through this emerging paradigm calls us into a loving and ever-deepening relationship with this creation, which still holds us and sustains us in spite of our not befriending it. Write the word "world" at one of the remaining points of the star.

As part of this experiential journey, it's important that you continue to stand back from your experience and take note of any insights and awareness that you have as a result of what I am inviting you to do. These questions may help you to think in that way.

- When you focus your open-hearted attention on the world, both of nature and of humans, how does that affect the way you see your personal dilemma?
- Could you imagine going to a great living thing like a tree, a stream, an eagle, or a mountain, and seeking guidance on the issues that you find challenging in your life right now?
- Will you do that?

I was aware as I brought to your attention the poem by Roo Borson that I was taking our journey into the realm of written text. Roo Borson is one more poet in the great tradition of creative and spirit-filled writers who have, through all the ages of the human journey, reflected on these larger questions of meaning and divine relationship. In the Christian tradition, we honor especially the writers whose work was selected for inclusion in the Bible. Roo Borson came along too late to be included, but the poet of the book of Psalms came in plenty of time! I wonder how I would have reacted to finding the poetry of Psalm 139 presented in the advertising space on the Toronto subway:

O God, you have searched me and known me.
You know when I sit down and when I rise up;
you discern my thoughts from far away.
You search out my path and my lying down,
and are acquainted with all my ways…

Where can I go from your spirit?
Or where can I flee from your presence?...
If I take the wings of the morning
and settle at the farthest limits of the sea,
even there your hand shall lead me,
and your right hand shall hold me fast.
If I say, "Surely the darkness shall cover me,
and the light around me become night,"
even the darkness is not dark to you;
the night is as bright as the day,
for darkness is as light to you.
(NRSV, verses 1–3, 7, 10–12)

If you feel drawn to the words of the psalmist, you might want to turn in your Bible to Psalm 139 and read all the verses of this wonderful poem/song. In the tradition and practice of "praying the scriptures," allow one word or phrase to stand out for you from the words here, or from the whole psalm. As you have time today, create a reflective space in which you can let that word or phrase address the issue that you placed in the center of the star. Now write the word "Bible" at the tip of one of the two remaining unnamed points of the star.

As your attention moves to the final point of the star, return to your tree. In your imagination, picture the fullness of that tree: the solidity and centrality of the trunk, the shape of the branches as they reach away from the trunk, and the foliage as it presents the tree to the light, bringing sustenance to the whole.

Until now, you may have only paid attention to the tree as it is visible above the ground. Now it's time to imagine the equal fullness of the tree where the trunk plunges beneath the soil and becomes an incredible network of roots that actively seek the dark and the water, as much as the branches seek the light and the air. Are you suddenly able to see the tree as a balance of the visible living thing above ground and the unseen vibrant entity below the ground? In this moment, allow that icon of the tree to be a symbol of your own life, which reaches and grows into the world, into relationships, toward the light; even as it roots, supports, and sustains itself in community and in tradition. Write the words "community and tradition" at the final point of the star.

There are many ways that you might exercise your reflective spirit at this point of the star. Let me propose one way in particular.

Every time I have led a small group study on Marcus Borg's book *The Heart of Christianity*, the session in which we write affirmations under the heading "Why I am a Christian" has been a very powerful one. For many people who are drawn to the emerging paradigm, this is not a familiar exercise. However, given the diversity of the culture in which we find ourselves living our faith and reclaiming our passion for The Way, I think it is an essential one. This is the point in this experiential journey where you can claim your membership and your authority in a particular branch of the human spiritual journey, which has, at its heart, a very particular way of knowing God, Jesus, and the Bible. When you claim membership in this community of transformation-centered Christians, you are bringing the wholeness of who you are, dilemmas and all, to a community where you will find some kinship of thought and spirit, and an abundance of God's grace at work in the lives of faith-filled friends.

That sounds like the end of a chapter, but it isn't quite. Our concern in this book is with a change in our paradigm: a change of lens that will allow us to see all that is familiar in a new and transformative way. Here's one way to think of that: you have been moving around a five-pointed star, experiencing resources for your own transformation. But what if it wasn't a star at all, but a tree? What was a star up to this point could as well be a view looking down from above on a tree that reaches out in clusters of five branches up and down its trunk. You can take your pen or pencil and transform the star into a tree seen from above. Your life experience has taught you enough about trees and stars to transform them in a moment. How much more you know about your own life!

May God's ever-transforming spirit abundantly befriend and encourage you in your own Christ-affirming path of insight and liberation.

---

## ABOUT THE AUTHOR

**Tim Scorer** is just completing a three-year appointment on the Ministry Leadership Team at Penticton United Church, Penticton, British Columbia, where he has had responsibility for small group ministry and faith formation. Prior to that he was for 24 years a member of the management team at Naramata Centre, Naramata, British Columbia, a retreat and education center of the United Church of Canada, where he worked in the areas of program planning and development, human interaction, leadership development, and spiritual formation. He has just begun to work with Wood Lake Books in support of their initiative to provide resources related to emerging visions of Christianity.

# Part Two

# key perspectives

# three

## New Creeds[1]

### Tom Harpur

*There is something that can be found in one place. It is a great treasure, which may be called the fulfillment of existence. The place where this treasure can be found is the place on which one stands.*

*Most of us achieve only at rare moments a clear realization of the fact that we have never tasted the fulfillment of existence, that our lives do not participate in true, fulfilled existence, that, as it were, it passes true existence by. We nevertheless feel the deficiency at every moment, and in some measure strive to find — somewhere — what we are seeking. Somewhere, in some province of the world or of the mind, except where we stand, where we have been set — but it is there and nowhere else that the treasure can be found. The environment which I feel to be the natural one, the situation which has been assigned to me as my fate, the things that happen to me day after day, the things that claim me day after day — these contain my essential task and such fulfillment of existence as is open to me. It is said of a certain Talmudic master that the paths of Heaven were as bright to him as the streets of a man's native town. It is a greater thing if the streets of a man's native town are as bright to him as the paths of Heaven. For it is here, where we stand, that we should try to make shine the light of the hidden divine life.*

Martin Buber, *The Way of Man*[2]

## Prologue

Growing up as a boy from a working class, Irish immigrant family in the east end of Toronto, I spent most of my early, non-school time playing in the narrow streets and the network of lanes behind the houses. These were the years of the Great Depression, which began a few months after my birth, and then of World War II which broke out a decade later. One of our favorite pastimes as youngsters, following hard upon an obsession with playing "Cowboys and Indians," was playing "alleys," or shooting marbles. There was every conceivable variation of theme: trying to see how many one could toss into a small hollow scraped in the ground about three paces away; how close to a specific wall one could roll the brightly colored glass or stone globes; who could win the most marbles by taking turns trying to hit the other person's large "glassy" or "agate." Each hit won one marble. At the end of the day, each of us would roll out the contents of his "marble bag" – my mum had made me one out of some leftover cloth from her home sewing, complete with drawstring – and examine the contents. It mattered a lot what the number, size, and beauty of the alleys added up to. It was an important stock-taking. A moment of truth and of reflection upon it.

I have recently reached a significant date in my life. Thankfully, I have seldom felt more well and energized and happy. But it's a fitting, biblical time, three score years plus ten, to reflect on and examine any "jewels" found on life's path thus far. I'm eager to share what has done more for my spiritual life and understanding than anything else over years of study, reflection, and an amazingly varied experience of life. It has to do with crucial, existential matters such as the true self-identity of each of us, our chief purpose in life, and the very core nature of the Christian message, indeed of all true religion.

The Bible's first creation account tells us that God made humankind (Adam) in God's own image. This *Imago Dei*, as it is called – the image of God – has been the occasion of a lot of commentary and controversy down the ages. The early Church Fathers saw in it a reference to our possession of free will, a reference to our supposed superiority to all other creatures, our alleged possession of immortality, or our gift of self-reflective reason. In the more mystical tradition of the churches both of East and West, however, the concept of the *Imago Dei* has played a crucial role as the point at which the soul is *capax Dei*, capable of knowing God and hence of entering into ultimate union with God. Not ultimate absorption as in some forms of Buddhism and Hinduism, but *union.*

I say this in total awareness of the way in which both Roman Catholic and Protestant theology since their earliest days have choked out this kind of "high view" of humanity in favor of a much gloomier, more dour estimate of our nature and proclivities. Obsessed with the notion of the "Fall" in the great myth of the Garden of Eden and its purported flawing of the *Imago,* many great Western theologians have emphasized almost gleefully the depravity and corruption brought by sin – for example, St. Augustine, Jerome, and Tertullian, in the first centuries CE; and Karl Barth and Emil Brunner much more recently. Indeed, Barth held that because of sin, humanity is totally incapable of any knowledge of God apart from revelation, that is, Holy Writ. Centuries of teaching only this view of the human has brought nothing but incredible misery and spiritual inertia, I now believe.

The proof is out there for all to see. In the United States, for example, a major mental health issue is that untold millions seem incapable of holding a reasonable sense of self-worth and self-esteem. This, in spite of the prevailing religiosity – chiefly ultra-conservative evangelicalism, plus the "civil religion" espoused by most U.S. presidents – which insists its message is one of abundant life and of unfettered affirmation of the supreme value of each and every "sinner" out there. But first, of course, as watching any evangelistic "crusade" on television will prove, the person who is to inherit all this "abundant life" has to be roasted over the fires of a literal hell and be fully assured of how unworthy he or she really is of God's grace. The overwhelming spate of self-help books, tapes, and videos now flooding the bookstores in North America is but a small symptom of what is truly a pandemic disorder, the negative results of a negative theology.

I believe the profound, biblical concept of our having been created "in the image of God," goes even deeper than some of the early Fathers and many of the more humane scholars in the past have said. To be made in the *Imago Dei* is to share now, in some way in this world, in the nature and essence of God. It is not just a capacity or a remote potentiality, but an inner reality. We have each been given "something of God" within us. To cite the opening verses of John's gospel, the Logos, which was in the beginning both present with God and belonging to the essence of God, was the "true Light" which gives its light to every human being who "comes into the world."

The vast majority of Bible scholars today agree that John's opening verses, The Prologue, consciously and deliberately echo the opening words of Genesis in order to show that a fresh start is being made. Thus, the references to the *Imago Dei*, in Genesis, and the statement that the divine light is bequeathed to every human being at birth, in the Gospel of John, are linked tightly together. Both assert the presence of the divine Spirit or an individuated "portion" of God in the human heart. This latter is a metaphorical manner of speaking, of course. God cannot be divided up.

Let me say it again. What this means in bold terms is that we are all, regardless of creed, color, or culture, children of God – "sons and daughters of God" – and as such, bearers of God's own divine life within. This is not some New Age, simplistic wishing, but the clear witness of the entire Bible, particularly of the New Testament, once the reader divests himself/herself from years of cover-up and/or distortion from traditional church preaching and teaching. I call this proclamation of the essential divinity of every human, Core Christianity. Though externally it might seem quite different from Eastern and other religions, Core Christianity is very much like them after all – a specific form of the Perennial Philosophy, which is embodied in every faith.

According to the Perennial Philosophy, the whole purpose of life is to find out who you really are – the offspring of God, bearing God within as your higher self – and to see what your purpose is; to become awakened to this knowledge and to let this Light shine through you for fulfilling your own potential and that of all others in community, until a much fuller, eternal union dawns upon a "distant shore." Years of study and experience have long convinced me that basic Christianity is about this "Christ Principle" or "Christ Consciousness," as some prefer to call it, which Jesus discovered himself and which he proclaimed as Good News or gospel for all prepared to receive it. In what follows, we'll trace out in greater detail the origins and nature of this message and examine its implications for churched and non-churched alike.

## THE BACKGROUND

*I say, "You are gods, children of the Most High,*
*all of you."*
Psalm 82:6

*Is it not written in your law, "I said, you are gods"?*
Jesus Christ (John 10:34)

Christianity today is in the grip of a crisis of monumental proportions. Nothing that has happened in the previous 2,000 years of church history has come close to the present convulsion and increasing chaos that is shaking the church's deepest foundations, a predicament that will almost certainly only worsen to the point of threatening the very existence of the hundreds of kinds of churches around the globe. The future – if you project on a graph the current decline of the church in Europe and in North America – looks worse than bleak.

Many, both inside and outside the fold, are now articulating this ominous prophecy. John Spong, retired bishop of Newark, New Jersey, and the most high-profile of all the doomsters, has titled one of his latest volumes *Why Christianity Must Change or Die*. In 12 theses, à la Martin Luther, only this time not nailed to a church door but trumpeted first in his book and on the Internet, Spong makes clear that he's not talking about superficial cosmetic changes or about minor adjustments to sundry quaint aspects of faith and order. What the bishop's theses state quite bluntly is that the changes required will necessitate a completely radical transformation of the content of the historic creeds. It's no longer a matter of simply trying to update the church's language, but of transforming the conceptual framework and the inner essence of what is believed and promulgated. The urgent need is to make the foundations of faith square honestly with modern thinking – especially when it comes to reconciling faith with science and the comparatively recent discoveries in psychology, biology, physics, and cosmology.

But in reading Spong and the others who seem to be saying "the church is dead" rather than "God is dead," as some theologians loudly argued in the mid-1960s, one can come away wondering why, when most of their points are so reasonable and seemingly so inevitable, this entire trend leaves the seeker-after-truth still feeling so strangely empty. At least to date, they hand on such meager leftovers after all their probings that any idea of the churches having some "Good News" to impart, or of fulfilling a mission of bringing peace and wholeness to the world, seems to vanish. Spong, for example, argues persuasively that a theistic God who is "out there" – a sort of heavenly Superman – ready to intervene in the world arbitrarily if we pray hard enough, no longer makes any sense. I agree. But, so far, he has done very little to even "sketch in" what his non-theistic God is or does. Certainly what is not needed or wanted is a cool, indifferent God essence or spirit who, on further thought, can best be described in abstract terms denoting something very like a cosmic ether, a vague force, or an impassive energy field. A more recent book by Spong is *A New Christianity for a New World*. His ideas of God may satisfy him, but they are unlikely to speak to many others. This is not the "God of the Gaps" for certain. This God is a gap itself!

The question, then, is, can one find anything fully solid to cling to, given the vortex of Spongian-type attacks upon the theological status quo, mixed with the skeptical assessments by theologians, such as the

Jesus Seminar's New Testament scholars, of the role of Jesus in the formation of the gospels? What, in the light of our questing, is the deepest
message of the scriptures, both the Hebrew Bible and the canonical
New Testament writings, particularly the four gospels? Has such a message got any timely, life-changing implications for modern young people
and adults as well? Can this message not just make a leap into the place
once taken by the traditional obsessions with sin, punishment, salvation,
and saintliness, but also wholly inspire members and non-members alike
with a fresh vision of what Christianity – and all the other major religious faiths for that matter – truly embodies?

This is the issue before us. To anticipate, the key thesis which will
shortly emerge more clearly is that there is indeed a different way of
looking at the earliest documents and at the teaching of Jesus as it is
traced in them. There is an aspect, a deep, underlying theme in all his
offhand sayings, his parables and sermons – and, of course, of his life as
lived – that has not received sufficient attention in Western Christianity.
Too much ink (and blood as well) has been spilled over the matter of the
divinity of Jesus Christ. The time has now come to look more closely
at what he and his followers taught about the divinity of humanity, the
"godness" of every human being who has ever lived. After thinking,
reading, and reflecting on this matter – while teaching at my old seminary, while covering religion around the world as a journalist, between
writing other books and regular columns on ethics and spirituality for
*The Toronto Star* for the past 30 years – I am even more fully convinced
than I was when I wrote *For Christ's Sake* in 1986 that Jesus' chief teaching was not about sin and certainly not about founding a new religion.
It was about the kingdom of God, God's active presence everywhere.
More specifically, it was about the kingdom as an inner reality – the
divinity of every one of us. God in our midst; God within.

To put it another way: What was it that Jesus discovered about himself? Did he feel that this discovery was for himself alone? Or was he
referring to that discovery when he said, "The kingdom of heaven is
within you?" Or again, when he said, "You shall do greater things than

these" (i.e., the works and signs of his ministry)? Or on those occasions when he said to the disciples, "You are the light of the world"?

## THE CREEDS

*I know that age to age succeeds,*
*Blowing a noise of tongues and deeds,*
*A dust of systems and of creeds.*
Alfred Lord Tennyson, (1809–1892)[3]

What causes me the most distress as I survey the signs everywhere that this new millennium is destined to be truly "The Spiritual Age," is the feebleness so far of the response of the church and of other faiths to this challenge. In what follows, the major focus is on the Christian church in its numerous manifestations, but not narrowly so. The parallels with other world religions are striking and must not be ignored.

Right now, extremely liberal denominations and their clergy risk being so concerned about communicating with the secularized world – a laudable aim in itself – that they frequently end up becoming a precise copy of it. Many differ little from the local Rotary or Lions Club, apart from their own inexorable passion for ecclesiastical garments and new twists on ancient ceremonies. Liberals are left with little or no Good News to proclaim. Occasionally, to give full credit where it is deserved, they manage to be prophetic on crucial social justice issues. That's good. Most commendable, in fact. But for the millions aching for inner peace and a vital relationship with God, the source of everything, they bring small comfort. They have lost what used to be called "the care of souls." People demand "bread" – in other words, spiritual sustenance, a sense of purpose, a sense of meaning and of their belonging to the cosmos. They are given stones instead. In the attempt to be relevant, many belonging to this wing have fallen into the morass Paul warned about in Romans: "Do not be conformed to this world…" The Greek says literally, "Don't be pressed into this world's mold."

If anything, the state of the ultra-conservatives and that of funda-mentalists of every kind is much worse. Taking the overall situation in North America, these groups make up the large majority and seem to be growing. They have great political clout in the United States, particularly. For example, the swift exit of Senator John McCain from the race for the Democratic nomination as presidential candidate for the November 2000 election was due almost entirely to his courage or rashness in attacking the right-wing, "born-again" Republicans who were so keenly engaged in opposing him. Because of their understand-ing of mass media and its importance in winning the hearts and minds of contemporary seekers, the conservatives almost entirely dominate the field of religion on television. They are behind the publication of an unending flood of books, many of them preoccupied with apocalyptic "facts" about the "End Times." The result is that the prevailing public image or concept of what it means to be a Christian today has been de-fined in terms of belonging to the "born-again" style of faith. Naturally, those outsiders who are put off by all of the simplistic rigidities tend to identify the whole of faith with this anti-intellectual approach and thus throw out everything – baby, bathwater, and the tub too, so to speak.

The fundamentalists' essential response to the profound intellec-tual, emotional, and cultural changes of this unique moment, this *kairos* in history, is to dig in ferociously and keep on repeating the things they have always said. Only they say them much more loudly and in-sistently than ever before. While there is nothing else today, no field of human thought or endeavor, that has not been forced to make huge, revolutionary shifts in basic concepts, structures, and tactics, religions in general and religious conservatives especially feverishly resist this reality. Using their main weapon, a so-called "infallible" book, the Bible (for which I have enormous love and respect), and interpreting it in their own, literalistic and uncritical way (which is really a 20th-century her-esy unknown in earlier times), they preach as their gospel an "old, old story," that now only makes sense if you suspend all rational thought completely.

Critics have spoken out regarding the so-called "dumbing down" of America. It's interesting to study the way in which modern mass media, especially on this continent but by no means only here, have so catered to the lowest common denominator that our culture is indeed becoming shallower and flakier by the day. But so far, nobody I'm aware of has really researched the dumbing-down of Christianity that has gone on at an accelerating pace over the past 60 years or so. As the old millennium finally drew to a close, the growing spiritual hunger of the "unchurched" and "churched" alike was matched step by step with a growing anti-brain, anti-intellectual approach being taken by the conservative stratum in Protestantism and Roman Catholicism alike. These "true-believers" have equated being true to the "faith of our fathers" with simplification, literalism, and black or white answers to any personal or social dilemma, from the so-called "hormone issues," to gun control, to raising a family, to politics in general.

On a recent trip, Susan, my wife, and I spent some weeks in northern and central Florida. We spent the time reading, walking, watching the dolphins, and doing research for my writing. Among other things, we deliberately attended a different church each Sunday for several weeks. The first was a charismatic Episcopal church in Destin. Next came a very large Roman Catholic congregation in the same town. These were followed by a Southern Baptist, a Methodist, and an United Presbyterian congregations in the same region. They were all packed, except for the Presbyterian. Every single one we visited was friendly. The people seemed happy and normal. What was extraordinary, however, was the similarity of the sermons. They all came from one mold. You closed your eyes and it could have been the same preacher in every instance. Each homily, apart from the odd illustration or two, could have been preached 75 to 150 years ago. It made no difference that almost everyone there had seen humans walking on the moon, that quantum physics had stood Isaac Newton on his head, that doctors can operate on the heart of a fetus, or transplant whole organs, or that astronomers and astrophysicists assert that there are billions of galaxies in a universe that seems to expand ad infinitum.

In short, the messages were utterly void of any sense of how vastly our thinking and outlook – our worldview – has altered. The concepts, the images, the basic meaning of the Good News being proclaimed were like an alien discourse. The sermons only took on coherence and sense within their own framework and on their own axioms. Your mind, as I've said before, had to be checked at the door, hung on the rack with your coat.

A group of men, including an atheist, a couple of lapsed churchgoers, and several others who are mainly Anglicans but who all find present worship and dogma not only problematic but even a major stumbling block to spiritual growth of any kind, meet once a month in our home. Calling themselves "The Seekers," they tackle head-on the issues raised by trying to remain believers at such a time as this. At a recent session, they each described their increasing inability to recite either the Apostles' or the Nicene Creed with any feeling of integrity. Like millions of others today, they are keen to know and serve God. But the creedal statements, created and gestated in a pre-Copernican world and articulated for the first four or five centuries by theologians and bishops whose worldview and language were those of the Hellenistic world, are simply no longer comprehensible or relevant today. Nor is traditional, orthodox theology in general, which, beginning with the myth of the "Fall" in the Garden of Eden, is founded upon wholly outdated ideas of Original Sin, Atonement by a wholly pure and innocent sacrifice given by God to "himself," and Salvation through being cleansed and "washed in the blood of the Lamb."

For many years, I have tried strenuously to take each phrase of the Creeds in a symbolic or purely spiritual fashion. I have done so partly out of a vague sense of guilt, partly from a strong desire to identify with the millions of Christians who have gone before us by clinging to the historic formulae or principles for which they often fought and died. At the same time, however, I have felt a deep bond with some words of the late scholar and teacher Bishop Stephen Neill. Neill, a man of honesty and knowledge, said, "There are times when the only part of the creeds that I feel at all sure and comfortable with are those historically based words, 'And was crucified under Pontius Pilate.'" We know of Pontius Pilate from other sources than the Bible. He was a genuine historic figure. I have often quoted Neill on this because I have come to know quite intimately the dilemma he faced.

I can say the opening lines about God creating the heavens and the earth, but once they begin to list such dogmas as the literal Virgin Birth or Jesus' Ascension into heaven "where he sitteth at the right hand of the Father," coherence and credibility come to an end. There are many millions still in the pews for whom this is also true. Many others cannot even get that far! Certainly, many people remain and join heartily in saying the Creeds in spite of their deep-down unbelief. They have made a "tacit deal" to ignore a lot. They know well that the propositions to which they're giving apparent, verbal assent, are built on ancient, untenable beliefs in a three-decker universe and in ideas of the seating protocols of Oriental kings or potentates from 1,900 years ago. Many merely mumble something and ignore the problem of trying to follow the commandment of loving God "with all your mind." Most are in a zombie-like state of consciousness anyway and just let the whole liturgy roll completely over their heads, unexamined and unexplained. Eventually, these people will either wake out of their trance and listen to what they are repeating Sunday by Sunday, or drop out in any case because of age, ill-health, or death. When this happens, there is little sign that the next generation will take over and/or continue in the faith once known to our "fathers." The institutional "death" of which Spong and others warn will then be upon us.

The most striking thing about both The Apostles' Creed and The Nicene Creed is what they leave out. For example, they say absolutely nothing about the key teaching of Jesus about the kingdom of God, which includes the entire ethic of social justice – the theme both of Old Testament prophets and of Jesus. This theme of the reign of the kingdom of God, which totally dominates the synoptic gospels – Paul gives it exceedingly short shrift, mentioning it only a few times in contrast to the scores of instances in Matthew and Luke – is simply not present in the creeds. The more one thinks about this the more astonishing it becomes. However, other omissions are just as difficult to explain: for example, the Sermon on the Mount's ethic of the Golden Rule, or the vital Jesus-teaching (and, of course, Pauline as well) about the way of love and forgiveness as the hallmark of Christ-like living.

One could go on. But even if you recognize the need to formulate some brief, basic beliefs into creedal-like statements for the sake of brevity and focus, the glaring imbalance of so much emphasis upon ideas Jesus never expressly taught compared with the complete absence of the chief issues which he constantly addressed screams out that there is something fundamentally wrong.

There is no doubt left in my mind that this is one more powerful reason why the ancient creeds should be retired from active duty and be replaced by others more truly authentic, honest, and clear.

In the novel *The Babes in the Darkling Woods*, by H. G. Wells, one of the puzzled young people in conversation with a country vicar says, "At the back of all, there surely has to be a creed, a fundamental statement, put in language which doesn't conflict with every reality we know about the world. We don't want to be put off with serpents and fig leafs and sacrificial lambs. We want a creed in modern English, sir, and we can't find it."

The following is a slightly updated version of a tentative "creed" that I wrote and published in 1986:

We believe, and put our trust in God, Creator and Sustainer of all things, from the farthest-flung galaxies to the most microscopic forms of life; God is above and around and within every one of us, and yet so far beyond us in transcendence that our minds cannot fathom the mystery and our only response is wonder and worship. And we believe God sent Jesus, anointing him in the power of Spirit, to declare by word and deed the gospel of personal and social liberation from the power of fear and all injustice and oppression. Though he was cruelly and unjustly murdered, God raised him from death and God's seal is set forever on Jesus' message and ministry. In him we know that God is love, and that forgiveness and acceptance are ours always. In him we are called to realize God's kingdom in our own lives and in the lives of others. In him we are called to join with God in making all things new. We believe God has granted to us and to all humanity the same Spirit that was in Jesus, creating community and empowering us to be like him. We believe in a dimension of existence yet to come. We seek to build God's kingdom here, but we also look beyond to a day when wars will end and God's New Jerusalem will be revealed. We believe. God help our unbelief.[4]

This "creed" makes no claim whatever to be perfect. No creed will be. But it shows the direction in which I believe we could move. I challenge readers to take the time to create a creed for themselves. Discuss it and improve upon it with others. Simplify!

---

### ABOUT THE AUTHOR

**Tom Harpur** is a journalist, TV host, and Canada's best-known author on the topics of religion and contemporary spirituality. He is an Anglican priest and Rhodes scholar who studied philosophy and theology at Oxford. He has written several bestselling books including *Prayer: The Hidden Fire*; *Finding the Still Point: A Spirituality of Balance*; *The Pagan Christ*; and *The Spirituality of Wine*.

# four

# The Great Work[1]

## *Thomas Berry*

History is governed by those overarching movements that give shape and meaning to life by relating the human venture to the larger destinies of the universe. Creating such a movement might be called the Great Work of a people. There have been Great Works in the past: the Great Work of the classical Greek world with its understanding of the human mind and creation of the Western humanist tradition; the Great Work of Israel in articulating a new experience of the divine in human affairs; the Great Work of Rome in gathering the peoples of the Mediterranean world and of Western Europe into an ordered relation with one another. So too in the medieval period there was the task of giving a first shape to the Western world in its Christian form. The symbols of this Great Work were the medieval cathedrals rising so graciously into the heavens from the region of the old Frankish empire. There the divine and the human could be present to each other in some grand manner.

In India the Great Work was to lead human thought into spiritual experiences of time and eternity and their mutual presence to each other with a unique subtlety of expression. China created one of the most elegant and most human civilizations we have ever known as its Great

Work. In America the Great Work of the First Peoples was to occupy this continent and establish an intimate rapport with the powers that brought this continent into existence in all its magnificence. They did this through their ceremonies such as the Great Thanksgiving ritual of the Iroquois, the sweat lodge and the vision quest of the Plains Indians, through the Chantways of the Navaho, and the Katsina rituals of the Hopi. Through these and a multitude of other aspects of the indigenous cultures of this continent, certain models were established of how humans become integral with the larger context of our existence here on the planet Earth.

While all of these efforts at fulfilling a Great Work have made significant contributions to the human venture, they were all limited in their fulfillment and bear the marks of their deeply human flaws and imperfections. Here in North America it is with a poignant feeling and foreboding concerning the future that we begin to realize that the European occupation of this continent, however admirable its intentions, has been flawed from the beginning in its assault on the indigenous peoples and its plundering of the land. Its most impressive achievements were establishing for the settlers a sense of personal rights, participatory governance, and religious freedom.

If there was also advancement of scientific insight and technological skills leading to relief from many of the ills and poverty of the European peoples, this advancement was accompanied by devastation of this continent in its natural florescence by the suppression of the way of life of its indigenous peoples and by communicating to them many previously unknown diseases, such as smallpox, tuberculosis, diphtheria, and measles. Although Europeans had developed a certain immunity to these diseases, they were consistently fatal to Indians, who had never known such diseases and had developed no immunities.

Meanwhile the incoming Europeans committed themselves to development of the new industrial age that was beginning to dominate human consciousness. New achievements in science, technology, industry, commerce, and finance had indeed brought the human community into a new age. Yet those who brought this new historical period into being saw only the bright side of these achievements. They had little comprehension of the devastation they were causing on this continent and throughout the planet, a devastation that finally led to an impasse in our relations with the natural world. Our commercial-industrial obsessions have disturbed the biosystems of this continent in a depth never known previously in the historical course of human affairs.

The Great Work now, as we move into a new millennium, is to carry out the transition from a period of human devastation of the Earth to a period when humans would be present to the planet in a mutually beneficial manner. This historical change is something more than the transition from the classical Roman period to the medieval period, or from the medieval period to modern times. Such a transition has no historical parallel since the geobiological transition that took place 67 million years ago when the period of the dinosaurs was terminated and a new biological age begun. So now we awaken to a period of extensive disarray in the biological structure and functioning of the planet.

Since we began to live in settled villages with agriculture and domestication of animals some ten thousand years ago, humans have put increased burdens upon the biosystems of the planet. These burdens were to some extent manageable because of the prodigality of nature, the limited number of humans, and their limited ability to disrupt the natural systems. In recent centuries, under the leadership of the Western world, largely with the resources, psychic energy, and inventiveness of the North American peoples, an industrial civilization has come into being with the power to plunder Earth in its deepest foundations, with awesome impact on its geological structure, its chemical constitution, and its living forms throughout the wide expanses of the land and the far reaches of the sea.

Some 25 billion tons of topsoil are now being lost each year with untold consequences to the food supply of future generations. Some of the most abundant species of marine life have become commercially extinct due to overexploitation by factory fishing vessels and the use of drift nets 20 to 30 miles long and 20 feet deep. If we consider the extinctions taking place in the rain forests of the southern regions of the planet with the other extinctions, we find that we are losing large numbers of species each year. Much more could be said concerning the impact of humans on the planet, the disturbance caused by the use of river systems for waste disposal, the pollution of the atmosphere by the burning of fossil fuels, and the radioactive waste consequent on our use of nuclear energy. All of this disturbance of the planet is leading to the terminal phase of the Cenozoic Era. Natural selection can no longer function as it has functioned in the past. Cultural selection is now a decisive force in determining the future of the biosystems of Earth.

The deepest cause of the present devastation is found in a mode of consciousness that has established a radical discontinuity between the human and other modes of being and the bestowal of all rights on the humans. The other-than-human modes of being are seen as having no rights. They have reality and value only through their use by the human. In this context the other than human becomes totally vulnerable to exploitation by the human, an attitude that is shared by all four of the fundamental establishments that control the human realm: governments, corporations, universities, and religions – the political, economic, intellectual, and religious establishments. All four are committed consciously or unconsciously to a radical discontinuity between the human and the nonhuman.

In reality there is a single integral community of the Earth that includes all its component members whether human or other than human. In this community every being has its own role to fulfill, its own dignity, its inner spontaneity. Every being has its own voice. Every being declares itself to the entire universe. Every being enters into communion with other beings. This capacity for relatedness, for presence to other beings, for spontaneity in action, is a capacity possessed by every mode of being throughout the entire universe.

So too every being has rights to be recognized and revered. Trees have tree rights, insects have insect rights, rivers have river rights, mountains have mountain rights. So too with the entire range of beings throughout the universe. All rights are limited and relative. So too with humans. We have human rights. We have rights to the nourishment and shelter we need. We have rights to habitat. But we have no rights to deprive other species of their proper habitat. We have no rights to interfere with their migration routes. We have no rights to disturb the basic functioning of the biosystems of the planet. We cannot own the Earth or any part of the Earth in any absolute manner. We own property in accord with the well-being of the property and for the benefit of the larger community as well as ourselves.

A sense of the continent being here primarily for our use has been developing throughout the past few centuries. We proceeded with our destruction of the forests until the terminal phase of the 20th century, when we found that we had cut down over 95 percent of the primordial forests of this continent. With the new technologies that emerged in the last half of the 19th century and the automobile industry that developed in the early 20th century, industrialization achieved a new virulence. Roadways, superhighways, parking lots, shopping centers, malls, and housing developments took over. Suburban living became normative for the good life. This was also the time when the number of free-flowing rivers began to decline. The great dams were built on the Colorado, the Snake, and especially the Columbia rivers.

Yet this was also the time when resistance began. The increasing threat to the natural life-systems of the continent awakened the sense of need for grandeur in the natural world if any truly human development was to continue in our cultural traditions. This new awareness began in the 19th century with such persons as Henry David Thoreau, John Muir, John Burroughs, and George Perkin Marsh; with John Wesley Powell and Frederick Law Olmstead; also with artists, especially Thomas Cole, Frederick Edwin Church, and Albert Bierstadt of the Hudson River School.

To the work of naturalists and artists was added the work of the conservationists in the political realm. These leaders brought about the preservation of Yellowstone National Park in 1872, the first wilderness area anywhere on Earth to be officially set aside for preservation in perpetuity. Later, in 1885, New York State established the Adirondack Forest Preserve, a region to be kept forever in its wilderness condition. In 1890 Yosemite National Park was established in California. In that same period the first voluntary associations were formed to foster a deepened appreciation of the natural world. The Audubon Society, founded in 1886, was concerned primarily with appreciation of the various bird species. The Sierra Club was founded in 1892 and the Wilderness Society in 1924. Both sought to create a more intimate relationship between the human community and the wild world about us.

These various groups were the beginning. The larger dimensions of what was happening could not have been known to those living in the 19th century. They could not have foreseen the petroleum industry, the automobile age, the damming of the rivers, the emptying of the marine life of the oceans, the radioactive waste. Yet they knew that something was wrong at a profound level. Some, such as John Muir, were deeply disturbed. When the decision was made to build a dam to enclose Hetch-Hetchy Valley as a reservoir for the city of San Francisco, he considered it the unnecessary destruction of one of the most sacred shrines in the natural world, a shrine that fulfilled some of the deepest emotional, imaginative, and intellectual needs of the human soul. "Dam Hetch-Hetchy! As well dam for water-tanks the people's cathedrals and churches, for no holier temple has ever been consecrated by the heart of man" (Teale, p. 320).

Throughout the 20th century the situation has worsened decade by decade with relentless commitment to making profit by ruining the planet for the uncertain benefit of the human. The great corporations have joined together so that a few establishments now control vast regions of the Earth. Assets of a few transnational corporations begin to rise toward the trillion-dollar range. Now, in these closing years of the 20th century, we find a growing concern for our responsibility to the generations who will live in the 21st century.

Perhaps the most valuable heritage we can provide for future generations is some sense of the Great Work that is before them of moving the human project from its devastating exploitation to a benign presence. We need to give them some indication of how the next generation can fulfill this work in an effective manner. For the success or failure of any historical age is the extent to which those living at that time have fulfilled the special role that history has imposed upon them. No age lives completely unto itself. Each age has only what it receives from the prior generation. Just now we have abundant evidence that the various species of life, the mountains and rivers, and even the vast ocean itself, which once we thought beyond serious impact from humans, will survive only in their damaged integrity.

The Great Work before us, the task of moving modern industrial civilization from its present devastating influence on the Earth to a more benign mode of presence, is not a role that we have chosen. It is a role given to us, beyond any consultation with ourselves. We did not choose. We were chosen by some power beyond ourselves for this historical task. We do not choose the moment of our birth, who our parents will be, our particular culture or the historical moment when we will be born. We do not choose the status of spiritual insight or political or economic conditions that will be the context of our lives. We are, as it were, thrown into existence with a challenge and a role that is beyond any personal choice. The nobility of our lives, however, depends upon the manner in which we come to understand and fulfill our assigned role.

Yet we must believe that those powers that assign our role must in that same act bestow upon us the ability to fulfill this role. We must believe that we are cared for and guided by these same powers that bring us into being.

Our own special role, which we will hand on to our children, is that of managing the arduous transition from the terminal Cenozoic to the emerging Ecozoic Era, the period when humans will be present to the planet as participating members of the comprehensive Earth community. This is our Great Work and the work of our children, just as Europeans in the 12th and 13th centuries were given the role of bringing a new cultural age out of the difficulties and strife of that long period from the sixth through the 11th centuries. At this time, the grandeur of the classical period had dissolved, the cities of Europe had declined, and life in all its physical and cultural aspects was carried on in the great castles and monasteries to constitute what came to be known as the manorial period in European history.

In the ninth and tenth centuries the Normans were invading the nascent culture of Europe from the north, the Magyars were moving in from the east, and the Muslims were advancing in Spain. Western civilization was situated in a very limited region under siege. In response to this threatening situation, medieval Europe toward the end of the 11th century began the crusading wars that united the nations of Europe and for two centuries engaged them in an eastward drive toward Jerusalem and the conquest of the Holy Land.

This period might be considered the beginning of the historical drive that has led European peoples in their quest for religious, cultural, political, and economic conquest of the world. This movement was continued through the period of discovery and control over the planet into our own times when the Western presence culminates politically in the United Nations and economically in such establishments as the World Bank, the International Monetary Fund, the World Trade Organization, and the World Business Council for Sustainable Development. We might even interpret this Western drive toward limitless dominion in all its forms as leading eventually to the drive toward human dominion over the natural world.

The immediate achievement, however, of the 13th century was the creation of the first integration of what became Western civilization. In this century new and dazzling achievements took place in the arts, in architecture, in speculative thinking, in literature. By raising up the medieval cathedrals a new and original architecture was created. In these soaring structures an artistic daring and refinement was manifest that has been equaled only in rare moments in the larger history of civilizations.

This was also the period of Francis, the poor man of Assisi who established in Western civilization both the spiritual ideal of detachment from Earthly possessions and an intimacy with the natural world. It was also the period of Thomas Aquinas, who originated Aristotelian studies, especially in the field of cosmology, in medieval Christian civilization. Within this context Thomas reinterpreted the entire range of Western theological thought. As the philosopher Alfred North Whitehead has noted, this was the time when the Western mind took on that critical keenness and reasoning process that made our modern scientific thought processes possible. In literature the incomparable Dante Alighieri produced his *Commedia* in the early 14th century, a time when Giotto was already beginning, with Cimabue, the great period of Italian painting.

The importance of recalling these shaping forces in the narrative account of Western civilization is that they arose as a response to the Dark Ages from the sixth through 11th centuries in Europe. We need to recall that in these and in so many other instances the dark periods of history are the creative periods; for these are the times when new ideas, arts, and institutions can be brought into being at the most basic level. Just as the brilliant period of medieval civilization arose out of these earlier conditions, so we might recall the period in China when, in the third century, the tribal invasions from the northwest had broken down the rule of the Han dynasty and for several centuries brought about a disunity throughout the empire. Yet this period of dissolution was also the period of Buddhist monks and Confucian scholars and artists who gave expression to new visions and new thoughts at the deepest levels of human consciousness. Scholars carrying the Taoist and Confucian traditions would later inspire literary figures such as Li Po, Tu Fu, and Po Chü-i in the T'ang period of the eighth century. Following the T'ang period the Sung period of the tenth through 14th centuries would bring forth such masterful interpretations of traditional Chinese thought as those presented by Chou Tun-i and Chu Hsi. Artists such as Ma Yuan and Hsia Kuei of the 12th century and poets such as Su Tung-p'o would complete this creative period in the cultural history of China. These are some of the persons who enabled the Chinese to survive as a people and as a culture and to discover new expressions of themselves after this long period of threats to their survival.

We must consider ourselves in these early years of the 21st century as also experiencing a threatening historical situation, although our situation is ultimately beyond comparison with any former period in Europe or in Asia. For those peoples were dealing with human adjustment to disturbances of human life patterns. They were not dealing with the disruption and even the termination of a geobiological period that had governed the functioning of the planet for some 67 million years. They were not dealing with anything comparable to the toxics in the air, the water, and the soil, or with the immense volume of chemicals dispersed throughout the planet. Nor were they dealing with the extinction of species or the altering of the climate on the scale of our present concern.

Yet we can be inspired by their example, their courage, and even by their teachings. For we are heirs to an immense intellectual heritage, to the wisdom traditions whereby they were able to fulfill the Great Work of their times. These traditions are not the transient thoughts or immediate insights of journalists concerned with the daily course of human affairs; these are expressions in human form of the principles guiding human life within the very structure and functioning of the universe itself.

We might observe here that the Great Work of a people is the work of all the people. No one is exempt. Each of us has our individual life pattern and responsibilities. Yet beyond these concerns each person in and through their personal work assists in the Great Work. Personal work needs to be aligned with the Great Work. This can be seen in the medieval period as the basic patterns of personal life and craft skills were aligned within the larger work of the civilizational effort. While this alignment is more difficult in these times it must remain an ideal to be sought.

We cannot doubt that we too have been given the intellectual vision, the spiritual insight, and even the physical resources we need for carrying out the transition that is demanded of these times, transition from the period when humans were a disruptive force on the planet Earth to the period when humans become present to the planet in a manner that is mutually enhancing.

---

## ABOUT THE AUTHOR

**Thomas Berry** entered the monastery in 1934 and earned a doctoral degree in Western cultural history in 1948. In that year he went to China to study Chinese language, culture, and religions. He was the director of the graduate program in the history of religion at Fordham University (1966–1979); and the founder and the director (1970–1995) of the Riverdale Center of Religious Research in Riverdale, New York. He is the author and co-author of numerous books, including *The Universe Story*, with Brian Swimme; and *The Great Work: Our Way into the Future*.

# five

# Consider the Lilies of the Field: How Should Christians Love Nature?[1]

## Sallie McFague

Should Christians love nature? Most have not over the last 2,000 years and many today still don't. In some circles, loving nature is pagan or what Goddess worshipers do. Of course, Christians should respect nature, use it carefully, and even protect it, but isn't loving it a bit extreme? *Should* we love nature? My answer is a resounding Yes. Christians should because the Christian God is embodied. That is what the incarnation claims. God does not despise physical reality but loves it and has become one with it. The Christian tradition is full of body language: the Word made flesh, the bread and wine that become the body and blood of Christ, the body of the church. Physical reality, earthly reality – bodies and nature – are central to an incarnational theology.

### PAYING ATTENTION

But how should we love nature? That is the more difficult and interesting question. Most people love nature in a general way and some even in a religious way. Most of us get a high from spectacular sunsets and cute panda bears; many of us have religious feelings in a cathedral of the pines. We all like to fuse with nature, enjoy oceanic feelings of oneness with it. But that is, of course, just another use of nature, a higher use than eating it or using it for recreational purposes, but a use nonetheless. Some Christians have loved nature – loved it as a way to God. The sacramental tradition, most evident in Roman Catholicism, Eastern Orthodoxy, and Anglicanism and including the wonderful voices of Augustine, Hildegard of Bingen, and Gerard Manley Hopkins, has told us, in Hopkins's words, that "the world is charged with the grandeur of God." The sacramental tradition assumes that God is present with us not only in the hearing of the Word and in the Eucharist but also in each and every being in creation. This tradition has helped to preserve and develop an appreciation for nature in a religion that, for the most part, has been indifferent to the natural world as well as justly accused of contributing to its deterioration and destruction. The sacramental tradition should be acknowledged as contributing to a sense of the world as valuable – indeed, as holy – because it is a symbol of the divine and can help us reach God.

The natural world is here, then, a stepping-stone in our pilgrimage to God – a means to an end. Its value does not lie primarily in itself; other lifeforms and other natural entities do not have intrinsic value. Rather, they are valuable as pathways connecting human beings to God, as ways we can express our relationship with God. Everything in the world can become a symbol for the divine-human relationship, as Augustine so eloquently says: "But what is it I love when I love You? Not the beauty of any bodily thing…Yet in a sense I do love light and melody and fragrance and food and embrace when I love my God – the light and the voice and the fragrance and the food and embrace in the soul…"[2]

But I would like to suggest a different way that Christians should love nature – a way in keeping with the earthly, bodily theology suggested by the tradition's incarnationalism, a way that allows us to love the natural world for its intrinsic worth, to love it, in all its differences and detail, in itself, for itself. Francis of Assisi epitomizes this sensibility in his praise of the sun, moon, earth, and water as his brothers and sisters. Emily Dickinson suggested this way of loving nature when she wrote to a friend that the only commandment that she never broke was to "consider the lilies of the field" – not to use them to decorate her yard or pick them for her table (or even for the altar), but just *consider* them.[3] How Christians should love nature is by obeying a simple but very difficult axiom: *pay attention to it.*

But how can we learn to pay attention to something other than ourselves? What does it mean to really pay attention? Iris Murdoch, the British novelist, gives a clue when she says, "It is a *task* to come to see the world as it is." We will bracket for the moment the thorny hermeneutical issue implicit in the phrase "the world as it is," focusing now on the "me" versus "other" issue – the problem of attending to another, any other. Murdoch's suggestion is that paying attention is difficult and contrary to how we usually see the world, which is, as she says, in terms of our "fat relentless ego."[4] She gives a personal example: "I am looking out of my window in an anxious and resentful state of mind, brooding perhaps on some damage done to my prestige. Then suddenly I observe a kestrel. In a moment everything is altered. There is nothing but kestrel. And when I return to thinking of the other matter it seems less important."[5] There is a natural and proper part of us, she adds, that takes "a self-forgetful pleasure in the sheer, alien pointless independent existence of animals, birds, stones, and trees."[6] The message is that we pay attention to difference, that we really learn to see what is different from ourselves. That is not easy. We can acknowledge a thing in its difference if it is important to us or useful to us, but realizing that something other than oneself is real, in itself, for itself, is difficult. To acknowledge another being as different – perhaps even indifferent to me, as for instance a hovering kestrel – is, for most of us, a feat of the imagination.

One of the greatest contributions of contemporary feminism is its celebration of difference. To date this has been limited principally to differences among human beings – recognizing that there is no universal human being nor even any essential woman. As a recent book on liberation theologies comments, "People only look alike when you cannot be bothered to look at them closely."[7] But how does one learn to celebrate difference; differences among people and differences among lifeforms? How can we know and accept real differences? The first step, we have suggested, is by paying attention. Art often helps us to do so. Art stops, freezes, and frames bits of reality and, by so doing, helps us to pay attention, as for instance in this haiku by a Japanese poet;

An old silent pond
Into the pond a frog jumps.
Splash! Silence again.

The poet has put a frame around this moment. As novelist Frederick Buechner comments on this haiku, "What the frame does is enable us to see not just something about the moment but the moment itself in all its ineffable ordinariness and particularity. The chances are that if we had been passing when the frog jumped, we wouldn't have noticed a thing or, noticing it, wouldn't have given it a second thought."[8] Art frames fragments of our world; paintings, poetry, novels, sculpture, dance, music help us to look at colors, sounds, bodies, events, characters – whatever – with full attention. Something is lifted out of the world and put into a frame so that we can, perhaps for the first time, see it. Most of the time we do not *see*; we pass a tree, an early spring crocus, the face of another human being, and we do not marvel at these wonders, because we do not see their specialness, their individuality, their difference. As Joseph Wood Krurch reminds us: "It is not easy to live in that continuous awareness of things which alone is true living…the faculty of wonder tires easily…"[9]

Simone Weil deepens the meaning of paying attention with her comment that "absolute attention is prayer." She does not say that prayer is absolute attention, but that absolute attention is prayer. By paying attention to something she says, we are, in fact praying. May Sarton, poet and essayist, comments on this phrase from Weil: "When you think about it, we almost never pay absolute attention. The minute we do, something happens. We see whatever we're looking at with such attention, and something else is given – a sort of revelation. I looked at the heart of a daffodil in this way the other day – deep down. It was a pale yellow one, but deep down, at the center, it was emerald green – like a green light. It was amazing."[10] By paying attention to some fragment, some piece of matter in the world, we are in fact praying. Is this what Alice Walker means when she writes in *The Color Purple*, "I think it pisses God off if you walk by the color purple in a field somewhere and don't notice it"?[11] Is this what an incarnational theology, an earthly, bodily theology, implies? Perhaps it is.

We are asking the question, how should a Christian love nature? The answer emerging is that we must pay attention – detailed, careful, concrete attention – to the world that lies around us but is not us. We must do this *because we cannot love what we do not know*.[12] This profound truism is contained in the phrase we have all uttered at some time: "If they really knew me, they wouldn't love me," implying that only love based on real knowledge is valuable. We must, as Murdoch says, try to see "the world as it is" in order to love it. To really love nature (and not just ourselves in nature or nature as useful to us – even its use as a pathway to God), we must pay attention *to it*. Love and knowledge go together; we can't have the one without the other.

## Two Ways of Seeing the World

I would like to suggest that a branch of science, nature writing, can help us learn to pay attention. The kind of paying attention that one sees in good nature writing suggests a paradigm for us. Nature writing is not scientific writing that hides behind pseudo-objectivity; rather, it combines acute, careful observation with a kind of loving empathy for and delight in its object. In fact, as we shall see, it is more like the interaction of two subjects than the usual dualism of a subject observing an object. Nature writer Edward Abbey describes it as "sympathy for the object under study, and more than sympathy, love. A love based on prolonged contact and interaction… Observation informed by sympathy, love, intuition."[13] The best nature writing has this sense of personal testimony and detail, what Murdoch calls engagement with the "unutterable particularity" of the natural world.[14] In the writings of Annie Dillard, Gretel Ehrlich, Barry Lopez, Aldo Leopold, and Alice Walker, we see this sense of personal call opening the self to the surprise and delight of deeper and deeper engagement with concrete detail, the particularities and differences that comprise the natural world. It is a way of seeing, a kind of paying attention, that thrives on differences and detail. It is also an interactive kind of knowing – the knower must be open to the known, be sympathetic to, and engaged by the known. It is a knowing that is infused with loving, a love that wants to know more.

Let me illustrate this kind of nature writing by contrasting two very different ways of seeing the world. The first example is Annie Dillard's description of a goldfish named Ellery. The detail in this passage – Dillard's paying attention to the particularities of Ellery – calls forth in her, and in me, a sense of wonder and affection.

> This Ellery cost me twenty-five cents. He is a deep red-orange, darker than most goldfish. He steers short distances mainly with his slender red lateral fins; they seem to provide impetus for going backward, up, or down. It took me a few days to discover his ventral fins; they are completely transparent and all but invisible – dream fins... He can extend his mouth, so it looks like a length of pipe; he can shift the angle of his eyes in his head so he can look before and behind himself, instead of simply out to his side. His belly, what there is of it, is white ventrally, and a patch of this white extends up his sides – the variegated Ellery. When he opens his gill slits he shows a thin crescent of silver where the flap overlapped – as though all his brightness were sunburn...
>
> This fish, two bits' worth, has a coiled gut, a spine radiating fine bones, and a brain. Just before I sprinkle his food flakes into his bowl, I rap three times on the bowl's edge; now he is

conditioned, and swims to the surface when I rap. And, he has a heart.[15]

Every time I read this passage I am unnerved by the juxtaposition of twenty-five cents with the elaborateness, cleverness, and sheer glory of this tiny bit of matter named Ellery. I am learning both by reading nature writing like this as well as from my own experience that the closer attention I pay to whatever piece of the world is before me the more amazed I am by it. It is not that I "see God in it" in any direct or even general way; rather, it is the specialness, the difference, the intricacy, the "unutterable particularity" of each creature, event, or aspect of nature that calls forth wonder and delight – a knowing that calls forth love and a love that wants to know more. "Amazing revelations" come through the earth, not above it or in spite of it. An incarnational theology encourages us to dare to love nature – all the different bodies, both human and those of other lifeforms, on our earth – to find them valuable and wonderful in themselves, for themselves. That is what an incarnational view assures us: it is all right to love nature; in fact, we should. We pray to God through knowing and thereby being able to love all the wild and wonderful diversity of creatures. The prayer is simple: "*Vive les différences*. Long live the differences."

A very different way of seeing the world is epitomized in the now-famous whole-earth picture of our planet from the NASA files – the photograph of the earth as a blue and white marble floating in black empty space, lonely and vulnerable. Unlike the subject-subjects kind of knowing in nature writing, it can be seen as an example of subject-object knowing. As one commentator notes, "This distancing, disengaged, abstract, and literalizing epistemology is quintessentially embodied in the whole Earth image... From a distance of tens of thousands of miles away, transcendent, serene, and unaffected, we survey the whole Earth at once."[16] Since the whole-earth image is for many people *the* ecological icon, this comment may seem strange. And it did initially to me as well, for I use it in my book *The Body of God* to raise consciousness about the fragility of our planet. But there is a somber underside to this bright, aesthetically pleasing image: it eliminates all detail, not only the smells and sounds and tastes of earth (the blood, sex, feces, sweat, and decay that make up the life of the planet) but also all the signs of deterioration, rape, and pillage that have resulted in holes in the ozone, topsoil erosion, and clear-cut forests. The view from space is of a clean, sterile, beautiful – and manageable – planet, rather than the going-to-pieces one we actually inhabit. The whole-earth view simplifies and objectifies the earth: it is the outsider's view, the spectator view, as in astronaut Russell Schweichert's description of it as "a blue and white Christmas ornament." The earth is a plaything, a beach ball, a yo-yo, a lollipop. This objectifying view underlies computer games in which the earth is destroyed on the screen but instantly restored by the reset button. We can do what we want with this earth, for in the astronaut's view, there are other possibilities, other planets, as we read on the *Star Trek* bumper sticker: "Beam me up, Scotty, this planet sucks." This view from space is also, ironically, claimed to be the "God's eye view": as we are, so God is also distant and disengaged from the earth, finding it pleasing only if all the mud and guts, all the blood and sweat, all the billions of creatures, from creepy-crawly ones to two-legged ones, are invisible. "The whole Earth poster decorating the wall of a Manhattan apartment is no substitute for a true belonging to place."[17] Indeed, it is not.

## THE ARROGANT EYE VS. THE LOVING EYE

Seeing Ellery and seeing the earth from space: behind these two very different ways of seeing, of paying attention, lie two different ways of knowing: what one commentator calls "the loving eye" versus "the arrogant eye."[18] We want now to reflect in some depth on the differences between these two ways of seeing. We are suggesting that a certain kind of paying attention, a certain kind of knowing, is how Christians ought to love nature. Let us now analyze this claim.

But we are immediately drawn up short: we are trying, as Murdoch says, to see the world as it is so that we can love it rightly. But how, what, *is* it? How can we "see the world as it is"? There is no "natural" view of nature. We know there is no innocent eye, that what we see is determined in large measure by where we stand. The importance of social location for interpreting the world is by now a platitude, but that does not make it any less true. We see from our *Umwelten*, our self-worlds, which are personal, cultural, even genetic. As two-legged creatures of a certain height, formed by specific personal histories as well as by different gender, racial, economic, national, and cultural realities, we each see the world differently.

Hence, when we turn now to an investigation of paying attention, of a certain kind of seeing and knowing, we must remind ourselves that all seeing, all knowing, is perspectival. The specific issue with which we are concerned – how should we love nature? – will necessarily be based on perspectival knowing. The question is, which perspective, which kind of seeing, is better for nature?

There are many kinds of seeing, many kinds of knowing, but the contrast suggested between the arrogant eye and the loving eye epitomized by the whole-earth image and the description of Ellery is a fruitful one for our purposes. The terms are from feminist philosopher Marilyn Frye, who describes the arrogant eye as acquisitive, seeing everything in relation to the self – as either "for me" or "against me." It organizes everything in reference to oneself and cannot imagine "the possibility that the Other is independent, indifferent."[19] The arrogant eye simplifies in order to control, denying complexity and mystery, since it cannot control what it cannot understand. Frye illustrates the arrogant eye with the example of how it has functioned to exploit and enslave women, "breaking" and "training" them so as to serve male interests. This breaking and training can be so subtle that the oppressed eventually willingly conforms to the wishes of the oppressor – as in the pimp-prostitute relationship – or, more commonly, the way the standardized visual image of women's bodies in the media induce women into extreme diets and even anorexia in order to conform to the arrogant male gaze. The arrogant eye is also the patriarchal eye, which, of course, is not limited to the male perceptual standpoint. All of us in the Western world share this gaze, especially as we move the object of the eye's focus from women to nature. Like women, the natural world has been the object of the arrogant eye: we have broken and trained other lifeforms – domestic, farm, and zoo animals – to do our will and have perceived the forests, air and water, plants and oceans as existing solely for our benefit. The natural world with its lifeforms has not been seen as having its health and integrity in itself, for itself, but rather in and for us. We can scarcely imagine what it would mean for nature to be considered Other in the sense of being independent of and indifferent to human interests and desires. We Westerners all perceive with the arrogant eye. If you doubt this, answer the following question: How important would creation be if we were not part of it? Can we honestly say, "It is good!" and mean it? Don't we always implicitly believe that it would be considerably less good without us, in fact, perhaps not much good? We never ask of another human being, "What are you good for?" but we often ask that question of other lifeforms and entities in nature. The assumed answer is, in one form or another, "good for me and other human beings."

The loving eye, on the other hand, acknowledges complexity, mystery, and difference. It recognizes that boundaries exist between the self and the other, that the interests of other persons (and the natural world) are not identical with one's own, that knowing another takes time and attention. In Frye's words, "It is the eye of one who knows that to know the seen, one must consult something other than one's own interests and fears and imagination. One must look at the thing. One must look and listen and check and question… It knows the complexity of the other as something which will forever present new things to be known. The science of the loving eye would favor The Complexity Theory of Truth and presuppose The Endless Interestingness of the Universe."[20]

The loving eye is not the opposite of the arrogant eye: it does not substitute self-denial, romantic fusion, and subservience for distance, objectification, and exploitation. Rather it suggests something novel in Western ways of knowing: acknowledgment of and respect for the other as *subject*.

Rather than the classic relationship between knower and known as subject versus object, the model here is two subjects: what I see is another subject (like me in some ways). What I know is another being with its own integrity and interests – and this model is extended to the natural world and its lifeforms. In other words, rather than the standard paradigm for knowledge being subject-object (with myself as subject and all others, including other human beings, as objects), we are suggesting two subjects. Feminist philosopher Lorraine Code puts it this way: "It is surely no more preposterous to argue that people should try to know physical objects in the nuanced way that they know their friends than it is to argue that they should try to know people in the unsubtle way that they claim to know physical objects."[21] This seemingly slight perceptual shift can have enormous implications. It means that the route to knowledge is slow, open, full of surprises, interactive and reciprocal, as well as attentive to detail and difference. And it will be embodied. The disembodied, distant, transcendent, simplifying, objectifying, quick and easy arrogant eye becomes the embodied, lowly, immanent, complexifying, subjectifying, proximate, and "make-do" loving eye. The pure mind's eye becomes the messy body's eye, and those lowly senses (the so-called female ones of taste, touch, and smell) are allowed back into the knowledge game.

In the West, however, knowledge has been associated almost exclusively with sight and, since Plato, sight has been associated with the mind (as in "the eye of the mind").[22] This kind of vision discovers truth by recognizing likenesses – universals – and by dissociating itself from the messiness, complexity, and teeming differences of the body and the earth. This view of sight connects truth with what transcends the earth: we can see the more universal and hence "truer" truth the further we are from the bodily. For this kind of truth, we need the God's eye view, the angelic view: we must objectify in order to simplify, we must distance ourselves in order to see the big picture. Recall the whole-earth image: we can see the whole object only from a great distance; and it is then easy to say high-sounding things about the earth, for instance, that it is a beautiful Christmas ornament. Of course, such statements have little to do with the actual mind-boggling unknown or little-known mud-and-guts complexity of the planet's lifesystems, let alone the baffling mystery of even one of its lifeforms, from an earthworm to a human being.

A very different kind of vision from the so-called God's eye view is suggested by the phrase "locking eyes." Imagine shifting your vision from the picture of the whole earth to the eyes of another person – not to look at him or her, but into their eyes. Sight is not necessarily the eye of the mind; it can also be the eye of the body – in fact, it rightly and properly is. When we lock eyes something happens: we become two subjects, not subject and object. Locking eyes is perhaps the ultimate subject-subject experience: it is what lovers do and what nursing mothers do with their babies. A version of it can happen with other animals, especially the eerie experience of locking eyes with a lowland gorilla or chimpanzee at a zoo. It is possible even with a tree or plant. It all depends on whether we can "see without staring."[23] The loving eye, paying attention to another (another person, animal, tree, plant, whatever) is not staring; it is, in Martin Buber's suggestive phrase, relating to the other more like a Thou than an It. There is nothing sentimental or weak-minded about this: it is simply a refusal to assume that subjectivity is my sole prerogative. Iris Murdoch puts it bluntly, "Love is the extremely difficult realization that something other than oneself is real. Love…is the discovery of reality."[24] The loving eye is not the sentimental, mushy, soft eye; rather, it is the realistic, tough, no-nonsense eye, acknowledging what is so difficult for us to recognize: that reality is made up of *others*. Love, then, is no big deal or a specific virtue reserved for Christians; it is simply facing facts. It is, in a nice twist, being "objective."

But as we all know, this is not what objectivity usually means. In fact, just the opposite. It has been reserved for the mind's eye, the distant eye, the arrogant eye, the eye that can objectify the world. This eye lies behind the Western scientific understanding of objectivity. From the time of René Descartes on, science has advanced on the assumption that what is known is passive and inert, laid out before the subject so it can be reduced to its smallest parts, studied exhaustively, and thereby known. As

Hans Jonas puts it, "I see without the object's doing anything... I have nothing to do but to look and the object is not affected by that... and I am not affected... The gain is the concept of objectivity."[25] Feminists and others have criticized this view of objectivity, seeing it as a mask for Western male privilege as well as for technological exploitation of women and nature.[26]

## THE SUBJECT-SUBJECTS MODEL

What is the alternative? There may well be more than one, but an intriguing possibility is the suggestion from feminists, ecologists, process philosophers, phenomenologists, and others that we pattern our knowledge, all knowledge, on a subject-to-subjects model, and more specifically, on friendship. This will involve the eye – the loving eye – but also the other senses, for it moves the eye from the mind (and the heavens) to the body (and the earth). It will result in an embodied kind of knowledge of other subjects who, like ourselves, occupy specific bodies in specific locations on this messy, muddy, wonderful, complex, mysterious earth.

But appreciation for the particular and concrete is not the way I began my acquaintance with the natural world. I am going to become autobiographical now, using my own experience with nature to illustrate how I've come to believe a Christian should love nature: as subject to subject, on the analogy of friendship. My love for nature began when I was fourteen years old, hiking in the White Mountains in Vermont. I was not captive to the Western Platonic-Cartesian-Scientific subject-object dualism (of which I was blissfully unaware) that I and other feminists have criticized. Just the opposite: I wallowed in oceanic feelings of oneness-with-it-all. I fused with nature: lying on mountaintops covered with billowing clouds, I sank into Wagnerian religious raptures. The New England transcendental poets were my favorites – I could sense Ralph Waldo Emerson's "oversoul" enveloping me as I relaxed into the arms of Mother Nature. I was one with nature. As a critic of deep ecology (a sensibility close to mine at that time) writes: "The correct metaphor for such fusion is of a lonely but megalomaniacal pond sucking up all the water of the world and becoming itself the ocean."[27] Indeed. I was not relating to nature as subject to subject but as the one and only Subject: I was the whole, the only one.

Gradually, over the years, I changed. I became "Elleryfied," interested in detail, in difference. I learned the names of some birds and wildflowers – a study that encourages paying attention to what is other than oneself. In fact, you can't identify a bird or a flower unless you pay close attention to detail. Such a simple desire as wanting to know the names of things is an opening to other attitudes toward the natural world. One day while hiking, I recall coming across a bi-footed, tri-colored violet, a rare and extraordinarily beautiful, tiny flower. It was all alone by the side of the trail. I had never seen one before. I squatted down to look at it closely and for a few minutes it was my whole world. I was transfixed by its beauty, its specialness, its fragility, and by the sense of privilege I felt to be looking at it. I was, I believe, seeing it as a subject; that is, I was relating to it with a recognition of its own intrinsic value quite apart from me. I was surprised and delighted by it and felt respect for it as well as a desire to care for it (in fact, I thought of putting some rocks around it to protect it from a careless hiker's boot, but decided this was too controlling). The violet was not a subject in the way you or I or one of the higher mammals is, but I could recognize its otherness and yet at the same time feel a connection with it. It was not simply an object to me. Rather, it had its own very special being, which surprised and delighted me even as I appreciated and felt empathy and concern for it. Which analogy is more appropriate for describing this experience – a subject viewing an object or a subject trying to know another subject?

Lorraine Code calls the subject-subjects analogy an ecological model of knowing because it assumes that we always know in relationships: we are not solitary individuals who choose to be in relationship with others, but we *are* in relationships, from before our birth until after our death.[28] Hence, the language of relationship – respect, reciprocity, interest in the particular, listening, openness, paying attention, care, concern – all this sort of language becomes relevant to how we know others. The way we come to know another, for instance a friend, becomes a model for ecological knowledge: it is a practical knowledge with the goal of responding to the other in terms of their own well-being. We want to know them better so we can empathize with and care for them more appropriately. It is a more-or-less knowledge, based on hints and nuances, open to surprises and changes, and infinitely more complex than knowing an object. Feminists have come to realize that knowing other women, especially across racial lines, involves this sort of thing – recognizing that the other must be taken as a subject in all her own irreducible particularity and difference. Knowledge of an African-American woman by a white woman, for instance, is proximate and always open to revision, because it is a practical knowledge, concerned first of all not with a theory about the other but with her concrete well-being.

To sum up: we have been asking how a Christian should love nature and have suggested that practicing the loving eye, that is, recognizing the reality of things apart from the self and appreciating them in their specialness and distinctiveness, is a critical first step. It is opposed to the arrogant eye, the objectifying, manipulative, and disengaged kind of knowledge that supposes that I am the only subject and the rest of reality merely an object for me or against me. We have suggested further that a helpful way to think about knowledge with the loving eye is in terms of a subject knowing another subject, especially on the analogy of friendship.

There are several things to note about this model. First of all, it is not the reverse of the subject-object model, but a *different* model. The subject-object model assumes a hierarchical dualism of one over another. It is the basic pattern for a number of other common hierarchical dualisms: male/female, whites/people of color, rich/poor, heterosexual/homosexual, West/East, North/South – and humans/nature. One solution proposed for this problematic pattern is to reverse it (female/male or nature/humans), but the difficulty here is that the domination intrinsic to this way of thinking continues. The arrogant eye remains; it simply becomes someone else's. The model we are suggesting is a different one, not the old one reversed. It is a relational model derived from the evolutionary, ecological picture of reality, a picture that underscores both radical unity *and* radical individuality. It suggests a different basic sensibility for all our knowing and doing and a different *kind* of knowing and doing, whether with other people or other lifeforms. It is a different posture and presence in the world, in all aspects of the world. It says: "I am a subject and live in a world of many other different subjects."

The second thing to note about this model is that what I know is many subjects. The model is not subject-subject, replacing the singular object with a singular subject, but subject-subjects. The other is a multitude, a myriad of subjects. If the other were one subject, we could know all subjects by knowing just one – all others would be forms or reflections of the one basic or universal subject. Presumably this would be the human subject with all other subjects simply variations of it. But just as feminists have insisted that there is no essential human being, no one type which can stand for all, so also we must insist that there is no one, essential subject that I know. In the subject-subjects model, I know a world of subjects, different subjects.

The third thing to note, then, is the *differences* among subjects. We have praised difference as our planet's glory (the heart of the daffodil, the color purple, the uniqueness of each human face), but difference also means that we will not respond to all subjects in the same way. The AIDS virus, just like a wood tick, is a subject in its own world. This does not mean, however, that when it attacks my body I should honor it or allow it to have its way. I should fight it (if "natural" can ever be used literally, it would be of such a response). The subject-subjects model could, however, in this case, help me see that the virus is not against me; as a subject, it is simply "doing its thing" in its own world. The model would help me to avoid seeing it as punishment: the world is not organized around me, for my benefit or my punishment. In an unbelievably complex world of billions of subjects, the sole criterion cannot be what is "good for me." In this instance, then, the model would operate to neutralize demonizing fantasies.

Chickens being raised for human consumption in inhumane conditions present a different level of subject, and my response would be different. In the subject-subjects model I might decide that the cruelty involved in commercial chicken farming is such that I will not eat chicken. Another possible response is to eat only free-range chickens or to work for legislation to improve the conditions under which chickens are raised. Vegetarianism is also an option, but not the only one (Native American traditions that have related to animals as subjects have also condoned hunting and meat eating).

## Care or Rights?

What is beginning to emerge from the subject-subjects model is a clue for an environmental ethic of care. At the present time, a lively debate among environmentalists concerns a "rights" versus a "care" ethic. A rights ethic seeks to extend the rights accorded to human beings since the Enlightenment – the right to "life, liberty, and the pursuit of happiness" – to all animals and even forests, oceans, and other elements of the ecosystem. A rights ethic functions on the model of the solitary human individual (originally the landed, white, Western male); it details what one such person owes to another similar one. This ethic is beset with a number of problems when applied to the natural world. Does the lamb or the wolf have the right to survive – does the wolf have the right to eat the lamb for dinner, or does the lamb have the right to protection against the wolf's needs? Can such an ethic address the complex issue of biodiversity or only the more simple one of individual animal rights? Is it an appropriate and helpful one for the natural world, given its human, individualistic base?

A care ethic, on the other hand, is based on the model of subjects in relationship, although the subjects are not necessarily all human ones and the burden of ethical responsibility can fall unequally. The language of care – interest, concern, respect, nurture, paying attention, empathy, relationality – seems more appropriate for human interaction with the natural world, for engendering helpful attitudes toward the environment,

than does the rights language. As with friends, we come to know and love
the natural world with an open and inquiring mind, trying to discern
what will be best for its health and well-being. Often there is no easy
answer, for it is seldom so clean a matter as one creature's rights over
against another's.

A case in point: logging companies engaged in clear-cutting old-
growth forests replant the areas with a monoculture – a single species of
fast-growing tree – claiming they are restoring what they have removed.
Thus, they have presumably respected the right of the forest to survive.
However, these monoculture forests are not only vulnerable to fire and
blight, but they lack the rich, complex diverse insect, bird, and mammal
life as well as underbrush and underground root systems of a natural
forest with its many different kinds of trees. In fact, they are not forests
at all, but plantations of single-species trees. The appropriate ethic in
this instance is not one of rights but of care – paying attention to what
truly constitutes forests and then providing the conditions to maintain
and restore them; for instance, selective tree cutting for intact forests and
reseeding for biodiversity in clear-cut areas.

But is all of this *Christian*? What makes the subject-subjects model
a Christian option? Is it commensurate with the radical, destabilizing,
inclusive love of Jesus? It appears to be, for Jesus is reputed to have made
the classic subject-subjects statement when he said, "Love your enemies."
Treat the person who is against you, perhaps even out to kill you, as a
subject, as someone deserving respect and care, as the Good Samaritan
treated his enemy in need. The subject-subjects model is counter-cultural:
it is opposed to the religion of Economism, to utilitarian thinking, to
seeing the world as for me or against me. So is Christianity. Christianity is
distinctly opposed to the subject-object way of thinking, to the arrogant
eye. If Jesus could say, "Love your enemies," surely he would find the
much milder statement, "Love nature," perfectly acceptable. If enemies
are to be shown respect and care, should not other lifeforms also, as
well as the habitats that support them? Loving nature this way, not with
mushy feeling or charity, but with respect for its otherness, its Thouness,

and with a desire to care for it, will not be easy. But loving other humans, especially enemies, is not either. Christianity is not an easy religion. As counter-cultural, it will make outrageous demands, like "Love your enemies" and "Love nature."

## MAP OR HIKE?

So what does all this come to? How should we relate to the natural world? More like to another subject than to an object, and to a subject, many subjects, who are very different from ourselves. This is extremely difficult. We can learn how difficult by looking at the analogy of how feminists came to realize that there is no such thing as woman, but only women. Early in the feminist movement, white, North American, middle-class women glibly used the phrase "as a woman"; later, they came to recognize that "as a woman" was a mask for their own particular, racial, sexual orientation, or class version of what it means to be a woman. To understand what very different women in various other social locations experience, white North American, middle-class women would have to become, as Maria Lugones puts it, "world-travelers," or as Elizabeth Spelman suggests, "apprentices."[29] In other words, they would have to give up the center, admit ignorance, pack their bags, and go on a journey, a journey that would require them to listen and pay attention to others. It is not enough to imagine how women in very different circumstances might experience their lives; rather, one must learn about the lives of these different subjects much as a traveler learns her way around in a foreign country or as an apprentice studies with an expert crafts-person. Might we need to do something similar with nature – that is, to consider ourselves travelers in the world of nature we do not know, apprentices who need to listen to the others in that world?

An example might help. Anne Sellar, a British feminist who spent six months teaching at an Indian university, hoped to instill feminist theory into the minds of her women students.[30] Instead, she learned from them about their lives, for their notions of family, feminism, and patriarchy were radically different from hers – not to mention the importance of dowries and of instructing village women about infant diarrhea. Nothing was more important to these women than family; and feminism was a bad word, symbolizing all they disliked about Western civilization – individualism, sexual promiscuity, and loss of femininity. Sellar became a world-traveler and an apprentice: she said she went to India with a map – a theory of how to teach the women about feminism – but ended up taking a hike, learning by paying attention to the lay of the land, ready for discoveries around the next bend in the trail, realizing that she was in an unknown place without a map, one that would require the full engagement of all her senses and skills.

Map or hike? Which metaphor is the better one for our relationship with the natural world? We have depended heavily on the map metaphor, for we believe we *know* what nature is. As Thomas Berry says, nature has become resource, recreation, or retreat for human beings: it supplies our needs, gives us a place to play, and refreshes us spiritually. But what if we saw it more like a different subject, one vastly different from ourselves with infinite particular entities and strange, wonderful lifeforms? What if we saw nature as "a world of difference"?[31] Then we might realize that we have to take a hike (without a map), become world-travelers, become apprentices to nature.

In other words, imagination is thin compared to the perception of other persons and real things. What we imagine a person or entity in nature to be cannot begin to compare with the depth, richness, detail, and complexity of the simplest object – even the heart of a daffodil, let alone another person. Looking at the world with full attention – any bit of it – should stun us, leaving us amazed and wanting to know more. We come to value the world and want it to prosper through local, particular knowledge, for the world as it is is more amazing, more interesting, than any theory or image about it. If we practiced this sort of attention we might come to say with Annie Dillard, "My God what a world. There is no accounting for one second of it."[32]

To return to the autobiographical and to conclude: I have found that the route to some of these insights is through paying attention to the particular, to what is, as it were, in one's own path – as, for instance, a bi-footed, tri-colored violet. Anything will do, as Ellery, the twenty-five cent goldfish, illustrates. In fact, the smaller the better in some respects. A little city park is probably a better place for one's lessons than the Grand Canyon. I took my last sabbatical in Vancouver, British Columbia, and every morning walked in a small city park – Jericho Park, an area of a few acres beside the bay. I came to know it very well. It has a duck pond and small wooded section. It also has lots of rabbits (probably unwanted released Easter bunnies), several kinds of ducks, many species of birds (including red-winged blackbirds), blue and purple lupines in the summer as well as blackberries, and even an occasional Great Blue Heron, raccoon, and red-necked pheasant. I always felt interest and even some excitement when I started out, because the sky and clouds varied every day, and I never knew what animals I might see. I came to love this small plot of land; its familiarity and its daily concrete, particular delights combined to make me feel at home there. My knowledge of the park was certainly not a mind's eye experience; rather, it was a body's eye one – my eyes reveled in the scurrying of a rabbit only a few feet away, the glory of a field of fuchsia sweet peas, the sight of a heron resting on one leg. And knowledge of this park involved my other senses as well – the smell of the salt water, the sound of bird calls, the touch of a flower's petal. These are the embodied senses, the ones that remind us that we are involved and open in our knowing: we cannot touch without being touched, or hear without listening to what comes to us. The initiative is not just ours. As I walked in this little park, soaking up its sounds and smells and sights, I came to know it – and love it – more or less as I would a friend.

But why bother with such unimportant, autobiographical, personal stories? What possible relevance can such idiosyncratic and seemingly minor incidents have for the well-being of a planet that is falling to pieces? Isn't this sort of caring for a small bit of the earth just sentimentality? Shouldn't Christians love nature in terms of the global picture – be concerned about the ozone layer, the rain forests, the greenhouse effect?

Shouldn't we love the "whole earth" rather than Jericho Park? Yes, surely, but there is a connection here; in fact, a critical one. No one, I believe, loves the whole earth except as she or he loves a particular bit of it. It is more likely, I suspect, that loving Ellery or Jericho Park – appreciating, respecting, and caring for them – will move one to care for the whole earth, than admiring the NASA image will generate the energy and concern to save Ellery and Jericho Park.

Here are a few thoughts along these lines from some wise people. From Alice Walker:

> Helped are those who find the courage to do at least one small thing each day to help the existence of another – plant, animal, river, human being. They shall be joined by a multitude of the timid.[33]

From the Veda:

> O God, scatterer of ignorance and darkness,
>     grant me your strength.
> May all beings regard me with the eye of a friend,
>     and I all beings!
> With the eye of a friend may each single being regard
>     all others.[34]

And from Rabbi Abraham Heschel:

> Just to be is a blessing.
> Just to live is holy.[35]

ABOUT THE AUTHOR

**Sallie McFague,** B.A., B.D., M.A., Ph.D., is distinguished Theologian in Residence at Vancouver School of Theology. Prior to that, she was Carpenter Professor of Theology at Vanderbilt Divinity School. Sallie is the author of several books including *Metaphorical Theology: Models of God in Religious Language; The Body of God: An Ecological Theology; Life Abundant: Rethinking Theology and Economy for a Planet in Peril;* and *Super, Natural Christians: How We Should Love Nature.*

# six

# On Being a Postdenominational Priest in a Postdenominational Era[1]

## *Matthew Fox*

Howard Thurman has written of a "soul-searching conflict of loyalty" that occurs in our lives. I certainly went through that kind of soul-searching in my move from the church of my ancestors to the Episcopal church.

### OUTSIDE THE RUSTY GATE

In February 1994 I had a dream that moved me to tears (something that happens rarely in my dreams), and I recorded it:

*Ash Wednesday, February 16, 1994*
*Dream last night (I cried in the dream) – I'm at an old gate, outdoors, made of iron. It is like a cemetery gate and I hear the statement (have I been teaching it?): "Everyone is here for a purpose. God has a role for everyone."*

*And then I hear a question: "Has my role been to make creation spirituality known?" With that I cry because of the simplicity of it and the clarity of it and (I think) because it says something about my life and its many choices, including the recent one to become Episcopalian and the Vatican's choice to dump me. And also because it suggests that maybe my life and life work have had some meaning after all.*

In reflecting on this dream, I suspect that being "outside the old gate" means being outside the church as I have known it and also outside the modern culture. Both of these structures are getting very old – indeed the gate is a *cemetery* gate, thus a dying church and a dying modern structure. There is grief work to do – ashes to bless ourselves with – as we want to give them a decent burial. Yet my vocation remains alive – I am *here for a purpose* and there is continuity in my work, that of making creation spirituality known. Indeed, all our vocations are alive. That is why we are still outside the cemetery gate and not within. Ash Wednesday is a prelude to Easter Day. The gate is an iron gate and it is rusting. This speaks to me of the modern age, which is industrial and whose metaphor in the 19th century was the iron horse, that engine that spanned the continent but destroyed the buffalo and the indigenous peoples' way of life and so much more. Now that era is a cemetery, a rust belt, and we are asked to let the dead bury the dead and move on. The key to our moving on from the modern era will be our heart work – the grief and the joy that come from doing the true work for which we are here.

I recognized the iron gate in the dream as being the gates that surround the Luxembourg Garden in Paris, located midway between the Latin Quarter and the Catho. The order and the institutional church rejected what I had learned beginning in my Paris days. The fact that I am expelled from the garden has obvious archetypal meanings; yet the garden is no longer a garden but a cemetery; and the gate is no longer beautiful and polished but is rusting. All this speaks to me of death and rebirth; of letting go and moving on; of grief work and – with the words that accompanied the dream – hope for the future. For my existence in the garden was for the same purpose as my existence beyond the garden. I am no longer protected by the *cloister* and the garden it represented, as in my novitiate days. But the vocation continues. The tears were of grief – for all that might have been (what if the Dominicans, instead of turning on me, had sent another brother out to work with me?). But the tears were essentially tears of joy and relief and beauty. For they did not flow because the gates were closed; they flowed at the moment when the voice said, "Your vocation has been to make creation spirituality known." Joy is deeper than sorrow. In spite of the expulsion, my vocation continues. Inside or outside, my vocation goes on. Everyone's does.

## Modern Era Yielding to the Postmodern in Religion

When I was dismissed by the Vatican, the first thing I did was sit down and meditate. In my meditation it came to me that the Vatican had made me *a postdenominational priest in a postdenominational era.*

What is postdenominationalism? What does it mean to be a post-denominational priest? I see postdenominationalism as postmodernism playing itself out in the religious sphere. A young artist from England said to me one day, "We are the generation that will understand your work." When I asked why, he responded, "Because creation spirituality is *postmodern.*" That got me scurrying to study the movement known as postmodernism. In the process I have learned that one helpful way for me to understand my journey is to grasp the difference between modern and postmodern times.

The modern era began with the invention of the printing press in the 15th century and extended to the invention of the electronic media in the 1960s. My generation has straddled the two eras. The modern era was characterized by anthropocentrism and cultural elitism – it was the time when Europeans sailed around the globe, encountered indigenous peoples everywhere and overcame them with military might and colonial control. The modern era dismissed other cultures as inferior because they were not book oriented and text oriented. Indeed, it elevated textual truths to the sum of all truths, as when Descartes declared that the soul was in the head and that truth was "clear and distinct ideas." The modern era was patriarchal with a vengeance and it ignored the body and the heart and the passions as sources of truth. It also dismissed the wisdom of beings other than the human (other beings have no souls, according to Descartes). Beholden to a physics of piecemealness, it honored parts more than the whole. In contrast, postmodernism is pluralistic and honors the wisdom of premodern peoples; it honors the whole body not equating truth exclusively with patriarchal headiness; it looks for the whole that is, for cosmology. As the physicist David Bohm puts it, "I am proposing a postmodern physics which begins with the whole."[2] In many ways my work in creation spirituality has been postmodern – to be *creation-centered* is to be cosmologically centered. Creation is about the whole. And to speak of spirituality is to speak of *our experiences of the whole*. Mysticism is nothing if it is not an experience of the whole. Awe is not piecemeal; it connects to all things.

Postdenominationalism is about pluralism and ecumenism in religion. It is about stretching our piecemeal religious boundaries and *setting aside our boxes* to the extent that they are neither challenging us nor nourishing us deeply anymore, or to the extent that they are interfering with the pressing earth issues of our time. Denominationalism mirrors the physics of the modern era, when we were taught a parts mentality and that atoms are rugged individualists that never interpenetrate. In the name of denominationalism we have, over the centuries, fought wars, tortured people and whole towns, excommunicated one another, hated one another, competed against one another, banished one another to hell for eternity, and more or less managed to miss the point of what Jesus of Nazareth was teaching: such behavior characteristics as compassion, justice making, loving your enemies, telling the truth. How many of our denominational differences today are no more than "the narcissism of minor differences," to use Freud's phrase? It is hoped that a postdenominational era will improve our efforts to live out the message of Jesus.

To me postdenominationalism means that denominations pale in comparison to nature, creation, and creation in peril. How can human beings come to the aid of creation? How can denominations come to the aid of creation? Consider how the ecumenical movement in this century among Protestants, Catholics, and Jews was born in the death camps of the Second World War. In the face of death, denominationalism wanes. So today, Earth itself has become a kind of death camp. As Lester Brown puts it, "Every species on the planet is in a state of decline." In so dire a state of emergency, the question is clear: What can religion do about this? Lapsing into denominational flag-waving and moat-deepening and wall-thickening and orthodox-litmus-testing is the opposite of what we need. Postdenominational means that denominations come second (or third...or last) and that other values come first. The richness of worship; the courage of spiritual warriors who will struggle for social justice and ecojustice. In short, holiness.

### Becoming Anglican as a Postdenominational Move

Does being postdenominational mean belonging to no denomination at all? I believe in the Protestant principle of prophecy and protest, and I believe in the Catholic principle of mysticism.

I think postdenominational means to belong to one and many. In my last summer as a Dominican I did back-to-back workshops with Unitarian ministers and Unity church members. Following the Unitarian workshop a woman stood up in the back of the room and said, "You are one of us. Why don't you join us?" Following the Unity workshop a man said, "You are one of us." What was the universe telling me? Before I heard that my dismissal papers had been forwarded from the master general to the Congregation of Religious in the Vatican, I had written the following in my journal:

[Summer, 1993]
*While grateful to all the offers for refuge and ecclesial homes proffered to me already by all my brothers and sisters in other Christian denominations, I believe my path at this time is to say yes to all and yes to none. What does that mean?*

*It means, I believe, that the times call for me to stand up as an ecumenical priest. (Is that not the real meaning of "Catholic," i.e., ecumenical or universal?) Thus I shall continue to pray and celebrate ritual with all those who care to pray and celebrate with me. Together, Anglican and Methodist, UCC and Unitarian, Unity and Lutheran, Native American and Jewish, Roman Catholic and other Catholic, we shall recommit ourselves to the pressing task today to provide new and ancient forms for our traditions of worship. I offer my services to those who desire them. This is so that the earth might be renewed, the people awakened, justice come alive and real, and compassion birthed. The Environmental Revolution calls us all, and Deep Ecumenism is a contribution religion can make to that revolution.*

*Now, instead of a vow of poverty, I make a renewed commitment to living a sustainable lifestyle and encouraging others to do so.*

*Now, instead of a vow of obedience, I make a renewed commitment to reinvigorating democracy and small communities.*

*Now, instead of a vow of celibacy, I make a renewed commitment to reverence in all my relationships, and if I'm blessed with a primary relationship, especially there.*

*We need renewable religion today, and "intermediate rituals" analogous to "intermediate technologies." Sustainable and nonpolluting spirituality. Simple living spirit-wise. Maybe this is behind the Spirit's work in removing Leonardo Boff, Bill Callahan, and other American priest-theologians from active priesthood. Maybe this is why the bureaucratic and hierarchical models of religion are fast being supplemented by base communities and intermediate ritual experiences.*

When I was dismissed from the Dominican order I felt that three options presented themselves to me:

1. hide under a rock (the Vatican's choice)
2. do what Fr. Leonardo Boff did: seek laicization
3. make a lateral move to another tradition in the Christian church

For me, and my culture, I felt the third option to be the most creative choice. I consulted only one Roman Catholic clergyperson on making this decision and he was a liberation theologian and elder Dominican, Fr. Albert Nolan of South Africa. He had been elected head of the Dominican order several years earlier but had turned the job down – the first time in its 750-year history that anyone had! – which says something of the wisdom of the man.

He told me that the Vatican's intention was to isolate me, that I should do whatever it takes to stay within a larger community. The Episcopal decision made all the sense in the world. This very much confirmed my own convictions, and at the same time it reminded me of a statement of Cardinal Arns in Brazil that "the future of the church is in ecumenism." In retrospect, I return to a statement of Père Chenu: "I'm all for dialogue with non-Catholics, non-Christians, atheists. The theology of today and tomorrow must make itself into a dialogue with those who think they are unable to believe." All my work in creation spirituality can be understood as an effort to get those who think themselves unable to believe to at least experience, and trust again. And true belief – as opposed to the mechanical reiteration of dogmas – arises exactly from that juncture of experience and trust. "For God is at home – it is we who have gone out for a walk," as Meister Eckhart put it. The Source of all sources (including the Source of all healthy belief) is at home with us. "Emmanuel," God-with-us.

With this lateral move on my part, I am practicing what I preach. The future does not lie with denominations but with base communities. Those very theological arguments that kept so many Protestants and Catholics literally at one another's throats for the past four centuries are passé. No one cares anymore. Can you name any 20-some-year-old who can tell you the difference between a Methodist and a Presbyterian, an Anglican and a Roman Catholic? Denominationalism is no longer an issue. And that is a good thing, for denominationalism, like racism and sexism and adultism, has to be held accountable for its many sins over the centuries. Today, though, we can admit that we are living in a postdenominational time. While traditions and local roots matter, these are all traditions spelled with a small t. They are relative; they are human-made (though often spirit-inspired in the past); they are socially constructed realities; they can be mined for their wisdom; and let go of.

On the night before the press conference in which the Episcopal bishop of California, William Swing, and I were to announce my switch to the Episcopal church and my reasons for it, I had a dream that seemed significant. The operative line in it was clear and lucid. It was from the gospel. "Shake the dust from your feet." This was Jesus' advice when he spoke about entering a house and wishing "peace upon it" and not getting peace in return. This pretty much summarized my struggle with the Roman Catholic church at this time in history. By going public with the Episcopal bishop, I was indeed shaking dust from my feet. Now the work could go on – not outside the church tradition or community, but very much within it. Yet in a more modest corner of that tradition. Speaking of modesty, my heart leapt during the press conference when Bishop Swing made the point in response to a question that "the Episcopal church does not exist to make other people Episcopalians." I look forward to the day when a pope will make a similar statement. We will all breathe more deeply on that day. But I cannot wait around for that to happen. There is too much work to be done and too little time to get it accomplished.

On April 23, 1994, I preached my first sermon as an Episcopalian in Grace Cathedral at the 11 o'clock Sunday mass. I began my sermon as follows:

This past week I received a letter from a retired 74-year-old Anglican priest in New York. He said: "Rome's loss is our gain. You have jumped the sinking ship of the Vatican for the leaky rowboat of the Episcopal church."...

The funny thing about being told that I've jumped from a sinking ship to a leaky rowboat is that I actually feel like I'm on very firm, dry ground. Earthquake prone – but dry. And that what I want to do is to go deeper into the cellar, into the kiva, into the underground, into the lower chakras of the cathedral, into the basement of this cathedral, for example, where the young school students sweat in the gymnasium, and to go there with young adults who are artists and ritual makers and can help resurrect and restore our traditions of worship.

Following the mass a woman came up to me and said, "I'm Roman Catholic and I disagreed with your decision. But I've read your books and felt I should come to hear you speak. During the mass I was hit right here" – she pointed to her heart – "first by a woman celebrating mass and second by your talk. Now I get it. You have to speak – you have so much we have to hear and your church won't let you speak."

## ECUMENISM AND POSTDENOMINATIONALISM

Ecumenism is postmodern and may even be another word for postdenominational. Worship is becoming more and more ecumenical. Shortly before I flew to Sheffield, England, to experience the special Anglican mass there, I did a weekend workshop in a large Presbyterian church in the inner city of Pittsburgh. They do wonderful work at that church in so many ways, but when I spoke about my upcoming hopes of experiencing renewed liturgy in Sheffield, the pastor himself said to me, "Come back and tell us what you have learned. Our liturgy needs such a boost of new ideas and new forms." When I looked at their worship service I realized it paralleled exactly the form of the mass in Roman Catholicism and the Episcopal church. "Yes, since the Second Vatican Council we have all shared the same basic rite," he reminded me.

Recently I met with a friend who has been ordained in the United Church of Canada for only six months. He told me that he is already feeling the pinch of being responsible for a liturgy that lacks energy. All this tells me that worship is already ecumenical – it is ecumenically boring, and the reason is the same in each denomination: it is not a matter of lack of goodwill on the part of ministers and priests, nor lack of work; it is a matter of our being saddled with forms from the modern era that prevent prayer from happening.

A postdenominational era will be eager to learn from premodern religions instead of proselytizing to them. I have learned so much spirituality from premodern religions. I remember being ushered into a classroom of sixth-grade Maori youngsters on my first visit to New Zealand in 1987. First the girls, then the boys sang welcoming songs in their ancient tongue. I was overwhelmed by the power of the songs and the power of these youngsters as they sang them. There would be no suicides in this group, I said to myself, thinking of the sad number of suicides that hit Native Americans at the same age. These people had managed to preserve enough of their culture in spite of the white colonialists that their souls were still strong and their song was strong medicine.

Eddie Kneebone, an Australian aboriginal, spoke to a roomful of artists that creation spirituality people had gathered in Melbourne, Australia, and showed us his painting. It was his – contemporary – but it was also very ancient: it depicted the life of the soul, the life of a person from conception through childhood, adolescence, adulthood, and death – which returned to conception again. He explained how in his culture one doesn't hang a picture on a wall; instead it is placed on the floor and all sit around it, as you would around a campfire. Since everyone has a different topography from which to relate, everyone has a different story to tell about the picture.

To speak of these ancient traditions as being preliterate does not do them justice. "Oral traditions" are not just "preliterate." (How would Catholics like to be called "pre-Protestant"?) Oral traditions are *oral*; that means they are sung from the depth of the very first chakra. That is their deep power and their deep gift to a culture such as ours that has invested all its power in the upper chakras. Oral traditions still have the lower-chakra power to get us down. This is sure to have a lot to do with the recovery of holiness in our time. Clarissa Pinkola Estés's book *Women Who Run with the Wolves*, wherein she exegetes ancient stories from her own multiple ancestral traditions, offers a superb example of the power and the wisdom of oral traditions. Robert Bly provides a parallel service in his exegesis of *Iron John*, an ancient myth from his Nordic ancestors.

Again, the wisdom from the oral traditions.

In many respects I have been living a postdenominational priest-hood for many years. The majority of my invitations to speak in recent years have not been in Roman Catholic settings but in churches of other denominations: Episcopal, Unity, Methodist, United Church of Christ, Unitarian, Presbyterian, and others. Indeed, the very last workshop I did as a Dominican was at All Saints Episcopal Church in Pasadena, California. It was a powerful experience, as many art-as-meditation leaders led groups of various kinds on Friday and Saturday. It was the following Monday that I received notification of my dismissal from the order. Once, at a Common Boundary conference near Washington, D.C., when I finished a daylong workshop on liberating the Cosmic Christ in all of us, a man with a long white beard came up and kissed me on the cheek. "I am a rabbi in New York City," he said, "and I feel closer to you than to most of my fellow rabbis." I remember my last year teaching at Barat College when a middle-aged Jewish woman who had taken several of my courses approached me and said, "You are a good rabbi." And I re-member the toothless old Indian man following a presentation I gave in New Mexico who said, "During your talk my ancestors came and sat on my shoulders and said: 'Listen to this man, he is one of us.'" And the Filipina Catholic sister who was raised by a family that practiced both Catholicism and the ancestral religion and who wrote that she finds in creation spirituality "what was ours in the past. The European Christian-ity that was brought to us had put aside our own way of worshiping God and we have been left alienated from our own tradition." Her desire now is "to recover our creation-centered spirituality and also to undergo the process of grieving for what I and my people have lost." So many people I have encountered from so-called third-world nations express similar sentiments on learning of creation spirituality.

Postdenominationalism recognizes the closeness we feel to one an-other when we are all engaged – no matter what our denomination – in the search for mysticism and the struggle for justice. Mysticism and prophecy are much, much larger than denominations. To know that is to be postdenominational. It may or may not mean we are still part of denominations, but the fact is that it is difficult to live without one. Communities and traditions are important – provided we write "tradition" always with a small *t*. We are indeed living in an age in which, as Walter Anderson puts it, "whenever we describe ourselves, we should add 'etc.'"[3] This "age of the fading boundaries" applies to our religious and denominational boundaries as well as to other boundaries. Does this help explain my experience of being a postdenominational priest and of embracing the Anglican tradition of Catholicism? Ought I, now that I am a Roman Catholic priest and an Anglican priest, just sign "etc." after my name?

Recovering Christians outnumber practicing Christians in the world today. Because so many people have been wounded by the church, we all need to apply Alice Miller's work on the wounded child to our various church experiences. I once met one of the world's truly unhappy priests as our guide in the catacombs of St. Sabastian in Rome. He kept putting down "the pagans" as he called them, and even said that Hindus, Native Americans, and other pagans worshipped the swastika – making no distinction between Hitler's swastika and the ancient symbols. His theology was as appalling as his history, but above all it was his persecution complex, his wounded-child-as-a-killer-adult, and his utter unhappiness that came through so loud and clear to all visitors. Have the catacombs and the 300 years of persecution in Rome rendered the Roman church ever so eager for Augustine's theology of church as Kingdom, for his theology of dualism and his emphasis on Fall and Redemption versus creation? It would appear so. Just as the church needs to heal its child wounded at the time of the Roman persecutions, so too the church needs to pay attention to the wounds it received earlier in the synagogue. As Rosemary Ruether has pointed out in *Faith and Fratricide*, anti-Semitism began very early in the church. It is present in the Gospels. But there it is present as a child hurt by its parent – not as a parent hurting children. The latter is what happened when the church took over the empire; one finds in St. Augustine, for example, references such as "those lustful Jews" and other anti-Semitic statements. Christianity will never grow up to its adult stature until and unless it heals its *wounded Roman* and its *wounded Jewish* child. And when it does this it will finally let go of aspirations to Roman imperialism (including, one could pray, its very names of *pontifex maximus*) on the one hand; and, on the other, what seems to go with all empire building in the West from Augustine to Bossuet to Hitler to Jerry Falwell – its anti-Semitism and abuse of Jews as scapegoats. Then, being rid of anti-Semitism, it might begin to learn what I have had the privilege of learning over the years: the deep, deep gifts that Jewish theology has to give to Christianity.

Indeed, if I were shipwrecked on an island and able to read only one theologian, I would choose the works of Rabbi Abraham Joshua Heschel. When I read him I feel I am the closest to the mind and heart of Jesus. After all, Judaism *is* the morphic field, the collective memory, the ancient matrix that not only nourished Jesus but the entire early Christian community, including the writers of the Gospels and Epistles of the Christian Bible. It amazes me to this day how deeply the dualistic teachings of an Augustine, for example, can penetrate the Christian religion while the holistic teachings of Jesus pass almost unnoticed.

Ecumenism with Judaism is part of the postdenominational mindset that can reinvigorate our species with spirituality. To this we should add ecumenism with Islam as well. And especially the Sufi mystical tradition, which is so rich in spiritual practices of dervish dances and other forms of healthy meditation. Is it mere coincidence that what Chenu called "the greatest renaissance in the West" – that of the 12th century – occurred under the impetus of the Islamic intellectual tradition that swept into Europe at that time?

Ecumenism with Buddhism and Taoism and Hinduism – in other words, East meeting West with its wisdom – is also important to a postdenominational and postmodern awakening. This is happening but usually on a personal scale, as individual Westerners go to Eastern meditation centers for their spiritual praxis. But I sometimes get frightened by what academia does to this interaction, reducing it so often to studying foreign languages and going over ancient texts. I would like to see more spiritual praxis and therefore "deep ecumenism" in the coming together of East and West. But, of course, if Western academicians are themselves not in touch with their own spiritual practice or that of the Western tradition, then connections that matter are hard to come by. The Dalai Lama recently put forth his own view on deep ecumenism when he said, "There are now no grounds for making distinctions between East and West. What we need now is a melting of minds, a coming together. Human compassion is the most important factor – not ethnic divisions, racial divisions, religious divisions."[4]

A few years ago when I was doing a workshop in Malibu, I was put up for the night in a beautiful home with a Buddha altar and statue. The Buddha and I spent the night alone together in that house, and I woke up with an insight that I shared with the retreatants that morning: namely, that Buddha lived a full life into his 80s and died a natural death. He knew midlife crisis and he knew serenity. Jesus, on the other hand, was a prophetic, angry, even impetuous Jew, and he was killed before his time when he was about 33. What does this mean? Judaism and Christianity have a life force about them, a prophetic imperative, that is essential; but Buddhism has a serenity and a sense of longevity that the West can use. My conclusion? We need both. Buddhism needs the West and the West needs Buddhism.

Postdenominationalism also means that denominations are far less important for spirituality today than are our *professions*. It is at work more than at church that the real moral – and immoral – decisions are being rendered about the health of our planet, our bodies, our children, our very souls. Work is the adult arena for spiritual decision making, whether we are talking about the waste our species spews into the earth, or the violence and titillating sex that dominates our television programming, or the inane political issues that get raised to fever pitch in order to drown out the real issues. It is in our work, as I argue in my book on *Reinventing Work*, that the moral issues of our lives play out. And, as I conclude in that study, it is in our work that spirituality itself will be redeemed. As the Bhagavad Gita teaches, "They all find perfection who find joy in their work."[5] The bringing of spirituality back to our work worlds will amount to a revolution in work, and it will also allow us to pay more attention to the great amount of inner work that needs doing in our time. In paying attention to this, we will find that *unemployment is not only unacceptable but unnecessary.* There is work for everyone, so long as we include inner work as integral to our definitions of work – something the industrial era failed to do.

Postdenominationalism recognizes that our church affiliations, as dear as they are or might have once been to us, are themselves more often than not *socially constructed realities.* The concept of socially constructed realities helps us to understand denominations – their limits *and* their grace. Our ancestors created expressions of their faith that today we call tradition. Awareness of this does not strip them of all their power. Nor does it mean that their differences do not count; only that idolatry of these differences and temptations to narcissism about them ought not to prevail. What I call "ethnic religion" is the lowest form of all religions, and in many instances it is at that first, collective level of religion that we fight our wars and battles. Northern Ireland seems a case in point. There religion is the outward excuse for a struggle involving class, jobs, political decision-making power. Fear rules and religion takes the brunt of it. To recognize our denominational expressions as socially constructed realities is to allow ourselves to move beyond them. Or, if we choose to stay, to stay with a kind of denominational humility. Charles Jencks believes that part of any postmodern movement is a practice of "double-coding," which is the "strategy of affirming and denying the existing power structures at the same time."[6]

Postdenominationalism, then, allows us to get over our superiority complexes when it comes to religion. To let them go. It means taking what we can believe in in conscience and moving beyond.

## PROTESTING CATHOLICISM AND PROTESTANTISM

In my own case I can now say the following: I am now, officially as of January 1994, a Protestant (Episcopal) Christian. What does this mean to me? It means I honor the principle of protest, of saying no, of prophecy therefore. When it comes to religion, this is what I protest: I know Catholicism rather well, having lived it out quite faithfully for 54 years, 34 of those in a religious order, 26 of those as a priest, 21 of those as a theologian (31 years of theological studies). I protest the following:

- clericalism
- ignoring of its creation spirituality tradition and mystics in seminary training in the order
- closing of churches without asking why no one wants to come to mass today
- pedophilia and its cover-up
- rigor mortis
- fascism
- sexual morality as taught by the hierarchy
- inquisition yesterday and today, and the fear of it spreads[7]
- infallibility
- papalmania and cult of personality
- links with the CIA, and the National Security Council under Reagan, in destroying peace movements, liberation movements, base communities, and liberation theologies[8]
- hypocrisy
- homophobia
- power!
- sexism
- fear
- sins of the spirit ignored while sins of the flesh are preached
- ignorance of its own mystical-prophetic tradition
- lack of curiosity
- resentment
- envy
- witch burnings
- complacency
- Vatican as a modern power base, not postmodern

- condemnations
- lack of accountability
- silliness of birth control, and consequent ignoring of global population crisis
- silly opposition to condoms, a position that can result in death by
  AIDS
- anthropocentrism: pride, arrogance
- treatment of native peoples and their religions
- colonialism and its sins
- sectarianism/tribalism/lack of "catholic" spirit
- anti-Semitism
- inability and unwillingness to stop its radical right fringe
- Opus Dei (the secretive spiritual lay order embraced by Franco and
  other fascists of this century)[9]
- bad people in high places: Torquemada, Cody, Ratzinger, and others
- Pius IX's Syllabus of Errors
- inability to admit past errors
- bad popes[10]

These are the shadow factors in Catholicism signaling the end of an era.
But I also protest things within Protestantism, including the following:

- its lack of premodern roots – indeed its conscious and deliberate
  ignorance of the medieval church with its great accomplishments in
  spirituality and theology and art
- its silly notions of predestination and biblicalism, as if the Bible didn't
  come through the believing community
- its preoccupation with texts, as if the "word of God" is words from
  human books and not every creature of God
- its being stuck in the modern era
- its headiness and patriarchal roots and banishment of the goddess
- its boring worship, based as it is on words, words, and more words
- its swallowing hook, line, and sinker the Enlightenment and capitalism

- its lack of a universal outlook, that is, its acquiescence to nation-state ideologies
- its fragmentation resulting in a papal-control compulsion at the local level
- its lack of mysticism
- its seminary system that owes more to Descartes and Kant than to Jesus and our tradition of mystics/prophets
- its substitution of sweetness and kindness and "fellowship" for prophecy and anger, moral outrage and healthy love
- its Eurocentrism

And so, I am clearly neither Catholic nor Protestant – or, if you wish, I am both Catholic and Protestant. I hope I bear within me the cosmic mystic of Catholicism and the protesting prophet of Protestantism. But to do this today, we must both draw from these two traditions *and move beyond them.* Who can predict what spiritual energy might arise and flow again were we to apply spiritual lessons of "letting go" to religion itself and were we to succeed in washing away religious imperialism and the competition that goes with it? Postdenominationalism is a kind of appeal to nonelitism in religion. The symbols and metaphors and rituals of a healthy religion will rise to the surface, and it is these, rather than denominations themselves, that will save our souls. Charles Jencks describes postmodernism's task as one that ought to "challenge monolithic elitism, to bridge the gaps that divide high and low cultures, elite and mass, specialist and non-professional, or most generally put – one discourse and interpretative community from another..."[11] Is this not all activity that postdenominational religion would be about as well? A bridging of the gap between high and low cultures (might we say religious sects), specialists and professionals, one community from another?

## WHY PRIESTHOOD?

But what about being a "postdenominational *priest*"? Why do we need priests? Walt Whitman had his answer to this question a century ago:

There will soon be no more priests: their work is done.

They may wait awhile, perhaps a generation or two, dropping off by degrees.

A superior breed shall take their place;

The gangs of kosmos and prophets en masse shall take their place.

A new order shall arise and they shall be the priests of man,

And every man shall be his own priest.

The churches built under their umbrage shall be the churches of men and women.

Through the divinity of themselves shall the kosmos, and the new breed of poets,

Be interpreters of men and women, and of all events and things.

They shall find their inspiration in real objects today, symptoms of the past and future.[12]

Rabbi Heschel had his opinion on the priesthood as well. He wrote: "The great dream of Judaism is not to raise priests, but a people of priests; to consecrate all men [sic], not only some men."[13] One wonders if this was not Jesus' aim as well, where "all men" meant "all women and men." M. D. Chenu used to insist that the New Testament priesthood was not about cult but about prophecy. Priests were to be prophetic. Thomas Merton also wrote about a radical revision of priesthood:

I think the whole thing needs to be changed, the whole idea of the priesthood needs to be changed. I think we need to develop a whole new style of worship in which there is no need for one hierarchical person to have a big central place, a form of worship in which everyone is involved.[14]

I agree with Fr. Bede Griffith and the study by James D. G. Dunn that he recommended so highly (Unity and Diversity in the New Testament) that the priesthood was not part of the early church. It was a second-century invention. And yet that still gives it a 1,800-year, if somewhat checkered, history. So there is some use to the priesthood, some power there. Yet the Quakers and others who have managed to transcend the priesthood offer some eschatological hope that we too will before long outgrow the priesthood as we know it in its clerical representations. I do believe, however, that human communities require leadership from among them, and that notion of spiritual leadership will not disappear. Granted that its abuse has been at times offensive even to religion, saying nothing of spirituality.

In my own case, I stay in the priesthood because I feel that, at this crossroads time in religious and planetary history, something useful might still be forged from that tradition. Especially if a new generation, one that is genuinely committed to a postmodern worldview and the value it puts on nonelitism, can reinvent the priesthood, making of it a source of authentic spiritual renewal and leadership. With women just recently entering the priestly traditions of the West, there is considerable hope that new forms and interpretations and training methods may be implemented to reinvent the priesthood.

In my own case, I felt that since I had been ordained 27 years previously, and since no decent rationale was given me for abandoning that leadership role that I believed I had discharged honorably over the years, I might as well stick it out to see what the next chapter would unfold. For me it is not at all a matter of clinging to the priesthood. After all, I "left the priesthood" before I was even ordained when I chose to go to the hermitage under threat from my provincial of not being ordained thereby. Thus I have all my priestly life been very little burdened by the office (I was helped in this by being primarily an educator and not a parish priest). But when the Sheffield group told me that I could actually assist their movement by remaining in the priesthood and becoming an Anglican to boot, I felt it was some good use to which I could put the holy oils.

As a certain farewell to my Roman Catholic history and as a courtesy to the man, I wrote the Roman Catholic bishop of Oakland on April 6, 1994, when I made my leave. In the letter I thanked him for his "quiet support" and concluded with the following paragraph:

> This decision has not been easy. But I believe that issues of ecological justice, native peoples' and women's rights, and reaching the young by way of new forms of worship are of sufficient merit that some of us, caught "between times," just have to make some uncomfortable moves. I do not feel I am leaving the Roman Catholic church but am rather embracing another expression of catholicism. I believe that the Vatican has made me a postdenominational priest in a postdenominational era, and I am responding to that reality.

Eight months later I received a personal response from the bishop in which he talked of his confusion and concern.

As I was making my move formally into the Episcopal church I received a phone call from Deborah Koons, the fiancée of Grateful Dead guitarist Jerry Garcia. It happened that just that month Jerry and I were featured in the same magazine, and on reading his interview I said to a friend, "This guy is a creation-centered philosopher if ever there was one." Deborah told me that they were planning their wedding and wanted me to be the officiating priest. I asked her how she knew of me and learned that they had been discussing my theology, especially that of *Original Blessing*. "Well," I said, "you have to understand that I'm not on very good terms with the Vatican these days." "Oh!" she replied, "an outlaw priest for an outlaw wedding!"

We were able to secure the support of the Episcopal church to hold a very private wedding in an intimate chapel in Marin County. Though I am not a great fan or frequenter of weddings, I have to say that I have never seen a more loving couple than Deborah and Jerry were that day. At the wedding I spoke on elements of a postmodern marriage, including the imperative not to bore each other (if we live in a cosmology, we will not be boring); on the need to see marriage as a creative act – a verb and not a noun – requiring the same daily effort at creativity as our art does; and on the importance of fun.

When I visited them at their home months later, I was touched by the utter child in Jerry – his enthusiasm for a new telescope he was setting up that afternoon, his relish at showing me the computer on which he painted and the work he was doing on an illustrated book of his childhood. Yet he was a philosopher in his own right and loved to talk theology.

I was honored that Jerry and Deborah continued to support me in my transition. They were in the last row of Grace Cathedral the Sunday morning I delivered my first homily as an Episcopalian; they were in attendance at my formal reception ceremony as an Episcopal priest; and they were present for the Planetary Mass in the basement of the cathedral. As Jerry put it to me on the day of my reception, "Religion is important to society. It has to be reinvented. We can't get along without it."

One and a half years later, Jerry died peacefully in his sleep at a rehabilitation center. Again I was asked to officiate as a priest, this time at his funeral. Synchronicity abounded at the service, beginning with the irony that it was held at St. Stephen's parish in Tiburon, and one of the Grateful Dead's earliest songs was called "St. Stephen." Deborah's strength was manifest in the heartfelt talk she delivered at the service about her and Jerry's love and relationship. Numerous other examples of wisdom arose from the friends and associates of Jerry, including a hastily written and passionately presented eulogy from the lyricist of the group, Robert Hunter, who delivered his gift like a bard of old. I made the point in my eulogy that Otto Rank describes three ways of healing in a society: therapy that heals one-to-one; art that heals small groups; and religious prophecy that heals the masses. The response to Jerry's work with the Grateful Dead demonstrated that theirs was a healing work both of art and of religious prophecy. It healed the masses. Its appeal was spiritual and mystical but also prophetic – it interfered with a culture that lacked joy and effective ritual. Jerry was a wounded healer, wounded by seeing his father drown in front of him when he was four years old and wounded by much in life. But his wounds contained his power, and he turned them to compassion for many. I learned from my brief but rich association with the Grateful Dead inner circle that I was one of many who felt indebted to Jerry for his brilliance and friendship. Knowing him was another gift of living in California. Before the service I was anxious, aware of how diverse the mourners would be in terms of religious affiliation and alienation, artists, special fans, and others. But during the service – as so often happens to me – peace settled in as the spirit of the group raised us all to heights of healthy grieving and remembering and laughter. At the last minute of the service, an inspiration came to me to invite the mourners to give Jerry one last standing ovation – this not just for his music but for his life. The applause was prolonged and deep, and I knew I had once more been blessed to assist some real people at real prayer.

## Planetary Mass

On Reformation Sunday, the last Sunday of October 1994, a wonderful event happened. In the basement of Grace Cathedral we hosted the first Planetary Mass in America. The posse was the priest and the posse consisted of 36 dedicated young people from the Nine O'clock Service (NOS) of Sheffield, England, who came to America for eight days to set up the service and put it on. I preached at that mass; the Gospel text was from John 1, which talks of the "Word" of God as the light through which "all things came to be." I spoke of all the things our century has done with light, beginning with a young scientist in his 20s named Albert Einstein saying, "All I want to do my whole life is to study light."

In the 20th century we have lassoed light in all new ways. The military harnessed light for its purposes: Dresden; Hiroshima; Nagasaki; MX missiles; napalm in Vietnam. The entertainment and news industries lassoed light for their purposes, first in black and white and then in color; business lassoed light in forms of computers, CD-ROMs, fiber optics, for its purposes.

The question we ask at the end of this century is the following: Can we lasso light so that the Sacred can more fully reveal itself to us? So that the "Word can become flesh," that is to say, "light," living and dancing in our midst?

I spoke of the meaning of Reformation Sunday, the Reformation representing not only a response to corruption in the dominant church establishment but also the religious response to the emerging modern era, an era opened up by the technological breakthrough we call the invention of the printing press. The printing press democratized the Bible, making it available to laypersons and others. It caused a religious revolution that was only partially successful in renewing religion. Why the failures?

The biggest mistake in religion in the modern era has been to confuse "the word of God" with human words or textual words in a book. If "the word was in the beginning," then clearly the WORD is bigger than human words or textual words. It preceded all words by about 14 billion years!

The creation-centered mystic Meister Eckhart said in the 14th century that "every creature is a word of God and a book about God." This carries us far beyond the overly anthropocentric idea of the Bible alone as the "word of God," a modern notion that emerged because of our fascination with texts at the invention of the printing press.

But now – with the emergence of the postmodern era – we can get it right. Because we have overemphasized "words" in religion, we have lacked a language for the mystical. Now we may have such a language – light itself – dancing, moving, living light. Physicist David Bohm says that matter is "frozen light." If matter is frozen light, then Spirit may be "melted, thawed, warmed up, and flowing light," and "flesh" is both! Our postmodern times were ushered in by another invention, that of electronic media, electronic music, light dancing, the harnessing of light. We have been gifted with a new language, a language for microcosm/macrocosm; for connecting to the universe again; past and future; for moving beyond anthropocentrism; a language that awakens awe and mysticism, heart and soul and body and, hopefully, body politic. Is the lassoing of light in our time not a special opportunity for a new generation to reinvent the "Word" that is with God and had been in the divine presence playing since the beginning of the world?

What were my feelings about the event of the Planetary Mass? As I sat on the floor amid hundreds of other worshipers, many of them young street people, I was deeply moved. Indeed, I was filled with joy and I am still, three weeks after the event, as I attempt to process my experience.

One thought awakened in me was this: Western culture has been running for two centuries on René Descartes's egoistic and heady statement: "I think, therefore I am." More recently, American consumer culture has altered this philosophy in its own unique way to: "I buy, therefore I am; I consume, therefore I exist." But as I participated in the Planetary Mass I sensed that a new philosophical era was opening up. Its shibboleth would be: "We celebrate, therefore we are." And of course, it is founded on a deeper truth: "We are, therefore we celebrate."

One thing I have learned from knowing the NOS community of Sheffield is that the alternative to capitalism does not have to be communism. It can be community. A community gets much more done and at a far cheaper price than does bureaucratic capitalism or bureaucratic communism or the modern state. For one thing, community allows giveaway to happen. These 36 people who came 10,000 miles for nine days of intense work to set up, put on, and take down the wonderful sacred space they created for the Planetary Mass did so for nothing. A lot of labor went into this effort and a lot of gift giving. It was truly a spiritual giveaway. Finances were handled by asking donors for contributions behind the scenes – not by asking anyone present at the mass. That makes for a much purer gift than is often the case.

In rediscovering the giveaway, the community was also rediscovering the authentic meaning of sacrifice. The idea of sacrifice has, I think, been severely tainted during the patriarchal era; it has been presented in an almost sado-masochistic setting in which, verbally or nonverbally, the message is: you are to sacrifice for me. But it is time to redeem that word sacrifice, which, after all, clearly includes the word sacred in it. Is anything sacred without sacrifice? Surely there is no love without sacrifice. Love inspires sacrifice and requires it, whether we are speaking of parental love or partnered love or love of friendship or love of art, work, environment, and so on. Sacrifice may just be another word for gift giving. There was a plethora of gift giving at this mass, ranging from the four Sufi dancers who twirled in the four directions of the room throughout the mass, to the singers and the rappers who gave their gifts with abundance; from the mixers and deejays with caps on backward, to the wild young man dancing madly under the strobe lights; from the designers of the mass to the leaders of it. All sacrificed (many took a week off from their jobs to come and work on the mass in San Francisco). This was evident. It helped to make the occasion special and spiritual and pure. A night of deep prayer.

I suspect it was this prayer dimension that most filled me with joy and is the reason I said to myself during the mass, "I could do this every night of the week." I joined the Dominican order 36 years ago in order to pray, to explore more deeply my relationship with the divine. I stayed in the order many years for that reason and to lead others in real and effective prayer. Yet, sad to tell, some of the dullest, most rote and dead liturgical experiences I have had in recent years have been at gatherings of Dominicans.

This was not the case at the Planetary Mass in the basement of Grace Cathedral. There was beauty going on wherever I looked. It was like being in a forest, where every direction displayed beauty and something interesting to behold. This included not only the singers, dancers, and rappers but also the projections on large video screens, on television sets, on a huge globe suspended over the beautiful altars (one a sun altar, the second a crescent-moon altar). On the screens were hummingbirds hovering, galaxies spinning, flowers opening, human beings marching, protesting, embracing, and polluting (sin was present and indeed renamed for us at the mass). Life was there in all its panoply of forces, good and not so good, human and more than human.

It was the opposite of dull, the opposite of boring. There was wonder everywhere – as in the cosmos itself. And beauty. Indeed, here microcosm and macrocosm came together magically. And why shouldn't they? Why shouldn't there be wonder and beauty everywhere when we worship? How has it come to pass that our civilization has practically managed to close down ritual and render it boring, especially in church? It need not be so. This mass was *interesting*, and to be interesting means to be about what goes on *inter esse*, between beings. It was that kind of experience – a cosmological one, wherein the relationships between things is named and celebrated and nothing is left out, especially not the Source of all things. Indeed, it was to thank that Source of all things that we gathered to pray at all.

A major feature of the Planetary Mass is that it is designed and executed not by theologians with Ph.D.'s in liturgical niceties but by a team of artists. That is why it works as ritual and as aesthetics. (That plus the fact that it has a solid, creation-spiritual theology to underpin it and give it depth and scope, including a connection to our ancestral mystical tradition.) What is art? What is the work of artists? A young artist, a painter who in fact attended the mass, wrote me recently about his vocation: "I think I've come to know that I paint in order to arrive at the point of surprise, to learn of myself."

The painter – literally – goes to the edge. In this case, of the canvas. Every artist goes to the edge. Is that what creativity is – "going to the edge"? To the horizon? To the frontiers? Or as Rank phrases it, to the *Beyond*? And why? To be surprised, first. And second, to surprise. And what is surprise? It's part of awe and curiosity and wisdom and fun and celebration and, therefore, compassion. It's also part of cosmology, for if cosmology is a study of the whole, the whole must include the edge and the surprise and the unborn of things, even the unexpected *between* things (thus, our word *interesting*).

But surprise is also transcendence. "Transcendence" comes from *transcendere*, to *climb across*. We all want to climb across new portals, be ushered into new rooms and vistas where our hearts and souls can experience awe anew and fall in love again. Artists assist us in this crossing over, this climbing over. The word climbing implies a certain arduousness to the task of following the artist's lead. Art is not itself the new vista; it is (merely) the door to the new perception. Like Jesus speaking of the kingdom – "do not look here or there" – it is among you. Art tells us what is deeply among us – not by its objectifying of some object but by its release of our powers of hearing, seeing, feeling, knowing anew. ("The blind shall see and the deaf shall hear and the lame shall walk.") In a new place and space. Art is a threshold experience. Artists carry us over the threshold – and leave us there. The rest is up to us.

This is reconstructive postmodern art. Spirituality is at its core. The invitation to climb across, to transcend. I had the feeling at the Planetary Mass that many people had come for transcendence – and that they indeed underwent a transcendent experience. In fact, that was the feedback I received that night and since. Following are some responses that I picked up from the mass.

From a woman Episcopal priest: "When I dance, I dance hard and when I pray, I pray hard, but no one had invited me before to dance and pray hard at the same time. It was dynamite. I want to spend the rest of my life working with these young people."

From a middle-aged woman: "This morning I went to church, sat in the pew, and prayed very hard. I felt good; this much of my soul was affected." Here she put her thumb and middle finger together to make an egg about two inches in diameter. "But tonight, tonight all of me was affected" (and here she threw her arms up into the air).

From a 23-year-old street person and writer: "I would come to this mass every Sunday. It was fabulous."

From a 20-some-year-old woman who is a secretary at a major publishing firm: "I have never been to a church in my life or to a rave. But ever since the mass three days ago, something has been vibrating in my mind. I have never felt like this before."

From a middle-aged woman theologian: "All my life I have read the mystics and I have never had the experience that Julian of Norwich writes about, that is, of seeing the cosmos in the hazelnut and Jesus in the hazelnut. Until tonight. At the consecration, when the universe was born on the video screens at the same time, I truly got it. It entered my heart: the Cosmic Christ is in us and we are all in the Cosmic Christ."

From a 27-year-old artist: "I was moved by the mass and liked it a lot. But every day since, a new level of vibrations has been going off inside of me. Its effect keeps growing on me."

From a 50-some-year-old executive: "The last time I went to communion was in the 1940s when I was nine years old. I took communion tonight. It was so moving."

I think the Planetary Mass represents a new, postmodern stage in human development. Postmodern worship has arrived. Asking the artists and the young to lead us in celebration is just common sense. It is a return of the repressed, for in the modern era neither artists nor youth nor mystics were asked to lead us in anything.

A community in Leeds, England, called REM sponsors an alternative Mass on a regular basis that includes visual media such as computers, video, and slides along with music. The music includes a voice-over about creation theology and has a strong beat that is quite premodern or indigenous in its flavor. A Leeds group called Synergy sent me their album, which includes elements of techno, dub, rave, house, and ambient music to dance to. I used this tape in three workshops recently, one in Boston, another in Orlando, and a third at Esalen near Big Sur in California. The response was very strong. After the workshop in Boston, one woman in her early 40s told me that in the middle of the dance she started to cry because she thought of her ten-year-old son who cannot stand going to church. Being Episcopalian herself, she was very concerned about his religious future. "Then, in the middle of the dance, I realized that here is a language my son will be able to pray in." Thus, her tears. Tears of joy.

At Esalen, a large man in his mid-40s approached me after we danced to this CD and celebrated a simple Eucharist: "I was raised Catholic and was deeply wounded by Christianity and left it years ago," he told me. "This was the first experience I have ever had of God in worship." Then he started to cry on my shoulder.

What we have here is a revolution. A nonviolent revolution. The return of celebration. This revolution will not be stopped. It is what the left lacks to the extent that it ignores the sense of the sacred. And, because healthy worship awakens a critical moral and ecological ethic that leads to action, it is also what the right lacks. Thomas Aquinas warns of the courage that true worship takes when he puts worship in the same category as prophetic justice making: "Magnanimous people put themselves in all kinds of danger for great things, for instance, the common welfare, justice, divine worship, and so forth."[15]

Worship ought to be the energy source from which a people heals itself and lets go and starts over. A space where a new politics as well as a new economics and a new art can begin. And a new priesthood. New and ancient ways to midwife transcendence. This postmodern worship makes all this possible and even fun.

## ORTHOPRAXIS

I believe that the renewal of forms of worship represents an exercise in orthopraxis. Orthopraxis is more important today than orthodoxy. Part of belief today is the conviction that we must walk our talk, that what we do is the only authentic measure of what we claim to believe. In the 19th century, John Henry Newman wrote a book called *Essay on the Development of Christian Doctrine* in which he underscored his reasons for leaving the Anglican fold for the Roman Catholic tradition. Newman's work needs to be supplemented today. Instead of debating the development of doctrine, it is time to implement *the development of polity*. Polity, which Webster's dictionary defines as "the form of government of a religious denomination," is about orthopraxis more than orthodoxy. Ours is a time, as liberation theologians insist, for paying more attention to orthopraxis. How can the church preach justice to others if it remains sexist or clericalist or racist or colonialist itself? Orthodoxy holds the danger of being idolatrous, especially when it comes at the expense of orthopraxis.

I sense that Newman's passion as a young theologian for the church standing up to the state was an authentic prophetic cry about the lack of orthopraxis in the Anglicanism of his day. His search for a period in church history in which he saw orthopraxis more appropriately displayed was commendable. While it is possible that John Newman and I have passed like trains in the night – he to Rome and I to Canterbury – there may be another way to look at our differences: that were he living in the latter half of our century, he too would have seen what I have come to see – that Rome is not on the right track for orthopraxis and that the Second Vatican Council, while it contributed to a healthy development of doctrine, has proved to be a failure at the level of development of praxis. It did not clean the Vatican house out; in fact, with the advent of computers and fax machines and instantaneous electronic communications, those who control the Vatican now wield more power than ever before in Rome's history. An openness is necessary to provide a more fluid and flowing avenue in which the Holy Spirit might operate. And this, after all, is the purpose of ecclesia in the first place, is it not? To be a space where the Spirit can move freely? Celebrate openly? And struggle justly?

We must make room for honoring local roots and local decision making. When we make room for development, we make space for evolution. This sense of space better fits the physics and cosmology of our times and the practical level of church organization, structure, and decision making. Thus it has the capacity to lead us in a postmodern era. A diverse decision-making apparatus needs to be in place for polity to evolve. Lay participation and decision making are requisites.

What is lacking in Newman's preoccupation with fourth-century ecclesial history is a concern about the polity of the earliest church. I believe that it is there, in the respect for the diversity of local churches, that we should look in a postmodern era. (Is diversity not a prerequisite for development?) The Christian churches before the imperial ambitions of first Constantinople and then Rome took over church polity respected diversity. Would that Newman had been as passionate about emulating the first-century church as he was about emulating the fourth-century church. (The polity of the Celtic church, so sadly dismembered by southern European Christianity beginning with the Synod of Whitby, was much looser and more closely mirrored the early church.)

Most Christians recite the Nicene Creed, which speaks of the Church being "one, holy, catholic, and apostolic." The meaning of what constitutes oneness or unity is at issue among them. Oneness cannot be enforced from above or outside. The cosmology of the postmodern era, a cosmology that teaches us that there is no one center of the universe but that the universe is omnicentric, can teach us healthy oneness again. If the universe is omnicentric, then no one space or place (Rome or other) holds the reins on all issues of polity. Rather, issues of unity and diversity need to be honored locally where they arise. This model of church has much in common with base communities of Latin America. It may be a less efficient model in the short run than that of Rome, but it allows more room for the Spirit to express itself.

A certain *humility* is needed by church itself. A humility not unlike that of any individual who sincerely sets about a search for truth, Spirit, and the God of both. A search that is never-ending and that is sure to be intensified as we move into a third millennium of Christianity in the context of ecological destruction, youth despair, population explosion, deep ecumenism, and Christians often being minorities around the world. More than ever, we need to listen to the Spirit who speaks through all avenues of church and society and try our best to discern our process of development from there. Newman's solution was too simplistic. The Protestant and Anglican reformation got some things right. The church does need ongoing criticism of a prophetic kind. Forms in which the church chooses to organize itself are and always have been subject to development and evolution, just like the rest of God's creation. Socially constructed realities are part of the human condition, as sociologist Walter Truett Anderson insists. The modern (as distinct from postmodern) effort of the Roman church today to be the center of the religious universe is doomed to failure, for it presumes a physics that is already passé. A genuine *development of polity*, one that mirrors some lessons learned from democratic institutions of the West, is a development to be welcomed.

Newman himself writes in the *Apologia Pro Vita Sua* about the "awful, never-ending duel" between authority and private judgment and how "it is necessary for the very life of religion, viewed in its large operations and its history, that the warfare should be incessantly carried on."[16] But there are multiple ways to carry on this "warfare," and it need not always be one authority versus one individual. Rather, blocs and groups and teams can support and healthily challenge one another. Newman maintains that "Catholic Christendom is no simple exhibition of religious absolutism" and that concerning infallibility, "both its subject-matter and its articles in the subject-matter, are fixed" with respect to "what the apostles held before us."[17] But when it comes to issues like birth control and celibacy in the 20th-century Roman Catholic church, issues of polity have been elevated to a position of preeminence if not downright obsession that is nowhere mirrored in the Gospel times of the early church.

"The unity of the Catholic Church is very near to my heart, only I do not see any prospect of it in our time," wrote Newman.[18] Is it any nearer in our time? Surely the efforts among Anglicans and Protestant bodies indicate some hope, as did the efforts by Pope John XXIII and Pope Paul VI. But I would say that the biggest obstacle to unity is Rome's disregard of orthopraxis when it refuses to allow polity to evolve and develop.

Bishop Swing, the Episcopal bishop of California, is one of those leaders who will allow and even encourage jumps to take place even in religion. This is evident in his genuine support of the NOS community and its efforts to jump-start our liturgical tradition so that it includes postmodern language and symbols. He demonstrated his commitment when he invited the NOS community to San Francisco, and in an article entitled "Let 'em Rave for God's Sake" that he wrote for the Episcopalian newspaper. In the article he defended the Planetary Mass against people upset by rumors they had heard about it.

> In 1994 there will be a minimum of 2,600 regular worship services in our Diocese and one Rave Mass, on October 30. We aren't recklessly abandoning our liturgical tradition. We are simply making a little room for young adults to offer their culture and music and lives to God. A recent survey of 50 young adults joining the United States Navy showed that 48 of the 50 had no religious affiliation and that 42 out of the 50 had never stepped foot inside a church. This, more than questionable decorum, is the scandal before us...
>
> It is clear that a lot of hostility is pent up around Fox and the Rave Mass. One person just called to say that she didn't want "that trash" around Grace Cathedral. She meant the young adults who might come to share in the Eucharist. Well, I'm committed to "that trash." In 15 years I have never received a phone call or letter berating this Church for its almost total spiritual neglect and abandonment of young adults. But when we take one step to respond to the youth, we suddenly are seen as dealing in trash. So be it. I am personally proud to be associated with a deep compassion for our ecology, with its respect for water, air, earth and young people as gifts from God and thus having abiding worth. Let 'em Rave, for God's sake.[19]

This kind of defense of orthopraxis is what will make a difference in ecclesial and religious history. It is a pity it is so rare in our time. I am blessed to have found it in the Episcopal leadership in California as well as in dioceses of northern England.

## THE END OF TWO ERAS

We should not be surprised, lost, or depressed because the "Roman Catholic era" as we have known it and lived it is rapidly coming to an end. The historical conditions on which it rested are fast melting away. Like Tillich, who says the Protestant principle ought not come to an end, but ought to take on new form, I think it can be said that the Catholic principle ought not come to an end but ought to take on new form. What is the "Catholic principle"?

It is decidedly not about popes or infallibility or sex as such. The Catholic principle, as I have experienced it, is about cosmology, mysticism, and wisdom. To me what is authentic in the word Catholicism does not apply to religion or church as such but to an attitude toward life that is universal, that is, cosmological.

The Catholic principle is our *Yes* to life just as the Protestant principle is our *No* to life's enemies, all that claims to be Life that falls short of it. Indeed, if we put these two together, a Protestant principle and a Catholic one, we are talking about a reconstruction of Western Christianity. We are also talking about what constitutes a deep spirituality, namely, our mystical and prophetic responses to life. This would move us from religion to spirituality. A postmodern era gives us permission to do just that: take what is worth saving from the burning building of Western ecclesial history and forge a simpler, more radical spiritual effort for the next millennium. A faith that has more in common with Jesus of Nazareth's teaching of compassion and with the Cosmic Christ's teaching of divinity everywhere in the universe.

If it is true that we are living through the end of the Protestant era *and* the end of the Roman Catholic era, and into a new postdenominatinal era, then surely we are required to take the *best* of the Protestant principle and the *best* of the Catholic principle and leave the rest behind. We must get on with the task of reconstructing Christianity.

Regarding religion's future, I made the following journal entry on August 2, 1993.

*The gap between religion and spirituality is growing ever wider and deeper. Of that I have no doubt. Religion seems to have less and less to do with Spirit, courage, joy, youthfulness, love, or compassion. And more and more people see this and recognize it. Is it at all possible to bridge that chasm and renew religion by renewing worship and offering spiritual praxis? Will all persons who attempt this get expelled as troublemakers?*

Whatever our religious tradition, I think all of us need to heed the warning of Rabbi Heschel: "Religion has always suffered from the tendency to become an end in itself, to seclude the holy, to become parochial, self-indulgent, self-seeking; as if the task were not to ennoble human nature but to enhance the power and beauty of its institutions or to enlarge the body of doctrines."[20]

Somehow I find it easy, in reading wisdom like this, to see Jesus' spirituality coming alive again.

---

## ABOUT THE AUTHOR

**Matthew Fox** is Founder and President Emeritus of Wisdom University (formerly University of Creation Spirituality). He is the author of 25 books on creation spirituality, the mystics, culture and science and spirituality. He is a lover of learning who wants to see education revitalized and a non-violent revolution (i.e. renaissance) occur in human culture by reinventing education, work, and ritual. He developed the (Techno) Cosmic Mass movement to revitalize forms of worship in the West. He lives in Oakland, California.

# seven

# Paying Homage:
# Being Christian in a World of
# Many Faiths[1]

*Bruce Sanguin*

*"We observed the rising of his star, and we have come to pay him homage."*
Isaiah 60:1–6; Matthew 2:1–12

I want to talk about two distinctive religious pilgrimages. One is ancient and the other is modern. The first is the ancient visit of Persian astrologers, the "wise men," to pay homage to the Christ child. The other is the modern pilgrimage of thousands of American Southern Baptists to the biblical land of Persia, now known as Iraq, to convert the heathen Muslims. Both are well meaning, spiritually motivated enterprises. But they represent two radically different models of faith and two different notions of how to get along with people who have a different faith from one's own.

The International Mission Board of Southern Baptists regards the current occupation of Iraq as a unique opportunity to win the souls of the Iraqi people for Christ. John Brady, the head of this organization has sent an urgent appeal to the 16 million members of his church. Jerry Vines, former head of the Southern Baptist Convention, has described the prophet Mohammed as a "demon-possessed pedophile." Franklin Graham, Billy Graham's son, who delivered the invocation prayer at George Bush's presidential inauguration, has described Islam as a "very evil and wicked religion." Jon Hannah, a missionary who has recently returned from Iraq, having distributed 1.3 million Christian tracts, has concluded, "The Muslim religion is an antichrist religion." They deliver food and clothing to the Iraqi people but, says this evangelist, these people need spiritual nourishment even more. That nourishment just happens to come in the form of the Southern Baptist belief system. This is one model of Christian mission and evangelism.

We have the Truth, capital T; their faith is nothing more than a lie, and therefore they must be undernourished. The primary purpose of being a Christian is to convert other people to our faith. The Muslim people quite naturally understand this for what it is – a holy war.

A different model is presented in Matthew's gospel. The Magi notice "a star at its rising." The symbolism is important. Here we have wise people scouring the night skies, not for signs that they have the Truth, but for signs of the truth wherever truth might choose to show itself. They have the wisdom to realize that the Holy One is not restricted to revealing Herself to only their people. They've taken their heads out of their own Bibles long enough to gaze up and out at what is the source of our fundamental unity, rather than at what divides us. The wise ones intuited what science has now confirmed, that the basis of the unity of all peoples of faith is biospiritual. We have come from the same place and are made of the same stuff. We are stardust, reconfigured in human form, inspired by the Creator. They gaze up at the stars and realize that a very special human being is about to be born, a child who is meant to transcend cultures, transcend religious differences, and point us all in the direction of a compassionate Father, the love which fired it all into being.

This star points them in the direction of Israel. They make the journey to Bethlehem in order to pay homage to the newborn King of the Jews. The poignancy of this story in light of the current mutual hatred between Iraq and Israel is not lost on us. Persia had a long history of kindness towards the Jews. When Cyrus of Persia conquered the Babylonian Empire, he allowed religious freedom to the Jews. Many returned home to Jerusalem to rebuild their Temple. The wise men inherited their wisdom from a culture of religious tolerance. Notice they go to Israel for a single purpose, to pay homage. They have no intent, or need apparently, to import their religious beliefs. They open up their treasure chests and offer to the baby gifts of gold, frankincense, and myrrh. Not a mention of religious tracts.

Every Saturday morning, Ann and I go to Granville Island Market to get our groceries. When we've finished shopping, I end up at the Tea Store. There is a pleasant young man who works there. He told me that he was interested in theology and he was thinking of enrolling in a particular theological college, which made it clear that he was heading down a fundamentalist path. I told him that I would like to give him a book to read if he was interested. He became extremely cautious and said he'd have to run it by his pastor. I realized that what I wanted to do for him was to save him from my own experience of fundamentalist Christianity. In the end, I decided against giving him the book. I had been given too many books over the years by those who thought I was in the grips of the antichrist, if not the antichrist himself. And how would my gesture be any different from handing out tracts quoting John 3:16? It's time the religions of the world, including our own, got over having to convert everyone to our belief system. The Magi offer an alternative.

What would ecumenical relations with other faiths look like if they were homage-based? What would it mean for Christians to make the long journey across strange cultural and religious landscapes bearing only gifts of respect for all that is sacred in other traditions? Just after the occupation of Iraq, people of my congregation visited Muslim mosques and worshipped with them. We invited Aziz Khaki, President of the

Muslim Federation, to address our gathering at Peace in the City. The Rev. Dr. Barry Cooke is organizing an interfaith event for this spring, which will feature persons from all faiths and of no particular faith, including the Dalai Lama of Tibet, Bishop Desmond Tutu, and Václav Havel. These are modern-day versions of the journey of the Magi. We need to be looking for and following the rising star of respect among different faiths.

It seems to me that we can learn from the Magi in another respect. Their wisdom extends to intuiting those people and political systems that are contrary to the very principles of life itself. In their encounter with Herod, they recognize a person and a political system that is anti-life. Herod embodies a paranoid worldview that is the enemy of all that is sacred. Where there is abundance, Herod sees scarcity. Where there is security, Herod sees imminent threat. Where there is love, Herod feels judgment. Where there exists the possibility of shared power and wealth, Herod uses his muscle to ensure a disproportionate amount falls his way. Where there is diversity, Herod imposes monocultures of his own creation. Where there is the threat of real democracy, Herod silences the people. Because of the Magi, the faiths of the world can withdraw allegiance from these systems and work together to articulate and enact an alternative vision.

As Christians, we express this vision in response to the revelation of Jesus Christ. We need to do this passionately and with all the conviction we can muster. We need to honor our sacred traditions, symbols, and narratives as sacramental; they have the power to open us up to the deep mysteries of God. The Magi were steeped deeply enough in their own tradition that they could make a pilgrimage into another culture and religion. They enjoyed the security of their own faith system sufficiently that they could pay homage to another. This, too, should be our model. I believe that the deeper we go into our own faith system, the closer we get to God, and the closer we get to God, the more we are informed by values of diversity, inclusivity, and respect for the inherent dignity of other people and faiths.

Notice that, after their encounter with the Christ child, the Magi "returned home by another road." We can take this as a metaphor suggesting that their encounter with the sacred center of another religion had a transformative effect on them. Matthew doesn't say, mind you, that they converted to Christianity after meeting the baby. Many of us make that assumption. They were probably Zoroastrians. They were so when they arrived and nothing in the story even hints that they became followers of Jesus afterwards. They went home. But they went home by a different road, meaning they allowed themselves to be influenced by the experience. The United Church of Canada (the denomination in which I minister) has missionaries around the world. But they don't go to their placements with all the answers. If you want a picture of what that kind of arrogance results in, read Barbara Kingsolver's *The Poisonwood Bible*. You may remember that the missionary insisted on baptizing the African people in the river. They thought he must be crazy, for they knew what he hadn't taken the time to find out – the river was filled with crocodiles.

There are two elders in my congregation, Kay Metheral and Muriel Bamford, who know what it is like to follow a rising star across different religions and cultures. Each spent a good portion of their ministries in India. They went with a set of skills, in their cases as nurses, skills that had been requested by the people themselves. If asked, they will tell you that they returned home by another road, profoundly affected by the experience, having received at least as much as they gave, and having found Christ in the people they served, whether they were Christian or Hindu. May the wisdom of the Magi prevail.

---

## ABOUT THE AUTHOR

**Bruce Sanguin** is minister of Canadian Memorial Church & Centre for Peace in Vancouver, British Columbia. He has been a United Church of Canada minister for 18 years. Before that, he was a practicing therapist, and he remains a member of the British Columbia Association for Marriage and Family Therapy. He is married to Ann Evans, who is also a marriage and family therapist. He is the author of *Summoning the Whirlwind: Unconventional Sermons for a Relevant Christian Faith,* which is available from Wood Lake Books.

# eight

# Radical Inclusion

*Anne Squire*

"What Jesus preached was 'the kingdom'; what he got was the church!"

These words from Don Cupitt[1] are a wake-up call to ask ourselves why the church is not practicing the radical inclusion of the kingdom described by Jesus, and what needs to change for the kingdom of God to be here and now.

"Radical inclusion" is the practice of including, in any community, those who are normally excluded. For Christian communities, Jesus is the model of someone who lived and taught "radical inclusion." For other faith groups, the model will be something or someone different, but radical inclusion demands that membership in the community in question be open to all.

### THE KINGDOM OF GOD AND THE LANGUAGE OF INCLUSION

What did Jesus mean when he talked of the kingdom of God? Before addressing that question, we must first look at the phrase "the kingdom of God" itself, because that very phrase raises its own issues of inclusion and exclusion. For many people today, any talk of a "kingdom" evokes images of an authoritarian, hierarchical organization with leadership to match. But the kingdom Jesus preached was the very opposite of this. Marcus Borg says that when Jesus spoke of the kingdom, he was evoking a new social vision, which included both the social and the political – an inclusive kingdom so different from that of Herod and of Caesar that the system of exploitation and domination experienced by the people of his day would be a thing of the past.[2]

Robert Funk reminds us that the language Jesus used also constituted a huge irony for those who sought the restoration of the Davidic kingdom. The kingdom Jesus preached was to be as this-worldly as David's, but quite different in its ethical implications.[3]

John Dominic Crossan acknowledges the dilemma which the word "kingdom" raises for many people.

> I am not particularly happy with the word kingdom as a translation of the Greek *basileia*, but it is so traditional that any alternative might be confusing... The basic question is this: How does human power exercise its rule, and how, in contrast, does divine power exercise its rule?... The Kingdom of God is what the world would be if God were directly and immediately in charge.[4]

Even if the word "kingdom" *does* raise damning images today, we cannot escape the fact that the teaching of Jesus focused on the kingdom of God and that any alternative to this translation disguises the shock value the phrase would have had when Jesus used it. The words commonly substituted are "kindom," "realm," or *basileia,* but none is as strong as kingdom. It seems better to redeem the word than to substitute another, and to concentrate on the differences between the kingdom of God and the kingdoms of this world.

## THE PROMISE OF RADICAL INCLUSION

Over 100 times in the gospels, Jesus speaks of the kingdom of God, giving us a picture of how welcoming it is. In God's kingdom, everyone is welcome. Indeed, Jesus extended a special welcome to anyone who had been left out of the society of his day.

In our most familiar prayer, Jesus names the two central concerns of the people of his day: bread and debt forgiveness. The coming of God's kingdom meant that there would be bread for breakfast, and the removal of debt, a burden too many carried because of the economic exigencies of the day. Jesus is quoted as saying, "Blessed are the poor, for theirs is the kingdom," but that kingdom, as described by Jesus, is not in heaven in the future but on earth in the here and now. This is what sets God's kingdom apart. Jesus insisted that God's kingdom is present and available to everyone. The leper and the blind man, the poor farmer and the rich young ruler, the tax collector and the widow, the Samaritan and the Jew, children and women, sinners and outcastes, Pharisees and Sadducees, even the lilies of the field and the sparrow that falls – all are part of God's creation and all are welcome in God's kingdom.

In a time when power and privilege were concentrated in the palace of a royal kingship and in the leadership of the temple, both of which practiced exclusion, Jesus challenged both with his vision of a new world order and a practice of radical inclusion. Jesus set the pattern of inclusion by teaching that many of the rituals and practices of the Jews of his day were extraneous to the kingdom. Circumcision, the laws of clean and unclean, and Sabbath observance were not mandatory for membership. He practiced an "open table," eating and drinking with those who were considered outside the pale. Indeed, John Dominic Crossan says that Jesus robs humankind of all protective privileges, entitlements, and ethnicities that segregate people into categories.[5] To cling to ethnic practices when God is offering a new vision is to forego what was being promoted by the new vision: right relationships, community, liberation, justice, and peace.

The stories and the parables of Jesus, as well as the sayings, condemn the practice of dividing people into "insiders" and "outsiders." What a shock it must have been to hear Jesus say, "Love your enemies"! How would it have felt to have Jesus praise the Samaritan as a better model of community than the priest and the Levite? The message of the king-dom was not only preached in the sermons of Jesus, but practiced and celebrated in his life as he ate with sinners, healed on the Sabbath, and encouraged women to think and learn, challenging the community in ways that were radical and shocking in his day.

The kingdom of God, as defined by Jesus, is a realm of radical in-clusion, a society of radical equality. It is a realm where justice and love replace systems of injustice. This is more than a personal matter. Systemic injustice, caused by unjust social and political systems, makes it difficult for the majority of earth's people to feel part of the kingdom. Abundant life in the kingdom means helping to make justice available to all. In the kingdom, distributive justice would replace retributive justice with a just and equal sharing of material things, and a just and equal sharing of justice.

For those who insist that the only way into the kingdom is through Jesus, there is a reminder that no one has the right to limit God's choice of who can inhabit the kingdom. In a multicultural, multi-faith world, we share the realm of God with those of other cultures and other faiths. Marcus Borg says that when Christianity lets go of its claim to be the only true religion and accepts its status as one of the great religions of the world, it has great credibility – not as a set of statements to be believed but as a sacrament of the sacred.[6]

Jesus also makes it clear that no one has the right to *speak* for God in the choice of who is in and who is out. In her book *Making God Laugh*, Anne Primavesi reminds us of the arrogance of those who claim to speak for God when all we can really do is speak *about* God or *to* God. She thinks that God must laugh when we speak about God's plans for us.[7] She says:

> The vision of God conveyed in the earth-centered life and teaching Jesus consistently transcends and subverts the tradi-tional ideas of God's plan for the world. Jesus' refusal to exclude others from table fellowship on grounds of their unclean status

constantly subverts our idea of how God's wisdom might categorize us.[8]

Primavesi, who was raised a Roman Catholic, left the church when she realized that its doors had been permanently closed to so many. She had learned that the kingdom has no doors or walls to exclude people. Instead, the kingdom has open doors and practices radical inclusion.

### THE PRACTICE OF RADICAL INCLUSION

How well is this vision of radical inclusion being practiced in the world today? In our communities there is evidence of unjust social and economic relationships, oppressive political leadership, biased race relationships, and as Walter Wink reminds us, "violence to maintain them all."[9]

Even in the church, which should be the very place where inclusion is best practiced, we discover, in different degrees in different communities, restrictions on the sacraments; exclusion of women from ordination; refusal to ordain or marry gays and lesbians; and barriers to the poor, the disabled, and the mentally challenged.

What exclusive practices still need to be challenged today and who is being affected or hurt by their continued existence?

### The poor

This exclusion stems from an unfair distribution of resources, an economic system that favors the rich, and a social system that stigmatizes the homeless and the destitute. What is needed is a political will to make the changes necessary.

### Women

Some denominations do include women in the ministerial leadership of the church; others refuse to accept ordained women and even fail to include the women in the decision-making processes of the church. The rationale these latter churches often offer is that Jesus was a man and chose only male disciples; they forget the important role women played in the ministry of Jesus and in the early church. Feminists have accomplished much in terms of opening doors that have traditionally been closed to women, but this is still a patriarchal culture.

### Children and youth
In speaking about children, Jesus made a point of saying that "of such is the kingdom of Heaven." Children and youth are not the church of the future; they are part of the church today and their opinions matter. The educational resources used by the church need to reflect their questions and concerns.

### Gays and lesbians
The current debate over the role of gays, lesbians, bisexual, and transgender people in both church and society illustrates one of the deepest and most hurtful exclusions in our society. Even though more and more people are becoming more inclusive in their outlook once they come to know people whose sexual orientation is different from their own, we still have a long way to go to make genuine acceptance the rule and not the exception.

### People of different races
Canada prides itself on being a tolerant society that affirms diversity. Yet racial intolerance is a part of too many neighborhoods. People are still classified by the color of their skin, by their accents and by their dress. Fortunately, the younger generation seems to be more accepting than the older one.

### First Nations people
First Nations people have a long history of being excluded from Canadian and American society. In a naive and misguided effort to help aboriginal peoples become a part of a newly developing society, governments and churches succeeded only in robbing them of their lands, their culture, their language, and their birthright. Even their children were lost

to them when many were taken from their villages and placed in residential schools where they were not allowed to speak their own language.

### People who are challenged physically, mentally, and emotionally

Although many congregations are making an effort to make their church buildings physically accessible to all, few are giving much thought to including those who are mentally or psychologically challenged. Openness to these kinds of differences will still require much practice, patience, and persistence.

### Saints and sinners

While Jesus said he came not to welcome the righteous, but to bring sinners to repentance, the church took it upon itself to decide which was which. Saints were only those so named by certain branches of the church. For "sinners," rituals of confession, repentance, and rehabilitation became barriers instead of open doors. Many of these concepts and rituals are challenged by the concept of radical inclusion. Especially challenged is the teaching that God's forgiveness can only come when a sacrifice has been made and that the supreme sacrifice was the death of Jesus on the cross. Understanding that there are no such limits to God's forgiveness means that both saints and sinners are welcomed into the kingdom.

### Christians in exile

A church which is radically inclusive will welcome those who are now living "in exile" from the church. People may be staying away because they have not felt welcome. Others may exile themselves because they can longer believe what the church has taught for centuries. Every congregation needs a safe place where people who might be labeled "heretics" can say what they really believe, and still be part of the community.

### Spiritual seekers

Many who can no longer accept the theology being preached in our churches still experience a spiritual longing for something they know they need. There is, among countless individuals on the fringes of the church, an ongoing search for a new spirituality that answers their need to understand the meaning and purpose of life. Those who seek and question should be welcome in the kingdom.

### All strands of ministry

A radical inclusion of all strands of ministry would mean that lay pastoral ministers, staff associates, and diaconal ministers would be more fully accepted and that ordained ministers would not be threatened by them. The ministry of the whole people is too important to allow ourselves to get caught up in controversy about status and privilege.

### Nature and the environment

The kingdom of God is more than a "people place." It is a realm where the earth is more than "landscape." As Anne Primavesi reminds us, the earth itself is alive; rather than just hosting life, it is a dynamic, self-organizing system.[10] As part of a larger system which existed without humans for millions of years, we need the earth more than it needs us. This realization changes our understanding of ourselves and relationship to the environment. No longer can we claim be the center and the caretakers of the earth. Instead, we see ourselves as recipients of the gifts of the earth – gifts without which we could not exist. Radical inclusion includes the earth itself.

### Science and technology

The kingdom of God has room for scientific discoveries. We live with a very different perspective on the universe than people had in Jesus' day. We have outgrown the three-tiered universe of the gospels. Galileo changed forever the concept that humans are the center and focus of creation. Ever since then, we have been trying to find the right relationship between planet earth and the kingdom of God. Science and technology are gifts from God to be used for the benefit of all people.

### Tradition and change

Theology of the kingdom has a place for tradition, but there is a need to distinguish between tradition that excludes and hampers, and tradition that adds to the concept of the kingdom of God as preached by Jesus. The creeds developed in the second and third centuries no longer speak to many people today. For example, the Nicene Creed focuses only on the birth and death of Jesus, leaving out the entire ministry of Jesus and his focus on the kingdom. There is a need to deconstruct much of our theology before we can reconstruct one that allows for both the useful new and the useable old.

## THE PROGRAM OF RADICAL INCLUSION

So how can we become the inclusive communities that Jesus proposed? For some, the way is simply in the doing – practicing radical inclusion in daily life and promoting it in community. For others, the very foundations of faith seem to shake when there is talk of becoming more inclusive. For them, it is not enough to say "Follow the example of Jesus," because that is what they sincerely believe they have been doing all along. Yet if their Jesus is the Christ of the creeds, they may have lost sight of the Jesus of the gospels. The Jesus who preached radical inclusion may threaten the walls they have built around their faith, and when someone threatens to breach those walls, they may become defensive of their current practice.

What we need in these situations is education about the early days of Christianity. The focus, then, was on sin and salvation rather than on the kingdom. We also need education about the new formulations of theology, which allow the church to re-create itself. Fortunately this is a distinct possibility.

The church constantly falls short of the ideals offered us in the gospel. It is – we are – a work in progress. But this process is inexorably driven by the fact [that], as Walter Brueggemann said, "The arc of the gospel is always bent toward radical inclusion."[11]

The theology that undergirds radical inclusion is as radical as Jesus and as inclusive as God's love, but it may require a paradigm shift in our understanding. Members of the Jesus Seminar believe that by recovering the Jesus of history, we can reclaim the reign of God in human affairs.[12] They also believe that those who would "save" the literal meaning of the gospel will "lose" it.[13]

Robert Funk, the founder of the Jesus Seminar, sums up the contribution made by these scholars:

> It is the vision that Jesus had of God's domain, not the myth of God incarnate, that is the bedrock of our discovery. The rediscovery of this vision was provoked initially by the collapse of the old mythical framework: the disintegration of the myth sent us in search of something beyond and behind the myth.[14]

That something turned out to be a new vision of Jesus and his concept of radical inclusion.

## THE CHALLENGE OF RADICAL INCLUSION

The main problem with exclusive practices is that they can become habits ingrained in our psyches and can come into play automatically, not just in the church but in all of our relationships, unless we learn to think the kingdom way.

Of course, the notion of radical inclusion as an antidote to exclusivist practices is not embraced by all. In the Episcopal church, USA, "radical inclusion" has been called the "working theology" of the denomination as it moves towards inclusion of gays and lesbians in its ministry. While many priests welcome this step towards greater inclusion, others see it as an outrage and the issue itself has become so contentious that it threatens the unity of the church. Just as divorce and remarriage, and the ordination of women originally met with much resistance, so too, this new expression of inclusion is seen as *too* radical by some.

All those who are more accustomed to be greeted with derogatory name-calling than with hospitality welcome this call for inclusion. This includes those whose race, gender, sexual orientation, political persuasion, disability, mental competence, and even their music, hairstyle, and clothing attract criticism and ostracization. The challenge for Christians is to learn to accept those on the fringe of society. Diarmuid O'Murchu reminds us that the right to protest, and more importantly the duty, is something we need to preserve and foster within a renewed spirituality of our time.[15]

## Conclusion

There is so much evidence today to support the "kingdom of God" emphasis in the teaching of Jesus that it is difficult to understand let alone justify the exclusions, divisions, and differences that accompanied the growth of the church. Today, with the church in decline and mired in outdated beliefs and practices, it would seem that we need to learn how to think the kingdom way of thinking, and to live the kingdom way of living. Every attempt to do so is an indication that the kingdom way is not a reduced version of faith but a fulfillment of the dream of Jesus for life in the kingdom now.

---

### ABOUT THE AUTHOR

**Anne Squire**, B.A., M.A., D.D., LLD., was the first layperson to be elected Moderator of The United Church of Canada (1986–88). That appointment recognized the leadership she has given in the ministry of the laity, in women's concerns, and in the understanding of human sexuality. Her teacher training has been used in curriculum development for the church, and in courses at Carleton University and the Ottawa Lay School of Theology. In retirement, she continues to write and to be involved in justice and educational issues. Anne and her husband Bill have three daughters, five grandchildren, and have celebrated over 60 years of marriage.

# nine

# Social Justice and a Spirituality of Transformation

## *Bill Phipps*

What could I possibly say? I was blank.

Sitting at my desk, I stared first at the piles of papers on the floor, on the chair, on the table. I stared at the piles of mail waiting my attention. I stared at the stack of newspapers, collected in my weeks away. It was the night before Easter Sunday. The church would be full. My body was jet-lagged. My mind was blank.

Our congregation is in middle-class, secure Calgary, Alberta. I had returned home from Sudan on Wednesday, after hearing horrendous stories of the slaughter of innocent people. As part of a delegation of church leaders, we were investigating the stories about villages near the oil fields being razed, and civilians of all ages being massacred. Talisman Energy, headquartered in Calgary, was denying such realities.

The stories were true. In one case, we sat in a circle in the bush hearing the detailed account of the fate of one such village. Taking the lead from the Paramount Chief, the other chiefs told of helicopter gun ships swooping down on their village, fire-bombing their homes and shooting the villagers as they fled.

One of us in the circle asked, "How many were killed?" The Paramount Chief said, "We don't think in numbers." Instead, the people named the grandmothers, children, parents. They represented each with a stone or a stick which they placed in the middle of the circle. We watched, stunned. With tears in our eyes, we watched this dignified process, these dignified faces. Margaret Atwood is correct: "The facts of this world seen clearly are seen through tears; why tell me then there is something wrong with my eyes?"

How could I preach to a congregation of secure, oil-friendly people after witnessing such pain inflicted to extract oil in a faraway place? But the refugee storytellers had not finished telling their story by naming the dead.

After further conversation, the surviving villagers straightened their backs and began to sing. A glorious sound filled the air. Again we were stunned to silence. Again we wept. These Southern Sudanese people would not be defeated or intimidated. Their songs rang not only with defiance, but with genuine hope.

I had my sermon after all. On Easter Sunday, 2001, I told that story of courage and beauty in the midst of fear, uncertainty, and horror. It is, after all, what Easter is really about.

★

Every Friday in Jerusalem, from 1:00 p.m. to 2:00 p.m., women stand in silence bearing witness to the power of non-violence. They are ridiculed by some, despised by others for their so-called betrayal and critique. They are the Women in Black. In silent vigil they have protested the Israeli occupation of Palestine, the establishment of settlements, and other forms of violence. They are primarily Jewish women, citizens of Israel, who believe that non-violent action is the only way to peace. They have been doing this action every Friday since 1988, during the first *Intifada*. There are now seven Women in Black groups in Israel, nine in Canada, and dozens more in 28 countries around the world composed of women of all faiths and of no particular faith. The vigils address violence of all kinds. A spirituality of creative non-violence inspires their collective witness.

★

Picture people of ten different faith traditions dressed in their "worship garments" standing on a stage in Calgary leading the concluding celebration of the Sierra Club's bi-annual conference. The conference theme was "People and the Planet." Position papers, workshops, and speeches involved participants in issues of sustainability. Our planet is sick. Human activity is largely responsible. We are strangling, choking, and poisoning Mother Earth. Instead of recognizing our total interdependence on the complex web of life, we insist on being masters of the universe.

The conference had validated, disturbed, and inspired people to action. The organizers had asked the Faith and The Common Good network to pull together an interfaith celebration of the gift of life and all its intricate beauty. Renowned entertainer and children's advocate Raffi sang songs of sustainability and hope. Each interfaith representative gave a blessing of the Earth from their own tradition and in their own language, and the whole assembly concluded by singing, with Raffi, *This Little Light of Mine.*

★

Bow Riverkeepers is part of the international Waterkeepers Alliance led by Robert F. Kennedy Jr. Their single-minded purpose is to ensure pollution-free waterways throughout the world. There are at least eight local affiliates in Canada. In the summer of 2005, the Bow Riverkeepers, led by Danielle Droitsch, paddled the full 657 kilometers of the Bow, beginning at the Bow Glacier in Banff National Park and ending where it meets the Old Man River in South Alberta.

Their goal was to draw attention to the precarious future of this precious river, which is the primary water source for well over one million people, including the City of Calgary. The experts tell us that the glacier feeding the river will be gone in less than 50 years. Currently the Bow is "maxed out." Irrigation for farming adjacent to the river represents the heaviest use of the river's water. Oil development and municipal needs follow closely behind.

Water is the lifeblood of our planetary home and we are bleeding. Life cannot exist without it, yet North Americans use it as though there were an endless supply. We treat it as a common commodity and are only now waking up to the fact that only three percent of the world's water is fresh, and much of that is inaccessible. Through overuse, misuse, and pollution, we are in danger of parching or poisoning ourselves.

Because of its importance, water has been recognized as sacred and integral to spiritual practice through the generations. The Waterkeepers Alliance seeks to touch the human spirit so that we may be transformed into honoring our rivers and lakes as essential parts of creation. The health of our water reflects our spiritual, political, and economic well-being. Waterkeepers throughout the world remind us that our hearts, minds, spirits, and actions need transformation – now.

★

Reflecting the deep connection between water and spirituality and the cry for transformation in our attitudes and actions, Scarboro United Church in Calgary hosted a "Celebration of Water" in the fall of 2005. The sponsor, ScarboroArts, is "committed to fostering spiritual enrichment and social transformation through the arts. We believe that the arts, at their best, expand human imagination and vision. The arts take us beyond our minds to touch our hearts and spirits."

The festival highlighted the beauty and plight of the Bow River, providing a complementary impetus to the call for action by the Bow Riverkeepers.

I believe that the arts (music, drama, poetry, words, visual arts, and more) not only reflect society and its values, but also can be powerful, prophetic voices calling us to action. In the introduction to his book, *Climate of Fear: The Quest for Dignity in a Dehumanized World,* Nobel Prize winner Wole Soyinka asks, "Is there a better venue than the arts to restore and inspire hope in the midst of darkness and despair?"

At their best, the arts touch the human spirit, going deeply into the place where compassion, generosity, and true illumination happen. By looking at the major issues of the day through the multitude of artistic expressions, true social transformation, and therefore action, is more likely to explode. Social action and spiritual transformation unite in seeking healing, justice, and peace in a world under attack from extreme consumerism, war, and greed for the Earth's resources.

★

The last issue in this context is that of the place of homosexual people in the life of Christian congregations. Increasingly, the genuine welcoming of people with various sexual orientations is challenging the church. Can the church, including congregations, be a safe place for people to be who they are and be able to contribute what they offer? I am grateful that many Christian communities are engaging this matter with openness, patience, and a willingness to listen. Being honest in these explorations is fraught with difficulty. Yet to avoid seeking full and equal opportunity, rights, and welcome for gay, lesbian and transgendered people, is unfaithful to the love and justice of the way of Jesus.

There are a multitude of excellent resources available, not the least of which are the stories of homosexual people themselves. There are now decades of experience in developing a process for congregational education that is faithful, biblically based, patient, and respectful of all people. As some congregations have undertaken this process of "welcoming" or "affirming," they have experienced a transformation of their life together as people of God. I have been privileged to be part of this road to discovery for 25 years. Indeed it is inspiring to witness the development of respectful relationships never before considered nor thought possible.

*

In each of these stories, a universal spirituality with a particular expression lifts up a spirituality of transformation, which leads to action.

A few decades ago, a movement inspired by Paulo Freira found resonance in our churches. It was called the "action/reflection" model of social transformation, of engaging faith communities in social justice work. The premise was both simple and challenging, especially for well-educated, middle-class, North American Christians whose faith is often located primarily in the head, before the heart and feet. Simply put, people were encouraged to engage in a particular action regarding poverty, housing, war/peace, health care, or race relations. After experiencing the social injustice leading to action, the people would gather to reflect on their experience. They would be led in social, political, and economic analysis of the issue. Critical to the whole process was biblical, theological, and ethical study and reflection on their "on the ground" experience.

In today's language, we would say that social transformation through action takes priority over correct belief. It is by immersing ourselves in the complex realities of planetary and human conditions that we begin to understand the true nature of incarnational and redemptive faith. The God of the Bible desires the active living of divine purpose over merely celebrating the idea of correct belief in the One True God. The testimony of David, Deborah, Amos, Isaiah, Esther, Jeremiah, Jesus, Mary, and Paul is unmistakable.

Micah 6: What does God require? Do justice, love tenderly, walk humbly with God.

Isaiah 58: Is this not the worship that I choose? To loose the bonds of injustice, to undo the thongs of the yoke, to let the oppressed go free, to share bread with the hungry, to house the homeless? *Then* your light shall break forth like the dawn and your healing shall spring up quickly.

Amos 5: God says, I hate, I despise your festivals and I take no delight in your solemn assemblies. Instead, let justice roll down like waters and righteousness like an ever rolling stream.

Matthew 25: Just as you did to one of the least of these [persons who are hungry, in prison, naked, stranger, refugee, sick] you did it to me.

In other words, true spiritual transformation is more likely to occur when we "act into belief" rather than when we try to "believe into action." Obviously, this is not always the case. Many of us have been inspired into action by beautiful music, a profound drama, a challenging sermon, or an engaging worship experience. But for middle-class people, such as myself, it is too easy to "stay in the head," wrestle with ideas, debate points of theology, and not quite get to the actions that will transform our lives. More likely it is when we face death, lose our job, experience violence, or act in solidarity with people who suffer injustice that we and our faith will be transformed.

Actions – how we live what we say we believe – are more relevant and important than what we say. Spiritual (not only social and political) transformation is more likely to happen through actual engagement than through seeking to attain correct belief.

In fact, there is much evidence to suggest that those who are adamant about correct belief are the very ones who build walls, start wars, exclude certain people, and condemn those who think and believe differently. Insisting on certain belief ("ours is the only truth") too often leads to the exact opposite of what such belief proclaims. ("We need to bomb them in order to save them.")

Insisting that correct belief results in spiritual and social transformation often leads to self-righteousness, arrogance, and living in a non-existent, idealized, and theoretical world. It also cuts one off from marvelous insights, wisdom, truths, and the experience of those who believe and think differently.

I remember standing on the shore of the frozen Decho (Mackenzie) River talking with George Barnaby, one of many thoughtful Dene leaders in the Northwest Territories. Looking out over the vast expanse spread before us, he talked quietly of the importance of the river, the land, and our relationships within creation. It was a deeply spiritual conversation. It touched new depths in this totally urban Christian. I have much to learn.

More recently, I treasure my regular conversations with Dow Marmur, Rabbi Emeritus at Holy Blossom Temple, in Toronto. He expands my understanding of Christianity's Jewish roots and gives me appreciation for an ancient faith that requires no "completion" or "fulfillment" in Jesus or anybody else.

Certainly, a stance that upholds correct belief provides one with clarity, and a world of absolutes and single purposes. By comparison, the action/reflection approach to spiritual enrichment and social transformation is messy. Just ask Jacob, Moses, and David; or Peter, Mary, and Paul. This approach to faith formation engages reality, lack of clarity, relativity, uncertainty, and nuance. It involves one with the realities of a sinful world, its complexity and our complicity. Inevitably, it involves doubt, compromise, frustration, and asking more questions than receiving right answers. It recognizes the vast array and beauty of belief systems. It accords respect and dignity to those who follow different paths to spiritual enlightenment and social change. It requires humility, acceptance, repentance, and forgiveness. I would suggest that our "spiritual" and "faith" heroes are more often known and respected for their compassion, openness, questioning, and listening to new truths than they are for correct belief, perfect practice, or elegant statements of faith.

From a slightly different perspective, Rebecca Solnit's book *Hope in the Dark: Untold Histories, Wild Possibilities* addresses the question of hope (and therefore, hopelessness) for activists who are discouraged. Sensing a certain paralysis of hope among activists seeking a better world, Solnit tells stories and offers analyses that encourage us to continue the imperfect struggle, with humor, imagination, and a willingness to act against the odds. She invites us to recognize that there are millions of people around the world working locally and globally toward social transformation. She connects spirituality to politics and sees manifestations of communion in unexpected places. She believes that walking the truth transforms the path.

Believing that important change or revolution begins with a vision in the imagination, which we then act upon, Solnit quotes Jonathan Schell in *The Unconquerable World: Power, Non-violence, and the Will of the People:* "Individual hearts and minds change; those who have been changed became aware of one another; still others are emboldened in a contagion of boldness; the 'impossible' becomes possible... the old regime, a moment ago so impressive, vanishes like a 'mirage.'"[1]

In an insight closely related to the straightjacket of correct belief, Solnit says, "Perfection is a stick with which to beat the possible...there is an increasing gap between this new moment, with its capacity for joy and carnival, and the old figureheads. Their grumpiness is often the grumpiness of perfectionists who hold that anything less than total victory is failure... This is Earth. It will never be Heaven."[2]

Moral purity, rigid dogma, correct belief, and perfectionism lead to either despairing frustration or destructive self-righteousness. We need to recover a theology and spirituality of both limitations and possibility. Nothing we accomplish is permanent. The good we do is but another light on the journey of history. We never comprehend the total picture. We are not the most important generation to ever live. In fact, I believe that humankind is not necessarily the pinnacle or chief end of creation. With humility and a spirituality of letting go of our inflated, arrogant view of ourselves, and by accepting ourselves as but part of creation, there is a greater possibility for genuine social transformation toward peace with justice.

Arguing against a mechanistic view of change (which scientific rationality encourages) Solnit reminds us that "History is made of our common dreams, groundswells, turning points, watersheds – it's a landscape more complicated than commensurate cause and effect."[3]

Therefore, we never know the total consequences of our actions. Many small, seemingly ignored actions, done by people motivated by compassion or horror at injustice, have changed history. Solnit tells about a women's peace group standing in the rain in front of the White House, attracting little attention. But Dr. Benjamin Spock saw them, and it became a turning point for him, a catalyst that changed him into a high profile activist for peace.

We act out of intuition, compulsion, even faith, and are transformed in the process. Out of the crucible of seeking the truth in love, of working for a more just and peaceful world, our beliefs are refined by the realities of our earthly condition. Consequently, they are more authentic, believable, and infectious.

One of my spiritual heroes, Archbishop Oscar Romero, understood these things. His is a dramatic story of personal, spiritual, and political transformation. As a priest, Romero was an intellectual, superbly pastoral, conservative, and somewhat quiet pastor to the wealthy elite of El Salvador. He was a "safe" choice as bishop. The hierarchy did not anticipate the radical transformation of this friend of the powerful. As bishop, Romero was confronted first-hand with the economic, political, spiritual, and military violence experienced by the poor and by the priests who served them. When he had to face the murder of "his" priests, the calculated war against the poor, and the oppressive reality with which the vast majority of Salvadorans had to live, Bishop Romero became outraged and began a journey of social solidarity with the poor. His theology, spirituality, and politics were transformed – literally turned upside down. He paid the price of walking the truth in love. While saying Mass, he was assassinated as he raised the Cup of Salvation.

When I was moderator of the United Church of Canada, I had the privilege of worshipping in that chapel on the 20th anniversary, to the day, of his execution. We who celebrated the Mass were from dozens of countries around the world. Visitors from France were there. Their daughter had worked with Romero and had been murdered before him. Later, hundreds, then thousands of us paraded through the street from the chapel to the cathedral downtown. Miguel, the local Baptist minister walking with us, pointed out buildings en route. "They used to shoot at us from the roof of these buildings," he said.

The ceremonies and celebration went on all day and evening. That night there was an all-night vigil in the square outside the cathedral. Performers and speakers, one after the other, addressed the crowd estimated at about 20,000. Around 2 a.m., it was my turn to stand under the full moon and look out over the candlelit crowd of babies and elders, teens and toddlers. I brought greetings of solidarity from the church and the people of Canada. They responded with humbling and exhilarating gratitude. It was a highlight of my term.

A few years before his death, Romero wrote a poem based on Micah 6:8 entitled, "Prophets of a Future Not Our Own":[4]

We accomplish in our lifetimes only a tiny fraction of the magnificent enterprise that is God's work.

Nothing we do is complete…

but it is a beginning, a step along the way, an opportunity for God's grace to enter…

We are prophets of a future not our own…

In keeping with the limitations and possibilities of contemporary reality, I believe our modest efforts for justice and peace are better if they are interfaith, if we fully respect and honor other paths of faith. No one has the corner on truth. We live in a multicultural world; if we are to be effective, our work for social change needs to reflect this reality.

The Faith and the Common Good Network, of which I am a part, represents a Canadian interfaith effort to engage in actions that promote justice, peace, and respect – common ground for the common good.

Recognizing our similar social ethics and shared social concerns, we have worked together on consumerism, health care, and ecological integrity. Working with people of various worldviews can transform and enlighten us. I believe such initiatives are the faith actions of the future.

Mahatma Gandhi said, "The highway to God is through action," and "Fearlessness is the first requisite of spirituality."

As the influence of so-called mainline churches recedes (it remains to be seen if this is a bad thing), and as issues of major social consequence grow, I believe we must take more risks, join hands with sisters and brothers of many traditions, and stand together in fearless witness to truth as we understand it in our limited fashion. By risking mistakes and by not deluding ourselves that we possess "The Whole Truth," we are more likely to make a valuable contribution to the common good. In the process of our actions, we will transform ourselves and our world. Our spirituality will deepen and we will learn we are children of holy purpose.

Reinhold Niebuhr once said, "Nothing worth doing is completed in our lifetime, therefore, we must be saved by hope. Nothing true or beautiful or good makes complete sense in any immediate context of history; therefore we must be saved by faith. Nothing we do, however virtuous, can be accomplished alone; therefore we are saved by love."

By sharing our stories, admitting our fears and failures, yet acting together once again, there is the real possibility that our spirituality will deepen and our world be transformed.

---

### ABOUT THE AUTHOR

**Bill Phipps**, B.A., LL.B, B.D., D.D., was Moderator of The United Church of Canada from 1997–2000. He is an International President of the World Conference of Religions for Peace, and Chair of the Faith and Common Good Network. Bill has been and continues to be an activist in the areas of economic justice, ecology, and aboriginal rights. He has traveled extensively, in various capacities, to Israel, Palestine, Jordan, East Timor, Sudan, Zimbabwe, Congo, and to all countries in Central America. Bill currently serves as minister at Scarboro United Church in Calgary, Alberta.

## Part Three

# emerging forms

# ten

# Worship: Pilgrims in the Faith

## *Mark MacLean*

Journeying by ferry to the island of Iona, off the western coast of Scotland, on a May Sunday morning in 2002 was a personal pilgrimage, a truly mystical affair. A fine mist hung in the air over the water. More deeply felt than the rumbling of the ferry diesels was a roar of the Spirit from ancestors long gone, a tradition burning forth, and the momentum of people preparing for worship. In every sense it was a mystical time, during which my own perception of time began to slip away. My family or "clan" originated from the island of Mull, from whence the ferry to Iona departs, and emigrated to the eastern cost of Canada, to the province of Nova Scotia, seven generations ago. There they settled in Hopewell, Pictou County, near the town of New Glasgow – an ocean away, but culturally a mere puddle jump. This new home for these hardy Presbyterians was shaped by their chapel, St. Columba, still in use today, and namesake of the chapel I was headed to that crisp May morning.

In the sixth century, St. Columba scrambled up the rocky shore of Iona and brought a message, a vision and the Spirit, to that small island, which would open a nation and the world through his faithful legacy. The Iona community and their unique and innovative worship have formed Christians for generations, providing a safe haven for all.

I arrived at the classic, pre-Gothic church for Sunday worship after walking across the island. The church was bursting at the seams and the music was led by an American woman, who played keyboards and who directed a group of young people in their early 20s, who sang and played rhythm instruments. The liturgy was deeply connected to tradition and to rhythmic forms from around the globe, which opened us all to the Spirit moving among us. This was not a dead liturgical tradition, but a living experience of the Spirit named in Jesus Christ and solidly grounded in the Creator. The preacher, a Warden of the community, was from the Presbyterian Church in Canada. She opened the Eucharist with words that were very recognizable to my heart, as we began to recite the statement of faith: "We are not alone…" These powerful words from the "New Creed" of The United Church of Canada, my spiritual home, pulled me from musings of my ancestral home, from the mystical touch of the island of Iona upon which I rested, from the time and pew in which I was sitting, to the Spirit. Lost to time and space, I rested in the Spirit, whose Word and song flowed through me.

*Ruah* is the ancient Hebrew name for the Holy Spirit found in the Hebrew scriptures or Old Testament. The Hebrews took their naming quite seriously, for a name did not simply designate a person; it was an actual representation of who they were. The name revealed the nature of the person; it was not simply a moniker. The name *Ruah* and its Latin translation *Spiritus* have a primary and secondary meaning. The primary meaning is "breath." Without breath, we cannot live. A breath is utterly intangible yet just as utterly required for life. Without *Ruah*, without *Spiritus*, without the *Spirit,* there is no life.

The secondary meaning of the term *Ruah*, along with its Latin and English translations, is "blowing wind." Again, we cannot see the wind itself, but its effects on the sail of a ship or on those who lived through the recent and horrifying hurricanes that hit North America are unmistakable. In essence, we can hear the meaning of *Ruah, Spiritus, Spirit* as "Breath of God," – intangible, yet its effects in and on the community are undeniable. This is not an intellectual concept. This is a deeply spiritual experience – this is the wind that drives us forward. *Ruah* is dynamic; it is the force of the wind; it is the generator of the community and bearer of life. *Ruah* is "God's Breath." This dynamic force is as intimate as the air we breathe. It is equally as necessary to the words we speak, sing, and pray, as it shapes our communities of faith in worship.

For a new generation of faith, our worship must capture this breath of God as the church moves forward and as Christianity is born anew. This new generation of faith is not one lost to the limited descriptions of demographics or sociological analysis. This is not a group we can easily market our wares to. This is a hungry, thirsty, spiritually sensitive and yet deeply critical collection of people who cross all boundaries of age, race, and gender. They are no longer bound by convention in lifestyle, or tradition in their daily existence, and yet they remember these things. Theirs might not be a conscious longing, or clearly defined memory, but certainly the church today represents *something*, both for those within it and for those at its edges. There still lingers a place in society for a system of belief that stood and perhaps may still stand for something that, at root, is positive and meaningful. How our worship represents this faithful convention and living tradition is the core challenge to the church in its mainline incarnation in our age.

It is essential that each worshipping community find a way to lift its faithful membership into that Spirit of God which binds our hearts. Our worship needs to flow in and through our communities, for *God's Breath – Ruah –* is central to our being and vocation.

The fact that we lost our sense of corporate worship as the central if not utterly essential moment in the life of Christian community points directly to the anxiety and concern present in so many of our churches and communities. Questions about leadership, lack of vision, membership, vocation, and isolation, escalate as the vivid, innovative, and creative worshipping lives of Christian communities evaporate. For the faithful who gather each week, and for those who may only faintly remember the story, our challenge is to provide this tradition of Word, song, and prayer, passionately and prophetically. We have a unique opportunity, in the midst of changing cultural norms, to offer the convention we name as Christian community, to the world, as a place of creative innovation, personal safety, moral support, and spiritual sustenance.

To be quite frank, worship is where our communities of faith hit the street. Of course, our outreach, community support, and activism are important and vibrant works of the church. Yet as vocal and prophetic as we may be, it is when two, three, or more gather at worship that our identity in community is named and can be experienced. Those who may want to remember the faith, or who venture to faithful community for support or simply to enter into something other than the daily grind, will experience the desire to linger or leave during these times of public worship. In my opinion, we have a limited window of opportunity in which to live into our tradition in a conventional and touching way. Our challenge is to provide a space for this new generation of faith to find a spiritual home, and to be willing to hear their voice when they arrive. It is through our corporate worship that this window is first cracked open so it can be flung wide for *Ruah* to blow through *them,* and *us.*

Looking to the future of worship in the coming years, it is important, I think, to reflect briefly on the state of things in the mainline worshipping context. Perhaps if we can establish some guidelines for this reflection in our respective communities we can comment on the *art of worship,* which is so essential in this discussion. In my opinion, this is at the heart of our concern, debates, and need. To reclaim worship as an *art form* cleans the slate and provides space for the Spirit to support our creativity and innovation. Our corporate worship must be authentic in its language and be able to acknowledge the natural ebb and flow of human experience, for if it isn't, we are more about bake sales and rummage sales than about the Holy Spirit.

The raging debate among our worshippers and worship leaders is how to remain relevant, contemporary, and "up-to-date." This discussion has spun out in a variety of ways, but the direction that has been most clearly laid out is, unfortunately, a negative one. To put it in perhaps simplistic terms, a great divide has arisen between the "traditional" and "contemporary"worshipping communities.The most destructive element in this conversation is that the language being used is as appropriate for discussions in faith communities as dividing a congregation down the middle using terms like "conservative" or "liberal." In short, the language simply does not work.We need to realize that the terms "contemporary" and "traditional" are in essence irrelevant as categories, because they have taken on solid, finite, and limited definitions. Numerous other labels should be dumped into the recycling box as well, including liturgical renewal, blended, style, seeker, tribalism, ancient-future, and emerging or emergent. Perhaps more misguided is the language of the demographer who uses monikers such as Gen X, Millennial, Baby Boomers, etc. This language simply does not do justice to our discussion, for it originates outside of the broad evolution of the Judeo-Christian liturgical tradition. It is like having a debate in Latin with a Greek speaker. Perhaps we can reflect briefly on the origins of these two worship "camps" before we move beyond them.

## WORSHIP AND COMMUNITY

Many who are reading this will balk at my use of the term "liturgical" claiming that it simply points toward a stayed, traditional, dying church clinging to what it knew as it expresses its last gasps. For some who have participated in the above debate, the term "liturgical" has indeed lost meaning or is associated with an antiquated form of worship. But in my opinion, nothing could be further from the truth. Used in its broadest and truest sense, the term "liturgical" does not refer to a *style* of worship. Rather, it is a word to be used in the context of the worshipping community, *regardless of style*. The term *liturgia* (liturgy/worship) cannot be separated from *ekklesia* (faith community/church).

These terms, borrowed from the Greek speaking Roman contexts of the early church, refer to people called by God (*ekklesia*) and their response to that call (*liturgia*). This is the work of people of faith on behalf of the world, our worship. I would be surprised if anyone reading this cannot find themselves or their worshipping community within this description of the two or three gathered in Christ's name. So now we have found a place to be together in our discussion. But where are we headed?

## THE LITURGICAL RENEWAL MOVEMENT

Since the groundbreaking work of the Second Vatican Council of the Roman Catholic Church, much has happened in the mainline Christian worshipping world. Within the mainline Protestant church, the movement toward "liturgical renewal" is clear. Organizations such as the World Council of Churches, the English Language Liturgical Consultation, the Consultation on Common Texts, and a myriad of multi- and bi-lateral denominational groups have arisen. The work of these groups of scholars and worship leaders has moved much of mainline Protestant worship to a very similar place.

The liturgical renewal movement has subtly influenced the basic structure of worshipping communities in mainline Protestant denominations throughout North America in a very quiet yet foundational way. The accepted norm for worship in these churches is now the practice of the Lord's Supper, Communion, or Eucharist. This is indeed a major shift in worship practice for the mainline churches, in which the Word as preaching was historically central and solitary. Most North American Protestant churches, at the regional and national levels, provide guidelines in the shape of worship books, pamphlets, or suggested forms of worship, for their respective local worshipping communities. Clearly, the use of these resources varies from community to community, but the shift toward the Lord's Supper as normative, or as the "completion" of a worship service, has occurred. This movement can be traced in numerous denominational worship resources, but the shift occurred formally in The United Church of Canada in the 1969 book of worship, *The Service Book*. This "ecumenically minded" form of worship, with the sermon placed more centrally in the worship service, became the "first" order of worship, as opposed to the now "second" order, where the sermon is placed at the end of the service followed by a hymn and the benediction.

This shift reflected a move toward a more balanced view of Word and sacrament (Holy Communion) as equally important in the worship of God's people, as led by the professional cleric. The increased attention to Holy Communion certainly moved the church in the direction of a renewed interest in the more sacred and ritualistic forms of worship. This included, generally speaking, an increased use of hymns and service music, a strong return to the cycle of the Church Year, and broad use of resources to support this perspective. Perhaps the most significant outgrowth of this work was the increased reliance on the weekly published written word, or Sunday bulletin.

Use of resources such as lectionaries, most specifically *The Revised Common Lectionary*; preaching aids based on the lectionary texts; common prayer resources; and shared ritualistic language around the sacraments, marriage, and funerals became commonplace. Clear use of the seasons of the Church Year, its festivals and ritual forms, such as candle lighting, seasonal colors and rites, has dramatically increased. The use of the alb in liturgical garb, as opposed to the traditional Geneva gown, and the move away from the "dog-collar" to the more elaborate stole, are consistent in this movement. Few mainline churches were without an Advent Candle Wreath this Advent, yet a scant generation or two ago this would have been unheard of in most Protestant churches. A myriad of worship resources providing prayers, pre-packaged worship services, and associated Sunday school and adult education-related materials have evolved from the use of standardized texts for Sunday. A framework for this worship on any given Sunday might look something like this.

### The Approach:

Prelude

Processional hymn or Hymn of praise

Opening prayer or Prayer of approach

Prayer of confession & assurance

Act of praise or hymn

## Service of the Word:

Hebrew scripture

The Psalm

New Testament

Hymn or anthem

The gospel

The sermon

## The Response:

Hymn

Prayers of the People/thanksgiving/intercession

The Lord's Prayer

Closing hymn

Blessing/Benediction

Sending forth

Postlude

This basic description of mainline worship in North America is certainly generalized, but I believe it fits the broad picture of the past 30–50 years of worship in this community. This worshipping format can be found in the majority of mainline Protestant churches, from the white rural church to downtown urban barn. The staff resources, size of choir, number of pipes on the organ, and seats in the pews may differ, but generally speaking this format characterizes the worshipping life of the "traditional" camp.

Preachers who used the lectionary text a short 25–30 years ago were considered to be "cheating," or not allowing the Spirit to move their work. For the past generation, those who selected their own text or biblical themes were accused of proof-texting or pandering to personal whim. Today, however, many preachers and worship planners have been through the lectionary cycle so thoroughly that they feel it has lost its prophetic and creative edge. Many have argued that this has contributed to a devaluing of the preaching task in the mainline Protestant tradition. Heavy reliance on fixed resources and liturgical aids has given rise to strong criticism that the liturgical renewal movement has undermined biblical scholarship and its effective presentation in preaching in the local church.

Strong criticism has also arisen within the mainline church that these "traditional" worship styles and formats have limited the creativity and relevance of worship for the modern and "postmodern" individual. Dissatisfaction has been expressed with the seeming inability of mainline worship to dialogue effectively with the experience of a new "pop-oriented" culture, which eschews authority, tradition, and structure. Overly ritualized trappings are criticized as separating the average person from the message of the gospel. Church jargon, irrelevant music, and antiquated language disconnect the everyday person from an experience of the sacred. Finally, the pietistic structure does not allow the person without the "inside" knowledge of the community, to enter into worship or the Christian community.

## "CONTEMPORARY" OR "EVANGELICAL" WORSHIP

This perspective and concern for relevant worship has moved segments of the mainline church in North America and Europe to look to the "Evangelical" tradition for resources, theological reflection, and worship styles. To refer to the "Evangelical tradition" is once again a misnomer. Generally speaking, the term is used to refer to worshipping communities that have arisen from the Anabaptist, Pentecostal, and Free Church communities outside mainline denominations. The use of the term evangelical to describe these groups has developed due to the high emphasis they place in their worship and community ethos, on "conversion," somewhat narrowly defined, to the Christian faith. These communities have largely developed outside of the liturgical renewal and sacramental traditions, and have relied on charismatic local leadership and cultural forms to define their worship pattern. This is the origin of the "contemporary" camp of worship leaders in the mainline denominations.

At essentially the same time as the liturgical renewal movement was being heavily resourced by mainline denominations, the Anabaptist and Pentecostal movements were active designing "culturally relevant" worship. Where the liturgical renewal movement developed frameworks for worship, evangelicals sought freedom. Where the renewal movement employed classic musical forms with printed worship bulletins, evangelicals supported pop-musical styles and new media. Where the renewal movement explored sacraments and the Church Year, evangelicals emphasized self-expression and emotional connection to the Spirit. Where the renewal movement sought broad usage of biblical texts through lectionaries, evangelicals expounded on single brief passages as chosen by worship leaders and preachers. And where the renewal movement entertained visions of a fluid, inclusive church, evangelicals drafted clearly defined theological and moral codes.

Music takes on a new and central significance in this worship style as a moment or opportunity to connect at an emotional level with the gathered worshippers. Preaching and worship are designed to speak to a more practical or commonsense focus in worshippers' lives. Scripture, music, and the movement of worship are defined in a more fluid and energetic process. Leadership includes worship bands, and lay worship leaders, and engages in a more intentional reflection on pop-culture, as a way to connect to "everyday" living. The focus for this contemporary worship becomes the "heart" of the individual worshipper, as opposed to the corporate community gathered. Deep emphasis is placed on discipleship, understood as "bringing people to Christ." Much of the musical styling (the selection of music) and worship design (including selection of scripture) is oriented to creating a theme-based message that will be experienced on numerous levels and, hopefully, accepted.

This contemporary worship is typified in the seeker or "praise and worship" style of worship, and on any given Sunday might look somewhat like this.

Opening music with opening prayers to the spirit
Praise music expressing adoration of God
   (upbeat short repetitive songs)

Music of the heart/self-connection
(energetic moving into reflective songs)
Intimacy with Christ
(Scripture – individual prayers undergirded by music)
Sharing of stories/personal testimony
(lay leader)
Music related to previous story/scripture
Intimate testimony – small groups sharing stories
Sermon (emphasizing message and discipleship –
individual responsibility)
Closing music (moving from reflective to
upbeat conclusion)

Again, this is a generalized description of a contemporary style of worship, which has developed into a formalized framework over the past 40 years, approximately.

## Moving Beyond the Split

These two frameworks for worship, liturgical renewal and contemporary, which I have presented in fairly concrete terms, represent two extremes. In recent years, both "camps" have employed elements of each other's styles in an attempt to enrich worship and, to a large extent, they have failed. "Ancient-future," "emerging," and "blended" worship styles are all loose attempts to incorporate aspects of these quite divergent styles of worship. The irony for both communities is that these styles are dated, outmoded, and neither adequately lifts the culture of the gospel in the midst of the dominant culture. For this reason, we need to release the arguments about worship style so that we can examine and honestly name the theological roots of these divergent worship forms. In doing so, that we can begin to see how what we say and sing has a deep impact on what the community at worship in fact *believes*. The liturgical renewal movement, with its roots in the bygone imperial history of the church, is criticized for lacking a direct and obvious ease with cultural vernacular, and thus, also for a lack of cultural relevance. This may well be true, but the liturgical renewal movement maintains the strong theological tradition of the prophet and pastor, which has carried the gospel forward for two millennia. The roots of the contemporary or evangelical worship movement are firm in a theology of individualist materialism, emerging from North American "pop-culture." This more emotive form may indeed more easily reach the "heart" of the worshipper, but it lacks authentic connection to community in dialogue with tradition. It is in essence not a prophetic or pastoral framework, but one of acquiescence to the dominant culture. Both forms of worship offer tools and resources that can aid our worship of God, but neither should be claimed as uniquely suited to address the mystery that is God's Spirit among us, as revealed and incarnate in Jesus the Christ. The new generation of faith sees past and through these models, but it sees dimly as in a mirror.

This is no criticism of this new generation of faithful Christians, but it simply names the fact that, at best, they need to "re-member" the faith. Most graduated from Sunday school, worship, and thus the active community of faith, as pre- or early teens, through confirmation. At worst, they have no experience of the institutional church, although I suspect that these people represent a very small minority of those who enter our doors. Our worship is where we will meet this new generation of faith and so we must be ready to accept this responsibility. They want the tradition, but they also need to be able to access it. This is not a stylistic question, but a theological and liturgical one. Our worship of God is about more than books versus projection, band versus organ, cleric versus lay. The only factor limiting creativity in the designing and leading of worship in the church is the leaders who do the designing and leading. We need not worship a screen, but we do need to screen our worship.

## AUTHENTIC AND ARTISTIC WORSHIP FORMS TODAY

The future of worship lies in deep authenticity and artistic forms. It "re-members" those who come to us in need of a spiritual home, and invites those in who are touched by something outside of the culture of accumulation, in which we now wallow. In his book *Remembered Voices: Reclaiming the Legacy of "Neo-Orthodoxy,"* Douglas John Hall employs historian Wilhelm Pauck's themes for identifying this school of thought, as a framework for evaluating theological movements. While I do not claim that the Neo-Orthodox movement has defined theological thought for the church, I will employ the five broad themes as a way to reflect on worship in the church today.

I use these five themes, with some adaptation, because they move beyond desire and style, which are defined by ego and culture. These themes point to deep forms of the Spirit and its artistic interpretation, which I have experienced in worship that has worked, firstly for me, and secondly, in corporate worship, as evidenced by the inclusive and spiritually rich nature of the communities in which it was expressed.

1.  **Revelation:** The question, in terms of our worship, is not what we have to say, feel, or wonder about the gospel, but what does the gospel have to say to us. Worship steeped in revelation takes seriously the incarnation of Jesus Christ as prophetic, pastoral, and priestly voice in dialogue with human experience. This worship honors sacrament as a mystery and moment of unity, among people of the Spirit created in God's image. Revelatory worship accepts human frailty and diversity as an essential witness to God's image among us. In this radical inclusion, we can experience the incarnation reflected, named, and realized in the community of Christ.

2.  **A new emphasis on the Bible:** By "new" I mean a radical retelling of the faith history and teaching of the story of salvation. This is not acquiescence to a simplistic literalistic interpretation of the text or loose allegorical "mythic" understanding of scripture. This new emphasis takes the radical challenge of the sacred texts as presented in their context, and drops it directly into our context as raw and real, as if it were written for us today. This "hermeneutic of relevance"

challenges us directly because of course the message of the gospel is written for us here and now.

3. **Historical consciousness:** We cannot go forward with innovation without knowing where we have come from. It is simple arrogance for any worship leader to discount the evolution of Judeo-Christian worship in general and in specific community. One does so at one's own peril. We do not want to recycle the mistakes of the past, while attempting to open the Word in fresh and new ways. There cannot be any final theology or worship style for the church universal. This requires the worship designer to explore the deep richness of the local community and of the historical church, in order to inspire and bear witness to the faith with a new and fresh voice.

4. **Influence of the Reformation:** From Pentecostal to Presbyterian, from Anabaptist to Anglican, we must all acknowledge the deep influence of the reformed movement on our worship and theology. Here is where we share our roots in protest and radical faith movement. Here is where we find the slim convergence that can allow us to bridge the historic and present divides of our faith communities. This reformed spirit is where we can begin to break down the false boundaries of denominationalism and theological division to claim shared history and to vision and reunite the faithful.

5. **Ecumenical character:** To this I must add the reality of our interfaith context. This reference is not to the movement of "ecumenism" that grew out of the late 1960s and early 1970s. Here is where we name in worship the unique identity of Jesus Christ, held up as giver of the Spirit and incarnation of God among us, Emmanuel. We claim ourselves in worship as Christians and share this identity with our brothers and sisters in the Christian faith beyond all boundaries, as imposed by human experience. In doing so, we acknowledge our unique Christian identity openly and honestly with our brothers and

sisters of every faith, and in so doing honor *their* distinct revelation of the creator God.

These themes can be used as a tool for evaluating worship, or simply as a means to reflect upon the task of creating worship. We have now moved beyond the limited language of style and function, to form and substance. We return to the open and fluid language of the community at worship – the *ekklesia* and *liturgia*.

As those who accept the intimate challenge of creating and forming worship in community, we must accept that, like all art, the form and substance of our creation is not always of our choosing. Perhaps a community and its history may authentically demand the integration of a worship band and the 32-foot stop of the organ in the same service. God forbid we might think we have to choose between drama and sermon as a celebration of the Word, or between projection and the use of classic hymn lyrics. For those who come to us from this new generation of faith, we offer our faith as openly in our worship as we are able, so that we might *all* grow past dim images in the mirror. The community at worship is a vast and diverse canvas and we cannot be about limiting its authentic presentation.

We must remember that this debate has been going on for a long time, since before we arrived on the scene, and will continue long after our leadership has ended. As the church explores a new vision of naming Christ in community through our worship, I propose that we hold on to the five broad themes mentioned above as guideposts on our shared pilgrimage in faith. Pilgrims know well that they are not the first to walk a road and they know well that they will not be the last. Pilgrims have a clear destination in mind but are always open to Spirit-filled, mysterious, and unexpected experiences along the journey. More importantly, true pilgrims revel in the rich stories of the other pilgrims around them, who are moving on their own distinct paths toward the same destination. Authentic, innovative worship moves beyond the concerns of bulletins and spreadsheets, instrumentation and multimedia, personality and taste, age and tradition, and points to the mystical realm of the Spirit.

Worship that stands against the imperialistic nature of our history welcomes and stands with the oppressed and the excluded. Worship that challenges the individualistic materialism of the "pop-culture" creates authentic communities that are relevant and innovative for a new generation of faith. With worship that takes seriously the experience of revelation, the radical nature of biblical faith, and that claims our shared historic path, we can look to the future with hope. Authentic worship names our unique heritage amidst our diverse reality, and openly shares the richness of the full human condition as spiritual gift.

I was not the only pilgrim present in that chapel on the island of Iona on that misty day in May and I will not be the last. I was not the only worshipper lost in the Spirit on that day and I will not be the last. Worship in Christ's name – which tears open hearts, breaks down barriers, and enlivens minds to be in faithful community – is inspired by and lives intimately within *Ruah*. We must breathe God's breath in our *liturgia* so we might truly be the *ekklesia* for the world.

## Sources

*A Wee Worship Book*. Wild Goose Worship Group, Wild Goose Resource Group. Chicago: GIA Publications Inc., 1999.

Barthel, Alan, David R. Newman, Paul Scott Wilson. *A Guide to Sunday Liturgy*. Toronto: The United Church Publishing House, 1998.

Hall, Douglas John. *Remembered Voices: Reclaiming the Legacy of "Neo-Orthodoxy"*. Louisville: Westminster John Knox Press, 1998.

Harding, Thomas, and Bruce Harding. *Patterns of Worship in The United Church of Canada 1925–1987*. Historical monograph, 1996.

Hawn, C. Michael. *Trends in Worship*. As taken from the website of the United Methodist General Board of Discipleship: http://www.gbod.org

*The Meaning of "Spirit" in the Old Testament.* John Paul II, General Audience, January 3, 1990. *Internet Office of the Holy See:* http://www.vatican.va

---

## ABOUT THE AUTHOR

**Mark MacLean** is presently serving the national office of The United Church of Canada, in Toronto, Ontario, in the role of National Worship Program Coordinator. Mark's work is to support the worship leaders of the United Church across the country, through resource development, peer networking and leadership development. Prior to this appointment, Mark was in pastoral ministry for ten years, and completed internships in Papua New Guinea and British Columbia. Mark has survived 20 years of rugby only to again don the blades and restart a rather ill-fated ice hockey career. Angela, his wife; Joseph, his son; and Jack, the English Setter; keep him grounded and inspired.

# eleven

# To Sing or Not to Sing: That Is the Question[1]

## *Bruce Harding*

*...it was you who formed my inward parts; you knit me together in my mother's womb. I praise you, for I am fearfully and wonderfully made.*
(Psalm 139:13–14a, NRSV)

Humanity is blessed with innate musicality. Although music is culturally specific, to the point that much of the world's music would not sound like music to us, the physical imperative to make music is a deeply ingrained part of who we are. It is a truly universal cultural phenomenon.[2]

*Let the word of Christ dwell in you richly; teach and admonish one another in all wisdom; and with gratitude in your hearts sing psalms, hymns, and spiritual songs to God.*
(Colossians 3:17, NRSV)

As Christians, the biblical call to sing is at the root of our musical practice in worship. For generations, particularly in Protestant traditions, we have lifted hymns of praise and lament to God, sharing in corporate song as a central, unifying act. The metrical psalms of the Presbyterian tradition, the great Lutheran chorales, the fervor and zeal of Methodist hymnody – all are a legacy of this great tradition of congregational, musical practice.

So what the hell is happening in worship today? I use the word "hell" quite intentionally, because it is certainly not heavenly! What has happened to the great tradition of congregational song? In many congregations throughout North America and Europe, singing has become a pitiful experience, a few voices straining to carry the tune while the majority dutifully mumble along, or wait in stoic silence for the song to end. We sing not because "we cannot keep from singing," but out of a sense of duty, merely because *it is tradition.*

In recent years, our secular culture has changed. Just as babies come out of the womb with an innate sense of how to breathe correctly, then gradually learn bad habits, our culture is now robbing us of the instinctive need to sing and make music. The ability to freeze music for all time on a recording, plus the various technologies for delivering recordings to us – from radio through to portable music players – are diminishing our need to make music ourselves in order to experience it. Television and the movies have become the chief source of personal entertainment, making evenings around the piano, accordion, or guitar with family and friends seems like a nostalgic relic of the past. We have become passive consumers of music and this passivity is affecting our congregational song.

Of course, worship trends in recent generations have also contributed to the decline of congregational song. We can't blame this entirely on the secular world! Performance culture has predominated among our church musicians, mirroring the rise of the cult of "the artist," especially through the 19th century,[3] and more recently the "global superstar" in the age of mass media. How many choir members have you known who stay home if they aren't singing an anthem that week? How many instrumentalists (and congregation members) expect that the congregation should sit quietly and wait while the postlude is played, then dutifully applaud? How much time does your choir devote to practicing the congregational hymns during its weekly rehearsal? Is the focus mainly on the anthem? Do your choir and other music leaders see their role primarily as leaders of congregational song?

Many churches have responded to the decline of singing by embracing popular culture, bringing "rock" instruments like drum kit, electric guitar and bass, and singers on microphones into worship, in the hope of enlivening music, keeping the music "upbeat." Opening praise sets of multiple songs begin the service, with every piece representing a similar theological stance of unbridled praise. But has this really solved anything? Is it not simply replacing one performance model with another? The fundamental question is: has congregational song improved?

Christianity itself is becoming increasingly countercultural. With the decline of Christendom, walking the path of Jesus has become a minority position in many parts of North America and Europe. But this is not something to mourn; instead, it is something to embrace and celebrate. At its heart, the message of Christ has always been subversive, a radical rethinking and questioning of societal norms. We are simply returning to the heart of the gospel, living out God's vision for a new community here on earth today, each in our own contexts and communities. In a similar manner, congregational song has also become subversive. We are simply returning to the heart of Christianity, rediscovering the joy, power, and passion of our collective musical voice. Here are some observations on the emerging paradigm of congregational song, some hopes and dreams as we sing our way into "the new heaven" here on earth.

### "All My Hope Is Firmly Grounded"[4]

Increasingly, congregations are becoming aware of how much our music grounds us in worship, of music's ability to create what Celtic Christians called "thin places."[5] Because of this ability, we need to be truly intentional about every musical matter in our worship service, so that every song becomes a vehicle for the presence of the holy in our midst.

Hymns and other forms of congregational song are a primary expression of our theology as worshipping communities, and must therefore be chosen wisely. Simply selecting a hymn because the congregation (or minister or musician) likes it is not enough. We need to ask questions of our songs: "What is the message contained in these words?" "Does the tune support the delivery of that message?" "Is the message and the energy of this song a good fit for this moment in our worship?" This does not mean that we should be narrow in our theological perspective, but rather that we should plan with awareness and with a good sense of context.

The manner in which we lead and accompany a song is equally critical. Every piece we sing in worship, from the shortest prayer response to a seven-verse hymn, deserves our full attention as leaders and singers. To simply toss off a song we don't particularly care for while focusing our energy on the type of music we personally enjoy does a disservice to the song and to the community. Every type of music provides an authentic connection with the Spirit for someone in our congregation. Therefore, we need to do all we can to bring *all* songs to life. Let the voice be the primary instrument for an African chorus; use the organ as the primary accompaniment for a grand tune like SINE NOMINE, to the hymn "For all the saints, who from their labors rest." Every song has an authentic or natural way of coming to life given a sensitive treatment.

## "YOU AND I BE THE SINGERS"[6]

The irony of our worship culture today is that *the worship wars* – the constant battle between supposed "traditional" and "contemporary" voices, between organ and "praise band," however you want to phrase it – *are completely irrelevant*. Increasingly, we are rediscovering that the only essential instrument for congregational song is the human voice. And when we focus on that corporate voice, on lifting it up and supporting it, all other issues fade away. It is not a matter of which instruments are appropriate for use in church, but rather a matter of which instrument or instruments are required (or not) for a particular song.

Many musicians are afraid to simply let people sing unaccompanied, insisting on, at minimum, playing gently underneath. But much of the global song coming into worship today, from Africa in particular, comes out of a context of a cappella or unaccompanied song. (This is true of many of the old Reformation tunes as well.) Listen to a recording of an African choir singing a song like "Sanna, sannanina," or to a recording from the Taizé Community of thousands of voices singing a cappella, and you will hear the pitch drop. This is natural, and perfectly fine. Experience shows that the more a congregation sings a cappella the stronger their singing becomes, because "there's no one else doing our job for us." An unaccompanied verse in a multi-verse hymn may result in a hesitant sound at first, but the volume quickly increases as people hear the sound of their own voices.[7] Duty quickly turns to delight when a sense of accomplishment and ownership over congregational song prevail. The mark of a Spirit-filled church is one in which the communal voice is at the heart and soul of worship.

When the congregational voice is primary, all instruments therefore have a secondary yet vital role. The most primal instrument for human musical expression is the drum, and the use of the drum in worship is increasing.[8] Drums and other percussion are a part of most musical cultures throughout the world; the physicality present in the combination of the breath of song with the heartbeat pulse of a drum has deep roots in our psyche. Drums are particularly helpful in maintaining the tempo and pulse of music while singing a cappella.

Acoustic instruments such as a pipe organ or piano are more effective than their electronic counterparts simply because it is difficult to accurately synthesize and reproduce the overtones of acoustic instruments. Electronic instruments *do* have a valued place in worship, but are best used to create new sounds not available acoustically, or to fill out the sound by adding instruments that would otherwise be unavailable (a "string pad" or "wash" for example).

## "LOST IN WONDER, LOVE AND PRAISE"[9]

Many of the ancient, grand hymns of the church contain a beauty and a depth of poetic expression that transcend time. The glory of a well-voiced pipe organ on a final verse, with the congregation in unison and a soaring descant from the soprano section of the choir, is an amazing gift from God. It is imperative that we remember *there is nothing wrong with our tradition*. It has fed our people for generations, and will continue to feed us in the future.[10]

Great hymns of the faith are filled with a deep sense of awe, wonder, mystery, and with the power of association with "all that has gone before," both in our own worship lives and with the communion of the saints. These are elements to lift up, cultivate, and celebrate, for they are at the heart of worship. If we simply sing these ancient songs out of a sense of duty, or if we remove them from worship entirely, we cut off our roots, and as a result our "branches wither above" (Job 18:16).

In our modern reality, however, in which many people in our churches have not been raised in the tradition, we cannot simply sing these songs because "that's what we have always done." We must choose wisely,[11] teach, and give people context so that these songs continue speak to us. According to legend, for example, John Wesley's favorite hymn or psalm was "I'll praise my Maker while I've breath," Isaac Watts' metrical rendering of Psalm 146. On his deathbed, Wesley could be heard still trying to sing the opening words of this powerful song: "I'll praise…, I'll praise…" Knowing this, the opening verse takes on a whole new meaning:

> I'll praise my Maker while I've breath;
> and when my voice is lost in death,
> praise shall employ my nobler powers.
>> My days of praise shall ne'er be past,
>> while life and thought and being last,
>> or immortality endures.

This is an important part of our task today, to open up our traditions with awareness and sensitivity, and to bring them to life, to help our congregations experience the awe and mystery of these ancient texts and tunes, to invite our people to sing in communion with the saints who have gone before us, in the spirit of the Great Thanksgiving.

## "O, Sing a New Song…"[12]

Of course, to simply dwell in the past will suck the life out of a worshipping community. We need that sense of both "roots and wings"[13] to truly be a transformational people in the world, and therefore we must also always be ready to "sing a new song." John Bell, of the Iona Community, describes this ancient, biblical imperative, calling it the 11th commandment:

> It is commonly believed that God gave Moses ten commandments.
>
> The possibility is that God gave eleven, but that Moses didn't have room on the stone tablets to engrave the final one, so God had to wait until David came along and let the forgotten decree be heard: "Sing a new song!"
>
> That this is a divine commandment and not a human option can be gleaned from the fact that the words *Sing a new song!* do not appear just once in the Bible, but are explicitly stated in Psalms 33, 40, 96, 98, 144, and 149.
>
> Echoes or intimations of God's expectation can also be found in Exodus, Numbers, Judges, Chronicles, Isaiah, Jeremiah, Zephaniah, Zechariah, Matthew, Acts, Philippians, James, and Revelation.[14]

Just as with many of the great hymns of our tradition, awe, wonder, and mystery also permeate newer music for the church. Music from the Taizé Community, newer hymns from the "Hymn Explosion" of the past 30 years, and praise choruses from the commercial Christian music industry can all invoke a sense of reverence, and of the divine. The important thing is to choose well, to look for music with depth and rich metaphor, and to lead it sensitively and with awareness of the power music has to take us to a deeper place.

## "Dance, Then, Wherever You May Be"[15]

Increasingly, we are also becoming aware of the importance of rhythm or pulse in worship song, regardless of genre. Our music leaders, however, are often playing catch-up when it comes to groove. Musicians who lead congregational singing are typically trained in conservatory traditions, which teach performance practices – such as an expressive performance style that emphasizes flexibility or ebb and flow in tempo – that are largely contrary to the needs of vital singing.[16] While flexibility is sometimes required in order for a musical line to breathe, a steady pulse can easily be overwhelmed by the desire to make a musical phrase sing, or to emphasize images in the text.

Running contrary to this is the pervasive influence of pre-recorded, secular popular music, and the effect it has had on the expectations of congregations. Drums and percussion drive the groove in the majority of popular songs, and the purpose of many popular music genres is to make people dance! Congregations today, therefore, respond to a strongly rhythmic style in all genres of church music, not just in popular musical styles. Groove and pulse reflect our own heartbeat and the rhythm of life itself. When hymns do not grind to a halt at the end of every verse, but rather have a measured, musical breath, when the pulse of a Taizé chant continues throughout all repetitions, people in the pews have an easier time settling into a song. The environment is set for success.

## "Calling Christians to Embody Oneness and Diversity"[17]

In the quest to be inclusive, many "progressive" Christians today are gutting our tradition with the best of intention for the sake of being open, non-offensive, etc. Language continues to evolve, and the song of the church also changes in response to current culture. But rejection in the name of inclusiveness leads to an equally problematic sense of exclusivity on the other end of the spectrum from the perceived "old way" of being. The radical edge, then, is in honoring diversity, both in our music and in our communities.

The hymn book of The United Church of Canada, *Voices United* (1996), is quite popular in the church and has been widely adopted by United Church congregations largely because its compilers understood the need for diversity of theological and musical expression. Old gospel songs such as Fanny Crosby's "Blessed assurance" sit side by side with newer expressions of the faith, such as Miriam Therese Winter's "Mother and God." Such tolerance for diverse expression has won the book many admirers, as well as serious detractors on both ends of the theological spectrum, and this is its genius. There is something for everyone within its pages, if people are willing to tolerate that with which they don't agree.

In contrast to *Voices United*, The United Church of Christ's hymn book, *The New Century Hymnal* (1994), has had a mixed reception with congregations in one of the most liberal denominations in the United States.[18] Both books contain a real diversity of new and old music; the difference is that the latter book went much further in "updating" older hymns to conform with newer sensibilities.

Diversity also moves beyond issues of language and theology into the musical realm. A diversity of musical styles and genres in our worship will likely more closely mirror who we are and who we wish to become as a people of God. And so traditional hymn structures can take their place alongside praise choruses and short refrains. Laments can share a place with songs of praise, reflecting both the diversity of the human experience and the complexity of our relationship with the divine.

Different musical structures serve different purposes, and so all have a place in worship. Hymn text structures and verse/chorus song structures are essentially linear; they develop theology and theme or tell a biblical story through multiple verses. Hymns and songs are rich, deep expressions of faith that feed our minds and satisfy our need for beauty, in particular when married with an equally marvelous tune. Increasingly, however, and in particular as Western Christianity comes into contact with Eastern faith traditions and music from other cultures, there is a need for cyclical structures. Shorter songs, which are intended to be sung many times around, be they gentle chants or lively African choruses, have a very different purpose. They are vehicles for prayer, for gentle contemplation, or for lively euphoria, an invitation into a sense of timelessness that linear structures by their finite nature cannot replicate. Timelessness in the midst of the busyness of modern life is a gift, if one can enter into it without concern about "when will this song end!"

Liturgically, cyclical structures are not better than linear structures; they serve different purposes. Hymn and song structures are incredibly effective at high points in the liturgy, when the cascading effect of image after image builds layers of praise. Hymns and longer song structures are also more effective for sharing scripture stories, since they are capable of delivering narrative. On the other hand, cyclical forms, with their flexible nature, are well suited to moments in which physical movement is required: processionals, when coming forward to receive communion, etc. As we become increasingly aware of the changing energy and needs of the liturgy, a greater diversity of song structures becomes essential to our communal worship.

Many newer forms of congregational song coming into use today also require an increasing diversity of delivery and new leadership skills. Dialogical forms, in which the congregation sings in dialogue with a song leader or with a choir, have deep roots in many global traditions,[19] and have already been in use for a couple of generations in Catholic churches. Songs such as Dan Schutte's "Here I Am, Lord" even build the dialogue into the text, a conversation between God in the verses and the people in the chorus. These kinds of songs call for different leadership gifts: no longer can the musicians simply accompany congregational singing; they must also "take up a voice" and participate. This new role can either re-energize music leaders, giving choirs and song leaders an even more integral role in worship, or it can scare the wits out of them.

Increasingly, we are also inviting the song of our sisters and brothers from around the world into our sanctuaries. Some congregations begrudgingly sing songs from other cultures only in translation; others rush headlong into all four verses of a hymn in transliterated Mandarin. We are so much richer for this experience; as a result, the global Christian community grows closer together. The experience of the Taizé Community in France – in which the use of multiple languages in worship, both concurrently and simultaneously, is common – is teaching us the beauty of other tongues. Songs generally sing best in their original language, and the experience of tasting unfamiliar syllables on our lips opens us to an experience of "the other," which reminds us that we are not alone, that worship and the Christian faith is bigger than our own perspective and experience.

There are dangers in teaching a congregation to sing in other languages in that we run the risk of excluding people from being able to participate. But these risks can be mitigated through common sense. In longer song forms, try singing only the chorus in the original language and the verses in translation. Always provide a singing translation, so that people can sing in the language they wish, and know the meaning of the words if they choose to try the original tongue. And, as with all new music, sing it often so that the congregation is able to take it to heart and make it a part of its own faith expression.

## "THIS ANCIENT LOVE THIS ACHING LOVE ROLLS ON"[20]

There is an increasing thirst today for music that is full of a variety of imagery for God: masculine and feminine, transcendent and imminent. God cannot be confined or even completely defined by language, and so the need for poetry and metaphor grows. There is an increasing thirst for songs that are deeply rooted in scripture and filled with the call for justice. And, most critically, there is a thirst for claiming Jesus Christ and his message, for being filled with the radical, inclusive, upside-down, countercultural essence of the gospel.

For our music to truly nourish us and send us forth to be God's people in the world, it must also be filled with a range of emotion and energy, a balance of head and heart, of new and old, of familiar and unexpected. For this reason, we must continue to sing the songs of the saints who have gone before us, exploring the depth of our traditions, in addition to embracing the new, the other, the unfamiliar. We need linear musical forms as much as we need cyclical forms. We need the grandeur of a pipe organ as much as we need the energy of the drum. Above all, we need to celebrate and to uphold the awesome power and beauty of that most fundamental musical gift: the human voice lifted in communal song.

To sing or not to sing: that is the question. Congregational song is the "make or break" issue of our day; there is nothing more critical to transformation-centered worship than the music we sing. May God continue to bless us in our journey as we strive to be faith-filled followers of Jesus Christ.

---

### ABOUT THE AUTHOR

**Bruce Harding**, Ph.D., is a church musician, composer, and church music scholar living in New Westminster, British Columbia. His particular area of expertise is Canadian hymn traditions. Bruce is a vocalist and multi-instrumentalist, playing electric bass, guitar, and flute. He is equally comfortable with classical, gospel, and global music of faith. Currently, he is the Managing Editor of the United Church of Canada's new hymn book supplement, *More Voices*. Bruce and his wife, Cheryl, are active as music leaders within the United Church in congregational ministry, in workshop and retreat leadership, and at concerts and other events.

# twelve

# Christian Education and the Imaginative Spirit

## *Susan Burt*

Exciting things are happening in congregations seeking an authentic Christian life in our culturally diverse and religiously pluralistic world. New settings, enthusiasm, and ways of being are emerging, as those at the grassroots respond to the changing dynamics of family, church, and community life. We are being motivated by a new story, an emerging vision that embraces search and meaning, not certainty. We no longer hold to the "jug to mug" model of teaching – an approach that is always telling and seldom listening, always trying to fill the other person up with our own understanding. Instead, we are listening for the word in others. We are also moving away from a literal and factual interpretation of the Bible. This approach to scripture has tended to emphasize the importance of a particular kind of Christian life so that "rewards" may be attained in the afterlife. It has also tended to see Christianity as the only way to life with God. Instead, we now recognize that the Bible was written by our spiritual ancestors, and that they used metaphor, imagery, poetry, and song to communicate the deep truths of God and God's way, in the context of their own lives. As a result, our focus has shifted from the afterlife, to an emphasis on transformed lives, communities, and world in this life, through relationship with God and each other. There is a growing understanding that the most effective context for Christian education is the Christian community, as it witnesses to the love, grace, and way of God, in the way it lives its life together and in the way it engages with the world.

This an exciting time to be involved in educating people of all ages in matters of faith, and to be assisting one another's efforts and imaginative spirit. In the words of Sean Gilbert,

> A stirring of the spirit and mind is taking place; a modest but important movement…for no longer, I think, is the emphasis on just trying to make some sense of the old story about a fall into sin, a blood sacrifice on behalf of us all (an atonement) or to make sense of a heaven beyond the grave, a heaven that bears little resemblance to this life… But through a Christ-given imagination, [we are] laying hold of something entirely new and yet still in accord with the gospel."[1]

"Imagination," says Edward Robinson, "is the essential means, humanly speaking, by which faith becomes possible." [2] However, Alan Jones also warns, "The work of the imagination is serious business because through it we build or destroy the world."[3] Our imagination can be wounded, impoverished, and stifled, as is the case with Arthur, in the vignette below.

### PLAYING "WHAT IF…?"

**Arthur:**     **God is a man, for sure.**

**David:**     What if God was the other sex?

**Arthur:**     **But God is a man!**

**David:** But can you play "What if"?

**Arthur:** **If God was a...huh!**

**Well, I don't know**
[laughs anxiously].

**don't know. Well,**

**I couldn't even imagine**

**God being a lady –**
**No sir** [laughs nervously].[4]

What has paralyzed Arthur's imagination? What might have stirred Arthur's imagination? What stifles our ability to play "What if..."?

"Language and imagery shape our self-understanding and view of reality."[5] Arthur's imagination and view of reality is impoverished because he has not been exposed in worship and in other educational settings to language, symbols, images, stories, and music that provide a variety of images of God. Arthur's imagination has not been fostered, nurtured, fed. Arthur is paralyzed, unable to play "What if...?"

Mary Ellen Ashcroft walked the streets of Rome, "visiting the Catacombs and the prison where Paul was chained," and played "What if?" She imagined walking with the women and men of the early Christian movement, people who had moved from the margins and had found a place of belonging in an inclusive community of love, justice, and service. She thought of the strong, decisive, committed women of the movement, leaders of the early church, teaching, preaching, and presiding at Eucharist.

The following day, the image she had formed was crushed by the "glory" and chill of St. Peter's. "Sculptures and paintings were layered high on the walls...Well-dressed men wielded power in their crimson robes...Thousands of pictures, hundreds of sculptures, and none resembled women in that early movement." Any representation of women had them looking downward, demure and meek, or pushed back to the periphery, "crouched in corners, looking way up at slickly dressed patrons of the church, at St. Peter, at Jesus, at God."[6] Not one image represented the strong, decisive women who followed and were transformed through interaction with Jesus and Jesus' radical ministry.

In despair Ashcroft asked, "Where are those lost women of our faith?"

Imagination stifled, imagination impoverished by "Christendom in all its glory"[7] The story of these "spirited women" would be lost if not for the imaginative spirit of women and men who combine biblical story, historical research, and imagination in order to "re-member" our history.

Take an audit of your worship and educational environment. In what ways do symbols, architecture, arrangement of furniture, language, and displayed images stifle or foster imagination? What is missing?

What can imagination do for us as we study, interpret, and respond to scripture? Educator Carol Wehrheim reminds us that imagination

- gives us ways to ponder new possibilities
- sets us on a path to seek hope
- helps us discover new meanings
- encourages us to see, hear, touch, smell, and even taste something in a new way
- places us where we can encounter mystery.

It is our imagination that propels us toward the God of all creation.[8]

The author of the letter to the Hebrews writes, "The word of God is living and active" (Hebrews 4:12). God continues to reveal, continues to speak today. The *Seasons of the Spirit* Theological and Educational Foundations paper asserts that, "The Bible contains meaning and mystery beyond the printed word," and that the curriculum seeks to "encourage children, youth, and adults to enter imaginatively into scripture, and to experience the message that transcends the printed words, inviting congregations and individuals to discern God's message for this time."[9] As we re-educate people, as we invite them to move from a literal-factual approach to scripture to a metaphorical and sacramental approach to scripture, we should not be afraid to declare "This story teaches us truths, but it may not be a story that is real," or, "I don't know if this story really happened this way, but the message is true."[10]

**"Erasing the lines and giving rise to the questions that are already there"**[11] Australian comedian Jimeoin once asked, "Do you ever wonder what the words on the page of a book do when you close the book?" We, too, might wonder what's between the lines, beneath the layers, and in the silences of biblical stories. When we imagine the "hidden" and give voice to the silences, the story is born anew. The Bible is full of characters wanting and needing a voice, wanting to be embodied. Imagination unbinds, unshackles. Poets, playwrights, musicians, and painters touch our hearts, open our feelings, stir our imaginations; they can be like mirrors that reflect, but also like windows that open to new ways of seeing. Their work can critique or challenge traditional assumptions. When we open ourselves to see as artists see, we free ourselves from the constraints of a "facts-based" view of reality.

> *The arts (visual, literary, dramatic, musical)*
> *nourish religious imagination,*
> *and because of that the arts are essential in forming faith.*
> Maria Harris, Christian educator

In the stimulating play *David's Rule*, the character of the "Storyteller," the narrator, takes the audience on a wonderful journey of the imagination. The audience is encouraged to move between the lines, to listen to the silences in the story of King David. At the end of the play, David visits a sorcerer. He recaps the story of his life, and, through the prompting of the sorcerer, wonders whether his younger sister, Hannah, should have been anointed instead of him. (When Samuel was asked by God to anoint the youngest, might God have been thinking outside cultural boundaries, while Samuel heard from inside cultural boundaries?) At that point, David recognizes that the sorcerer is his sister Hannah. Hannah brings her community to meet her brother. The audience learns that she had wanted to join David in exile, but being a girl was forbidden to do so. So she went anyway, becoming an "outcast" from her family. Ultimately, she discovered that it was her own freedom she sought. Along the way, she met others like herself, who did not have a home. Some were carriers of wisdom, who taught her new ways and the "laws that lie beneath the law." She learned songs for "making and songs for changing, songs for summoning and songs for concealing." As the women walked together, Hannah learned ways of seeing and skills for doing. She laid claim to the cave, in which Samuel visited her. She gave him soup and watched him as he went out to die.

In this play, Hannah tells David that she changed her name from "Han," to "Not Han"; and then to Nathan, the prophet of justice who challenged David about the murder of Uriah. For a time, Hannah enjoyed the disguise and the power of being a man, but then reclaimed her own name, her own identity, and her own way. Over the years, she built a community, a community of people without a place in the world, all the time living her story just a little behind the story of David, even making a home for Tamar. From Tamar, the community learned compassion and wisdom, and Tamar and Hannah wrote a song, "Hannah's Song":

My soul cries out.
To you, O God, we sing.
Lift up the weak and let them speak
And heal each broken thing.

Break down the walls.
Unlock the chains that bind.
Let all who cling to pow'r and things
Be changed or left behind.

Fill us with strength.
With us your Spirit fill,
To live the laws that give all life,
Resist all laws that kill.

We will not rest.
Our dreaming will not pause,
Until your Rule to break all rules
Is Law to end all laws.

My soul cries out.
To you, O God, we sing.
Lift up the weak and let them speak
And heal each broken thing...[12]

David then offers Hannah the crown. But she doesn't want it. Hannah has imagined a different way than the way handed to her. Hannah has imagined a new way of being together as human beings, and as people in relationship with creation. She has built the world.

Through research and imagination, Scott Douglas has told a story behind the story and created for me, and I am sure many others, a path for transformation.

## Imagining New Ways of Being

In her painting "Last Supper, No 1," Margaret Ackland presents a view of the followers at the table with Jesus, from a perspective that looks over the head of Jesus. Ackland says about her work,

I'm hoping that it will look like something that was very, very intense, and spiritual – a time when God was actually connecting with humanity. That it will have that very powerful and intimate feel to it, as a depiction of that subject should be. That it would look completely natural, for all the children, women, and men are all there together. It is an image of inclusion.[13]

The story is told of a three-year-old and a "theme conversation" during worship. The worship leader, commenting on Ackland's work and inviting the children to reflect on the painting, asked the children to think of women being at the table with Jesus at the Last Supper. To this the three-year-old child exclaimed, "Yes, and children too." Through Ackland's painting, and the prompting of the worship leader to imagine, this three-year-old discovered a deep truth about God's inclusive way.

Bringing our imaginations, emotions, voices, and experiences to every biblical story; giving voice to the silences and peeling away the layers will enliven the story and give it meaning for today. One way to bring imagination, emotion, voices, and our own experience to the story is to invite children, youth, and adults to imagine or place themselves into the story, but as characters not already identified. In the story of the Prodigal Son, you could invite learners to imagine characters who may have been in the household and may have witnessed the events of the story – when the son left home and when he returned home. The possibilities include the mother of the two brothers, the sister of the two brothers, a grandparent of the two brothers, a friend of the older son, a cook or other servant in the household, a farm laborer who works for the family, a friend of the younger son, the girl who was planning to marry the younger son, the owner of a neighboring farm, the manager of the father's accounts.

To imagine and interpret the story from the various emotions and experience of the characters, you might invite the group to arrange itself as in a tableau. Ask them to consider where their characters would be standing. What would the characters be doing or saying? Have them be in this tableau as the story is read, pausing, if you like, for interaction between the characters.

After the drama, you could take time to debrief and share new insights into the story. Some questions might include: How did you feel? What did you think? What did you want to say to the father? …brother? …younger son? Reflective questions should be geared to the age and life experience of the participants. Youth and adults might consider such questions as: What new insights into the story did you get from taking the part of this person? If your character was called upon to give a toast at the feast, what would he or she say? What do you think life would be like for your character the day after the feast? Using three sentences, how would you summarize this story? Reflective and open-ended questions stir imaginations.[14]

Working with an image such as *The Forgiving Father*, by Frank Wesley, can also reveal some deep truths, as well as the emotions of the story traditionally titled "The Prodigal Son." Wesley, drawing on Indian cultural images, pictures the father as part of the Brahman culture; the son is depicted as an "outcast." In an educational setting, a leader might ask participants to work in pairs to "mirror" the image. He or she might ask: What do you feel in your body? What do you notice? Who is taking the weight…the burden? Put yourself in the embrace. What does it feel like to be supported, and rest in this grace?

*Our deepest truths are non-cognitive,*
*rooted in the realm of the imagination.*[15]

### THE POWER OF THE IMAGINATION – TO BUILD OR TO DESTROY

The Syro-Phoenician woman (Mark 7:24–30) dared to imagine/re-vision God's way beyond cultural and religions boundaries. She "erases the lines and gives rise to the questions already there," wins liberation for her daughter, and builds the world.

The friends of a paralyzed man (Mark 2:3–12, Luke 5:18–26) dared to go beyond cultural and religious boundaries, and re-vision God's way. The paralyzed one is, according to the religious laws "outside" the grace of God and needs to atone for his sin in the "correct" ways. Jesus also dares to imagine beyond the cultural and religious boundaries, and re-visions God's realm. This interaction brings liberation and wholeness, and "builds the world."

Heather Murray Elkins, in a story about a vase, describes the fierce imagination of Korean women, which builds the world. She describes how a vase, which her father brought home from the war, sat on the shelves, tables, hutches and corner cupboards of her childhood. She says of this vase:

> Its presence is felt before its story becomes part of a woman's way of knowing...
>
> Its story is one of the few explanations he ever offers his daughters of the things he's done or seen.
>
> War had shattered Korea, a country called "Morning Calm." Armed forces from several nations engaged in fierce, brutal struggle, yet within a people who have survived countless invasions, the cultural will to survive persists. The vase is hard evidence of their passion for life. My father holds it in his hands, turning it as he tells his story.
>
> After the shelling stopped, village women would cautiously hunt for artillery shell casings, discarded in the fighting. Each casing was reshaped, polished, and etched. Sometimes silver was beaten into the sides, shaped like blossoming flowers. A weapon turns into a vase. An instrument of war is re-formed into a vessel of life. The trash of war is transformed into treasure, then traded for food, medicine, and the means of life. A thing of threat becomes a thing of beauty.
>
> Long before the biblical text of swords and plowshares was forged in our hearing, this earthen vessel taught us a truth. The strong hands of women are needed to turn weapons of death into instruments of peace. Fierce imagination, coupled with passion for beauty and compassion for life, are the primitive tools necessary for this kind of construction: hallowing the human, altar-ing the world.[16]

The vase and the story behind the story fed Elkins' imagination and vision of God's realm.

God dreams of a world at peace – God's creatures and creation living in peace and harmony. Isaiah gives prophetic voice to that vision:

God shall judge between the nations, and shall arbitrate for many peoples; they shall beat their swords into plowshares, and their spears into pruning hooks; nation shall not lift up sword against nation, neither shall they learn war any more (Isaiah 2:4).

The wolf shall live with the lamb,
the leopard shall lie down with the kid,
the calf and the lion and the fatling together,
and a little child shall lead them (Isaiah 11:6).

Christ-given *imagination* motivates practices that transform and build the world. Fierce imagination, such as that displayed by the Korean women, will lead to working toward a more peaceful and just world. Fierce imagination and persistence, such as that displayed by the Syro-Phoenician woman and the friends of the man who was paralyzed, will lead to "imaginative acts of compassion,"[17] that build a world in which all live in harmony and equality. Fierce imagination, as displayed in the prophetic voice of Isaiah, will lead to lives lived in relationship with each other and all creation. Such is the nature of a "transformation-centered Christianity."

So how might we provide spaces and opportunities to encourage such imagination, passion, and compassion? In what places are these gifts honored and nurtured in our Christian education practices? What do we need in order to foster "Christ-given imagination"? What changes for us personally, and in the world at large, when we imagine all people as truly valued neighbors, rather than as a rivals or strangers, or "lesser than…"?

Those with creative imaginations provide us with visions of new ways of being together as human beings, as church, as people in relationship with creation. But we need to heed Alan Jones' caution: Images that become concrete are dangerous, and imagination is not always kind, caring, gentle, and compassionate. Our images need to be questioned and, perhaps, revised; "believed and disbelieved at the same time."[18]

*Imagination is central to education.*
*Imagination, the ability to think the new, is an act of survival...*
*the saving work of theology requires new imaginative visions.*[19]

## COLLABORATING AND CONSPIRING TOWARD TRANSFORMED LIVES

For many years I used "shepherd" as a metaphor for the practical ministry of Christian education. A shepherd works on the margins, a shepherd walks with her sheep, guiding, tending, nurturing, and caring. A shepherd confronts and challenges anything that puts sheep at risk. A shepherd gets dirty – gets involved. Kathleen Billman, in "Pastoral Care as an Art of Community" offers a different metaphor, and a powerful image. It is the image of midwives, in particular, two Egyptian midwives, Shiphrah and Puah; women who collaborated and conspired to bring forth new life and hope. "Conspiring means literally 'breathing together'"[20] and co-laboring to bring forth life. Collaboration, "is more than partnership. It is the development of a shared vision of justice and deep care and then the taking on of hard tasks, co-laboring, to bring visions to reality...mutual care at the deepest personal and political level."[21]

The metaphor of the midwife "conspiring and collaborating" to bring forth life and hope is a helpful image of what we do together in Christian education: Conspiring – breathing and collaborating together to equip, enable, empower each other to bring the biblical story to [new] life, to imagine and search for meaning in our time and place, and to then respond – to imagine and build the world. It is the development of a shared vision.

In order to equip, enable, and empower the laboring mother, the midwife must first "attend." Preparing for attending, attending personally, and observing and listening are key principles in bringing any new thing to life.

When it comes to Christian education, preparing to attend includes preparing our space using symbols, art images, music, and ritual, to engage imaginations. Cover a box or table in the color of the season of the church year; add objects that have symbolic meaning for the session or the season of the program; bring recorded music, if possible music and songs that will be used in the session.

In *The Heart of Christianity*, Marcus Borg talks about the role of "thin places," those places where we experience transforming encounters with God. As Christian educators in "formal, intentional" learning environments, it is important to create an environment that can inspire or nurture a deep awareness of God's presence and of the sacred, and that fosters the imagination. Just as setting, place, and space is important, so too is taking time to prepare and plan to implement process.

Begin with an opening ritual that calls all participants together as a community of faith, with Christ at its center. Use symbols, images, music, and prayer to center the group and as a way to set the focus for each session. Move the group into biblical engagement by making connections with life experience. Creatively and imaginatively engage the text, listening for God's word to us in our time and space. Then, look at ways to respond to new learnings, new understandings, and reflect on ways we might live as Christ's disciples and as citizens of God's realm. Conclude with a worshipful closing, celebrating new learnings and transforming moments, and sending one another out to lives of justice and compassion – in the way of Christ.

Curriculum resources will offer help and support transformative educational processes and practices. Christian educator Deidre Palmer offers the following as effective Christian education processes for which to look when selecting curricula.

Effective Christian education processes:

- encourage participants to speak and share their own experiences of life and faith;
- convey the idea that both teachers and other participants are involved in a mutual learning process – that each participant has insights to share;
- make significant connections between the Bible and our own lives. They encourage people to reflect on the activity of God in their lives, the lives of others, and world around us;

- engage the whole person – emotionally, physically, intellectually, spiritually;
- contain content related to contemporary world events, conveying to participants that God is concerned with, and active in, the world in which we live.

Preparing to attend, and attending, will require that we practice listening, as Benedict says in his rules, "with the ear of the heart to thoughts and feelings that come from the heart of others." It will also mean asking open-ended questions that make it clear to children, youth, and adults that there are no "wrong answers," because we can't really know what happened. Our wonderings or imagining can help us to find the truths of the story in our own time and place; they can help us to discover what the story reveals about God, and God's way; what it reveals about Jesus, our relationships with God, and our relationship with each other and creation. There is always more than one answer to an open-ended question. Questions such as the following will prompt the imaginative spirit.

- I wonder what happened next in the story?
- I wonder what they said when they returned home?
- I wonder if they "did not tell anyone"?
- For whom is this story "good news"?
- What questions does this story raise for you?
- What truths did you discover in this story?
- What do you think the story reveals about who God is? …about who Jesus is?
- What does this story suggest about the way we might live as disciples following in the way of Jesus?

In questions such as these, children, youth, and adults are invited to "erase the lines and give rise to the questions that are already there." It is in the questions, in the not-knowing, that learning occurs.

Remember also that questions do not necessarily need answers, and it is important that we create environments where questions and doubts can be openly and respectfully asked and explored. You might provide sticky notes for group members to display their questions on a mural or around an image. At the end of a season or program, you might spend time exploring some of these questions together, or you might bring some of the questions into your sessions in other weeks. As you listen "with the ears of your heart," you will find ways to connect with these questions at appropriate and helpful times. At all times, honor and receive the questions, perhaps making your mantra, "It is not the answers but the questions that will lead to new discoveries, creative imagining, and transformed lives."

We will enable transformed lives and enquiring minds that will bring Christian growth when we can confidently offer responses such as, "I don't know, but that's a good question. What do you think?" "Does anyone want to say something about this?" "Maybe we can all think about this and come back to it later." This approach is also helpful when the imagination of the group goes in a direction you might not expect.

Preparing to attend will also involve laying aside preconceived notions, assumptions, biases, and predetermined conclusions[22] in order to suspend judgment and the need to have the answers, to suspend the need for an outcome. Over a decade ago, at a *Whole People of God* writers' event, I, along with all the writers and editors present, was invited to draw a slip of paper from a bowl. On each slip of paper was written a saying. The paper slip I chose is still pinned to my bulletin board. Its message reminds me, daily, to let go, to suspend, and to be open to transformation: "Let go of preconceived notions and prejudices. Expect surprises, expect miracles."

Preparing to attend requires taking time to nurture our own imaginations, "making it possible to enter into the mystery of God's creation and God's realm."[23]

As you encourage freeing the mind, freeing the imagination, consider the ways creative imagination is awakened. Our imagination

- may be nudged when we observe or participate in any of the arts: literature, music, visual arts, or dance
- can be nourished when we play

- can be brought forth in meditation and prayer, particularly if we allow time for silence
- can be nurtured as we serve others
- can be heightened when we spend time with children, allowing their imaginations to feed our own
- can also be fed when we allow artists to see as they see.[24]

When we exercise our imaginative spirit, we move the biblical story out of literalism, factuality, certainty, and fixed answers, and into the unknown. The story is born anew – a liberating, healing story, revealing deep truths, and an invitation to "discern God's message for this time."

*Today and tomorrow*
*the Bible will need teachers who are passionate as well as literate,*
*savvy as well as scholarly, street-wise as well as book-wise,*
*and who can, without degrading it, make the Bible come alive as living myth,*
*relevant, disturbing, and still capable of taking our breath away.*[25]

As Christian educators seeking meaning not certainty, and fostering the imagination as we strive to make the "Bible come alive, relevant, disturbing, and still capable of taking our breath away," we need to spend time nurturing, awakening, and exercising our own imagination, so that we, too, can enter into the mystery of God's creation and God's realm.

Using visual art as a starting place, here are some ways to begin to nourish your imagination.

- Select a piece of art. Perhaps an art poster from *Seasons of the Spirit*. Choose an image with a person in it. Place it flat on a table, or the floor. Walk around it and gaze at it from many angles. What is the person in it saying to you as you move around the poster? How does the message change as you move from the bottom of the poster, painting, or photograph, to the top? From side to side?

    As you do this, you are exercising your imagination by looking at a work of art from angles that you couldn't were it displayed in a gallery. Trying out new perspectives prompts our imagination to take hold.

- Sit in front of the image with a child. Close your eyes and try to erase the image of the piece of art from your mind. Ask the child to describe the picture to you and listen carefully. What does the child see? How does the child name what she or he sees? What does the tone of the child's voice tell you about the picture?

  Seeing the art piece through the eyes of a child can open *your* eyes to new sights. Our imagination allows us to sit on the margin between reality and mystery and to watch and listen.

- Display the image on a wall. Stand in front of it and mirror the pose of the person it depicts. What words come naturally to you in this pose?

  Our imagination comes into play not only through what we imagine, but also through how we move. Allow your imagination to grow as you dare to move into new ways of standing, walking, sitting, and resting.

- Gaze at the image. As you do so, imagine the person in bright sunshine. How does the change of setting change the figure in the art? Place the person in other settings, such as a field of wildflowers or a busy city street, to see what happens.

  Our imagination helps us to change the background of life, to substitute an alternative. Without this part of our imagination, we have no hope in God's future for all creation.

- Place the image where you can sit comfortably and gaze upon it. Slowly, look at each part of the picture. Take note of the colors and the use of light and dark. What is included in the picture? What is not? What motions do the lines (solid and broken) suggest? What gives depth to the picture? What kind of message without words does this picture give you? If the picture were untitled, what would you call it?

  Reading a painting or sculpture in this way takes us deeper and deeper into it. This depth feeds our imagination and grows our ability to enter into the mystery of the work of art.

Choose one of the above activities today, and another activity tomorrow. Repeat the same activity the next day, if you like, or select a new one. Devise your own activity to activate your imagination another day. Keep your imagination alive. Cherish this gift from God. Nurture it in others as you lead and as you live.[26]

By fostering imagination through the use of language, symbols, setting our space, imaginative engagement with the text, and Hebrew and Christian tradition, we can, with Hannah and Tamar in the play *David Rules,* "break down walls. Unlock the chains that bind."[27] Transformation-centered Christianity propels us into transformative acts of love, compassion, and justice.

Use your imagination to give yourselves settings, and characters, and action. "Make it in your mind. For what you make in your mind is only a step away from real…"[28]

Come on, let's S T E P!

---

### ABOUT THE AUTHOR

**Susan Burt** is Coordinating Editor of *Seasons of the Spirit,* an international, ecumenical, and lectionary-based Christian education and worship resource. Susan has been involved in Christian education all of her adult life, at the grassroots and professionally. She has worked in children's ministry for the Uniting Church in Australia, Synod of South Australia, and as Australian editor of *The Whole People of God* Christian education and worship resource. Susan lives in Adelaide, South Australia, where she is a member of Christ Church Uniting Church, a theologically progressive community that seeks to celebrate the best of the old with the possibility of the new.

# thirteen

# Pastoral Care for the 21st Century

## *Donald Grayston*

The reflections in this chapter have three main sources: my 42 years of ordained ministry, my 15 years of university teaching, and my 17 years of directing a spiritual direction training program.

The first source of my reflections is my ordained ministry, which began on September 8, 1963, the Feast of the Nativity of the Blessed Virgin Mary, in St. Mary's Church, Kerrisdale, in Vancouver, British Columbia. I was ordained a deacon (in the church of God, rather than just the Anglican Church, an important point; it is through our experience in one of the portions of the divided Body of Christ that we find our place in the whole and undivided Body).

My greatest single learning from this source? Work with the people who want to work with you, instead of spending your energy persuading the people who *don't* want to work with you (or are not ready to work with you) to work with you! Obvious now, obscure for many years!

The second source of my reflections is the 15 years I spent teaching religious studies at Simon Fraser University, also in Vancouver. There I learned, for example, that about a quarter of the students who take an introductory course in religious studies do so because they are "looking for a religion for myself." In my initial view, this was a bizarre way to find a religious tradition for oneself; but given how contemporary students have been formed by the mighty powers of consumerism, it makes perfect sense that they should do some consumer research to prepare themselves for comparison shopping.

I also learned that the Christian meta-narrative, the big story of Jesus and his community, the story that governed so much human thinking and feeling for so many centuries, in so many places, had been displaced, sidelined, marginalized. You have *your* story, and I have *my* story. But what is *our* story? From the time of the emperor Constantine's legalization of Christianity in the fourth century, until the end of the Second World War (my choice of date), Christians operated in Christendom mode. This involved either an explicit or implicit relationship between church and government.

People in Canada, for example, even with no established church, thought of themselves as living in a Christian country. The common story, often honored more in the breach than in the observance, was the Christian story. The lack of an *our* story today, for the population in general, has resulted in, among other things, the relocation of what I call *the community of meaning*, the community that tells and retells the story that gives meaning to my life in a compelling way, from the church to the couple-in-intimate-relationship. Lover and beloved have a common story, an *our* story, often celebrated with a choice of *our* song, *our* aperitif, and so on. So long as love lasts, the intimate partners delight in telling and retelling their story to each other.

It was particularly in this context that I discerned the strong presence of the spirituality versus religion dynamic, which is so powerful in our culture. It points to intimacy as central to the meaning of spirituality, and thus of spiritual formation.

The third source of my reflections is my experience since 1988 of directing the Pacific Jubilee Program in Spiritual Formation and Spiritual Direction (www.vst.edu, under the section devoted to the Chalmers Institute) and my involvement in the wider work of Jubilee Associates (www.jubileeassociates.ca). Spiritually hungry people, lay and ordained, female (mostly) and male, Christians and otherwise, register for these programs, mostly in midlife, for many reasons. Some have a clear sense of call to be a spiritual director for others – an anamchara, a soul friend – a call often awakened in them by others seeking them out for spiritual consultation. Others wonder if they have such a call, and seek to test it out in a supportive community. Still others simply seek a disciplined and in-depth approach to their own spiritual formation and re-forma-tion. They seek a functioning spirituality that will take their little canoes through and past the rapids of midlife and into the at-least-occasional still pools (which is not to say that there is any guaranteed age after which there will definitely be no rapids!).

My interaction with the hundreds of people who have taken the Jubilee program has shaped and re-shaped me powerfully. As I have heard their personal stories, and linked them to my own, I have encountered what I believe to be the beginnings of both a new way of telling the old Christian story, and a new and wider story, which Christians and others will some day be able to tell as their common story. (Thomas Berry says that this will be in some way the story of the earth, a new creation story, one shared by all major faiths.)

From these three sources, then, I draw much of what has come to me as I have reflected on the shape, the demands, the dynamics of pastoral care in the 21st century.

## Pastoral Care and Adult Christian Education

My first thought about pastoral care as such is that it can no longer be separated from what we have called Christian education. In earlier times, we thought of pastoral care as how the community, or, more often, the priest/pastor on behalf of the community, responded to crisis, tragedy, or moments of passage (birth, marriage, sickness, death). That it was the responsibility of the ordained person rather than the community to respond in moments of pastoral need was engraved on my mind the day of my ordination, when the bishop read the prescribed charge from the *Book of Common Prayer*. Specifically, it warned me that if I "lost" one of the lambs of Christ's flock, then a "horrible punishment…must ensue"! In the years since I first heard that ghastly warning (I doubt today that the bishop himself believed a word of it!), there has been much positive movement, with an increasing understanding that the *community* has the primary role in pastoral care, with the ordained person acting *on behalf of* the community, and working with the community to increase *its* capacity for pastoral ministry.

Christian education was something different from pastoral care. Christian education meant Sunday school, confirmation class, perhaps the odd adult study group or a midweek morning Bible study group for women whose children were in school, or finished with school, and who didn't work outside the home. Just to refer to that pattern reminds us of how much our society has changed, particularly in relation to the lives of women. As years passed, however, there was again positive movement, with the advent of such programs as baptism preparation, marriage preparation, Sunday morning education for all ages, and so on. However, pastoral care and Christian education are still seen as separate enterprises by most, both clergy and laity.

Where they come together, in my understanding, is in *spiritual formation*, broadly understood. The public ministry of Jesus combined healing and response to persons in need or crisis (pastoral care) with a teaching ministry addressed both to the many (the multitude) and the few (the disciples, and within that group, the apostles). The ministry of Jesus, however, was as seamless as the robe he wore to his crucifixion, not something segmented into "pastoral" and "educational" sections. Jesus himself had been fully formed into a whole human being, in the sense in which I am using the term, by his own Jewish tradition, and by his ability to be present to the historical moment in which he lived, and to the others who lived, as he did, in the same moment. If we accept this view, then we have gained some understandings on the basis of which we can move forward, in a pastoral + educational context, towards *integrative spiritual formation* as the essential matrix for congregational membership and adult Christian discipleship.

Let me begin to flesh this out by sketching an approach to confirmation (or admission to adult membership) that this integrative approach would suggest. (Later I will consider the initiation of adolescents.) Typically in recent years, adults coming to faith and wanting to be full members of the congregation have been given a few weeks of classes in which they have received an introduction to the Bible, to the doctrines of the creeds or their equivalent, to church history and the distinctives of their own denominational tradition, to the dynamics of worship as offered in their denomination, and to other expectations of responsible church membership, including ethical behavior and financial stewardship. I immediately acknowledge that there are many congregations where a much more imaginative approach to the Christian initiation of adults has been offered. In such congregations, the preparation for adult initiation will sometimes have included what I am now going to propose as the essential emphasis: *spiritual practice.* Adults in such a program will be taught to pray, to meditate, to go on retreat, to do *lectio divina,* to fast, to tithe, and to do the daily *examen* of conscience (or, better, as George Aschenbrenner, SJ, suggests, *examen* of *consciousness*). They will also be introduced to pilgrimage (an ancient practice experiencing a resurgence in our time), to a spiritual and ethical exploration of sexuality, and to the mandate required by scripture of every believer – that of doing justice, as well as loving kindness, and walking humbly with God (Micah 6:8).

And how long will this take? In one sense, a lifetime. In the more immediate sense, it will take as long as it takes. By this I mean that we have to let go of the unrealistic expectation that the classic six- to 12-week courses we have offered in the past will be sufficient in the future to permit adults to be formed in the Spirit in a way in which our historical moment requires. I see, instead, a formation program meeting on a weekly basis (either on Sunday morning or midweek) for some years, with confirmation/the initiation rite itself coming at some point in the middle of the process, not at the end. If we have not already done so, we need to move past the confirmation-equals-graduation phenomenon, whereby the 12-year-olds of former days who had memorized the Apostles' Creed and the use of the liturgical colors were confirmed one day and gone forever from the life of the church the next.

Beyond this, I see the opportunity for "field placements," as it were, in a social justice context and in an interfaith context. I see adult catechumens committing themselves to a stint as a volunteer in an NGO working with refugees, for example, and then returning to the formation cohort, sharing their experience, and with the assistance of the group, integrating that experience both with the biblical tradition (the Israelites in exile, Jesus as refugee in Egypt), and with an assessment of their own particular gifts for ministry. I see them choosing another religious tradition, taking part in its worship, interviewing one of its teachers or leaders, reading about that tradition and its relationship to Christianity (very different, for example, as between Judaism and Buddhism), and again returning to their formation cohort for an experience of integration. Certainly for my undergraduate students, mostly young adults, but including some older adults, the interview with a leader or teacher of a tradition other than their own consistently proved to be the highlight of the foundation course in religious studies which I regularly taught. And are you thinking that all this would be asking too much? All I can reply is that, observably, the churches that ask the most of their members receive the most, whereas those that ask the least receive the least. Again, I see in the formation cohort a prime context for self-assessment of gifts for ministry, and an implied openness to the assessment of gifts by others in the cohort (cf. 1 Corinthians 12–14).

To return for a moment to pastoral care in its traditional meaning, it would be through this identification of one's gifts for ministry that the community would find itself endowed, I dare to believe, with as many members concerned for the caring ministries of a congregation or de-nomination as were needed. Similarly, I believe, a vital program of spiritual formation would bring forth as many teachers as the educational needs of the congregation required.

This is where my earlier comment about working with the people who want to work with you comes into play. Clergy, other church staff, and congregational leaders have spent, in my observation, too much time trying *to move the congregation forward as a whole.* This has meant that, in many cases, the rate of forward movement (not change for change's sake, but real spiritual growth along the lines of Ephesians 3:16–19) has been governed by the response of the most conservative or even recalcitrant members. Our present moment requires of clergy in particular an increased intentionality, a readiness to resist the sentimentality and pressure to practice bonhomie, which is characteristic of so many mainline parishes. This would allow them to focus the use of their time and energy on working in depth with awakened and awakening adults. Over time, this approach will have its effect on the congregation as a whole. As the level of spiritual practice rises, and as the spirituality of the adults-in-formation deepens, so will the congregation as a whole experience its life in Christ as a fuller comprehension, "with all the saints, [of] the breadth and length and height and depth" of Christian discipleship (Ephesians 3:18).

## Spiritual Formation and Adolescents

I turn now to the situation of adolescents, which will take us, first, to a consideration of rites of passage. In my university teaching, I regularly met adolescents, mostly male, in their 30s and 40s. Why? Because neither the mainline churches nor secular society have any culturewide rituals of passage that communicate effectively to boys and girls that they are now men and women. How then to address this need?

In writing above about the spiritual formation of adults, I was thinking of persons 17 and older. Here I want to reflect on the possibilities of two moments – the ages of 12 and 16 – that offer huge potential for addressing the need of adolescents for rites of passage.

Typical 12-year-olds in our culture have entered puberty in a physical sense, and increasingly in a social and sexual sense. They may well continue to be outwardly cooperative with their parents, but inwardly they are very conscious of their own individuality and increasing independence. ("I am *so* different from my mother and father!") If the church engages adolescents at this age, and gives effective ritualization to the meaning of the age, it communicates to this age cohort that the church (unlike their parents and teachers!) understands and respects them, and provides a basis on which to approach their spiritual formation between the ages of 12 and 16.

This ritualization could take different forms, but it would certainly include a reference to the episode of Jesus in the Temple (Luke 2:41–52), in which Jesus sits with the teachers, listens to them, asks them questions, and thereby models the adolescent-adult relationship that is the basis for the congregation's engagement with young folk of this age.

The age of 16, I would then suggest, is the minimum age for a rite of entry into adulthood, and invites a different kind of ritualization. In my own church, the Anglican Church of Canada, a baptized 16-year-old can vote in parish elections, be elected to any office in the parish, and is expected to contribute to the financial needs of the parish. A 16-year-old in Canada can also get a driver's license, and in many provinces, leave school legally. A very high proportion of teens, whether or not they are active in the church, have by the age of 16 become sexually active, or are well on their way to becoming so (most often without their parents being aware of this). Together or separately, these quasi-liminal experiences are all that most teens have to mark the transition from adolescence to adulthood.

This being so, the church has a golden opportunity to work with teens and parents to develop a coming-of-age ceremony, after which the boy or girl would be considered and treated as an adult in the congregation – a young adult, yes, but an adult. In my last congregation, St. Oswald's in Port Kells, just south of Vancouver, we began to move in this direction by celebrating a coming of age for two teens: one girl and one boy. Women in the congregation took the lead in developing the ritual for the girl, and the men for the boy. On both occasions, which took

THE EMERGING CHRISTIAN WAY &gt; 227

place during the Sunday morning liturgy, there was hardly a dry eye in the place.

Manifestly these rituals had analogies with the Bar and Bat Mitzvah rites celebrated in the Jewish community. I stress, however, that neither of the rituals we created required a faith-commitment from either of the young folk involved. The awakening of a truly personal faith-commitment cannot be scheduled or programmed, which is why the wholesale confirmation of legions of 12-year-olds during the baby boom resulted in such a minimal return. Children were confirmed at 12 and were gone by 13, many of them resenting that they had been, in their view, forced by their parents to make public affirmations which in truth they either did not know whether they believed, or in fact had actively (though inwardly) rejected. If, however, we celebrate the coming of age of young people at 16, simply seeing the ceremony as an opportunity for the congregation to offer its love and support to them, this leaves wide open the later opportunity for a truly adult profession of faith, and its celebration and ritualization in an adult rite of confirmation.

What, then, should happen between the ages of 12 and 16? I suggest that there are four areas that are critical for the church and its teens to work at during those years. They are spiritual practice, sexuality, social justice, and pilgrimage.

Young teens are entirely capable, with guidance, of exploring every dimension of spiritual practice mentioned above, in my discussion of adult spiritual formation. A creative program in the United States, the Youth Ministry and Spirituality Project, has in recent years taken this approach, with very satisfying results (see its website at www.ymsp.org).

As regards sexuality, it should be clear from my earlier comments that we need to expect to be exploring this with a youth cohort who will be, for the most part, already sexually active in varying degrees. Whatever our own feelings or convictions about the morality or appropriateness of sexual activity among unpartnered teens, it is simply a reality which we need to acknowledge and engage. The challenge here goes well beyond safe sex, an issue that all young people experimenting with their sexuality face in our culture. The church's challenge is to help them integrate their developing sense of sexuality and sexual identity with their developing sense of spirituality and discipleship. This has always been the case, but what is different now from previous recent generations is that many or most of the teens will be sexually active. I believe, in fact, that the church must make its goal in this area helping its young people (and indeed all its members) to live out their sexual lives without shame, guilt, or fear; as well as helping them to understand sexual relationship as simultaneously an encounter with the sacred. This points to a future time, in which we will have developed a Christian tantrism, a way of integrating sexual practice with spiritual practice.

As regards social justice, what I said above about volunteering with justice organizations is even more applicable. All children and young people have an acute sense of fairness, which is the foundation for a mature sense of the needs of others for justice.

As regards pilgrimage, the years between 12 and 16 are prime time for taking young people on traditional Christian pilgrimages, which could include Jerusalem, Rome, Canterbury, Iona, Santiago de Compostela, as well as contemporary destinations such as Taizé; and anti-pilgrimage sites, such as Auschwitz or Hiroshima. Alternatively, these pilgrimages could be to places sacred to other traditions, such as Bodh Gaya or Polonnaruwa for the Buddhist tradition, or Lac Ste. Anne and other sites sacred to members of the First Nations.

Spending 48 hours away from the comforts of home is usually enough to open the eyes of most North American teens. Beyond that, they also get to experience the paradox of pilgrimage (you can't come home until you leave home); as well as the seven steps of pilgrimage identified by Phil Cousineau (awakening, call, departure, companions on the way, the labyrinth – I call it "the crunch" – the arrival, and the bringing back of the boon). It is the classic form of seeking God – and finding oneself.

In sum, then, I propose an integrative approach to spiritual formation for adolescents which would include the following elements:

- a ritual of entry into adolescence around age 12;
- an experiential curriculum for adolescents aged 12–16, which would include units on spiritual practice, sexuality, social justice, and pilgrimage;
- a coming-of-age ritual around age 16, and;
- confirmation or equivalent at age 17 or older, in response to the awakening of personal faith in the individual.

Most of these thoughts came to me as I struggled in the parish with the human realities behind them. A couple of years ago, I was delighted to discover a formation program that incorporates virtually all of these elements: *Journey to Adulthood*. The name says it all, and I highly recommend the program to you (for more information see www.leaderresources. org).

### SPIRITUAL DIRECTION AND CHRISTIAN PRACTICE IN CONGREGATIONS

Finally, some reflections on the place of spiritual direction or companioning in this integrative process. Like pilgrimage, spiritual direction has experienced a renaissance in recent years. Historically undertaken mostly by clergy, lay spiritual directors are now both more numerous and fully accepted. When I first began to work in what is now the Pacific Jubilee Program, I discovered that a number of people were taking the program not so much because they felt a call to be a director but because they saw it as an opportunity for disciplined, systematic spiritual formation, with a focus on spiritual practice. In other words, they were looking for what I recommend be available in every parish and congregation. For this reason, we changed the structure of the Pacific Jubilee program from an integral 18 months to two distinct program years, with Year I focusing on spiritual formation, and Year II focusing on the skills and perspectives needed to be a spiritual director.

Spiritual direction has blossomed, to put it briefly, because we live in a 500-channel society. No longer can a generalized form of direction – which used to suffice and which was mostly delivered from the pulpit

– respond adequately to the enormous *variety* of ways we live our daily lives. Given that no two people are exactly the same, seekers are saying, in effect, "Will someone accompany me on the journey I am *actually* taking?"

More often than not, spiritual direction is sought by people seeking a new direction for their lives. Yes, they are seeking God, but they are also trying to become themselves. After all, God can seem very distant to the person who doesn't know exactly who *he or she* is to begin with. This is not a new thought, of course; it's at least as old as the *Confessions* of St. Augustine. Typically, then, the search for identity and the finding of identity leads to spiritual practice, spiritual practice leads to formation, and, for the one who has been formed, formation leads to ministry. The process is a movement from receiving to giving.

This connects with my observation that in the years since my ordination, people's motivations for belonging to a congregation have changed radically. Forty years ago, people belonged to a congregation because their parents did, or because it was good for business, or because of any number of other less-than-basic reasons. Of course, some people still come to church on Sunday mornings for those very reasons. But many others who are coming to church for the first time, or who are coming back to church after a period away, are looking for a community to belong to in which there is no dichotomy between religion and spirituality. Bizarre though it may sound, they want a *spiritual* religion and are largely ready to be invited to the challenging kind of journey of spiritual formation that I have sketched out in this chapter.

Congregations, then, need to make spiritual direction known and available to their members. Congregations can offer group direction, occasional direction, days or weeks of direction, prayer partnerships, or direction as a component of programs of spiritual formation, as well as the classic one-to-one form of direction. People are hungry for a religion that involves experience more than theory, a way of living the Christian life that offers balance between heart and mind.

I find full support for this in Marcus Borg's book *The Heart of Chris-*

*tianity.* In chapter 10, "The Heart of the Matter: Practice," Borg defines practice in the following way.

> I mean all the things that Christians do together and individu-
> ally as a way of paying attention to God. They include being part
> of a Christian community, a church, and taking part in its life
> together as community. They include worship, Christian forma-
> tion, collective deeds of hospitality and compassion, and being
> nourished by Christian community. They include devotional
> disciplines, especially prayer and spending time with the Bible.
> And they include loving what God loves through the practice of
> compassion and justice in the world. (p. 189)

This kind of practice leads to the formation of Christian identity. It involves the capacity to initiate and sustain relationships, including our relationship with God. It involves seeking healing for whatever wounds we have suffered and forgiveness for whatever hurts we have inflicted on others. It involves learning how to touch "the deepest level of the self, the heart" (p. 191). As the Eastern Orthodox Church traditionally puts it, it involves descending with the mind (not *from* the mind) into the heart, and there, praying. It brings us, God willing, to a place where we know – not just think, not just feel, but *know* – that we are created by God, each as a child of God; and that we are loved by God and accepted by God, unconditionally.

This is both important and difficult in our time, because the Chris-tian way is not the way of secular society, which is the way of consumer-ism and accumulation. This being so, a Christian identity becomes what Borg calls a "counteridentity," an alternative identity to the one formed by the majority culture (p. 192). To sustain a Christian identity, then, car-ries a particular challenge for us who live in a society that trivializes or marginalizes the Christian faith, even while it sometimes pays lip-service to it. Borg's conclusion to his chapter on practice is both simple and profound.

Christian practice is about walking with God, becoming kind, and doing justice. It is not about believing in God and becoming a good person; it is about how one becomes a good person through the practice of loving God. (p. 205)

The challenge to Christian congregations in the 21st century is to move beyond the segmentation of ministries towards an integrative approach to the formation of healthy, adult Christians. Such Christians will seek out and exercise caring ministries, teaching ministries, and ministries of compassion, justice, spiritual direction, and intergenerational bonding and reconciliation.

The church is waiting for us to get moving on this. And whether it knows it or not, the world is waiting for us, too.

---

## ABOUT THE AUTHOR

**Donald Grayston** is a theologian and spiritual director who lives in Vancouver, British Columbia. A retired priest of the Anglican diocese of New Westminster, he taught for 15 years in the Humanities Department at Simon Fraser University. Director since 1988 of the Pacific Jubilee Program in Spiritual Formation and Spiritual Direction co-sponsored by Vancouver School of Theology and Jubilee Associates, he is also vice-president of the International Thomas Merton Society. His previous publications have been concerned with Merton, pilgrimage, and the Holocaust.

# fourteen

---

# Spiritual Discernment

*Nancy Reeves*

I had been booked a year previously to give a day-long workshop on the Saturday, and then to preach on the Sunday. Since it was a Unitarian Universalist congregation, the Sunday reflection would be half an hour and the contract specified the topic "Spiritual Decision-making for Our Highest Good." Three days before the weekend, the order of service arrived by e-mail. Much to my surprise, the reflection was titled "A Path Through Loss." I rummaged through the briefcase I had just packed and found the contract. "Yup, they've changed the topic," I thought. "I wonder why."

The congregation's secretary answered the phone and, after I introduced myself, the following conversation took place.

"My contract says 'Decision-making for Our Highest Good,' I began, yet the order of service has me down for 'A Path Through Loss.' Has something happened to make the loss topic more appropriate?"

There was a brief pause. "Didn't *you* make the change? When I was typing it up yesterday, someone came in and told me you had changed your mind. I think either of your topics would be of interest, so I put the new one in."

"I didn't talk to anyone from your fellowship. And I've prepared the spiritual discernment reflection. Who was it who spoke for me?"

"Oh dear, I'm so sorry. I should have checked with you, but they seemed so adamant. Come to think of it, I can't remember who it was. Shall we go back to the first topic? I've printed all the bulletins, but we can just announce that there was a mistake."

"You can't remember who told you I had changed my mind? Hmm. Have you had any loss in your community recently? Is there a reason you can think of that the loss topic would be better than spiritual decision making?"

"No losses that I know of. I apologize. I've never before changed a topic without speaking directly to the person involved. But it seemed so right when they told me."

"Hmm. Okay, I think I'll stay with loss."

That Sunday I told a large group of children a story about the many things that can be a loss for us, the various needs people have when they experience loss, and some ways to help someone who is grieving. Later in the service, I told stories to the adults about the impact grief and spirituality have on each other.

When the service was over, a group of adults made a beeline for me. One woman said, "Thank you so much for teaching our children and ourselves. You know the six-year-old who was leaning on your right knee? Her mom died yesterday of cancer. We've been supporting the family for the past year and everyone thought she had months more to live. It was a shock when she started deteriorating just two days ago. We didn't expect them to come to worship today and when dad and daughter arrived, we didn't know what to say. Then you taught us how to be helpful."

A man added, "I was with the children. When we got to our room, one boy said to the daughter, 'I know your mom died yesterday. What can we do for you?' The children spent the rest of their time listening to her talk about the death. It was wonderful."

Before I could respond, the adult group parted to let a man through. He threw his arms around me and said, through tears, "I woke this morning feeling so lost. All I could think of was that I needed the support of my faith community. So we came. I knew the reflection was on decision making, which didn't interest me. But then you talked about loss; just what we needed. Thank you, thank you!"

Later, as I was packing up to leave, the secretary came to say good-bye.

I asked her, "Have you remembered who told you to change the reflection topic?"

She looked at me with wide eyes: "No, and I asked the people who were in the main office. They said no one came in while I was working on the order of service. It was just what we needed, but we didn't know it then. It was the next day that she went into medical crisis. We had already changed the topic and had printed the bulletins."

I try to be receptive to the Spirit's leadings. God knows my limits, though, and if I had "heard" that the reflection topic needed to be changed, I probably would have balked, having been taught that contracts are powerful things. So the secretary was the one that first responded to divine guidance. When she told me that the change seemed "right" to her, I felt a corresponding rightness. God was guiding, but I didn't know why.

## SPIRITUAL DISCERNMENT VS. DECISION MAKING

When *I'd Say Yes God, If I Knew What You Wanted* was released in fall 2001 (Northstone Publishing), I expected to spend a few months giving talks on the book and then return to my clinical psychotherapy practice, in the area of trauma, grief, and loss. Instead, my life has been turned inside out and upside down. Four years later I am still speaking on the topic, traveling 70–80 percent of the time throughout North America, the U.K., New Zealand, and Australia. I have taught spiritual discernment as a credit course in a number of seminaries, and other educational institutions are using my book as required or suggested reading for spiritual formation. What follows is based on my conversations with thousands of people about their contact with the guiding power of God.

Decision making is quite different than spiritual discernment. In decision making, we use the talents and skills within us to make a particular choice. We may do this alone or with other people. Spiritual discernment implies that God is also involved in the process and choice, and leaves room for messages or leadings from the Holy One.

The decision or choice which is ultimately selected might be the same whether the individual used decision making or discernment. The difference lies in their willingness to be guided by the divine. Spiritual discernment is undertaken not just to make good decisions, but to develop a richer relationship with God.

Many people of faith view spiritual discernment as a procedure or tool – something to be done when making a major decision. If, instead, we view discernment as an *attitude*, we will discern always, and always be receptive to divine guidance. The smallest choice may have a ripple effect that does great good or harm.

### Children's Discernment

In my discernment workshops, I ask people to remember a choice they made where they experienced divine guidance. God may have gotten through to them in many different ways, such as a feeling or sense of rightness or peace, a dream, a voice they "heard" speaking within them, a particular book that seemed to call to them, a message spoken by another person.

Over the years, as participants have shared their guided decisions, I have come to realize that a great number of these experiences occurred in childhood. Usually, there was no one to speak to the child about these leadings. Sometimes adults told the children that they were lying or making up their "God touches."

Several years ago, some friends and I were at a Taizé prayer service. As we were leaving, six-year-old Tabitha said, "Wasn't it great when the Spirit came down to those people."

"I must have had my eyes closed," I replied. "Could you tell me what you saw?"

"It was when the people who were hurting went and kneeled around the big cross on the floor. Some were crying. Then the Spirit came down and stroked them. Some knew the Spirit was there and some didn't. It looked like white love."

Children already experience God even before an adult first speaks to them about things spiritual. As adults caring for children in our personal or professional lives, I believe we can best assist their spiritual growth by acknowledging, honoring, affirming, and giving words for the child/God relationship that is already developing. We are to be spiritual directors or accompaniers rather than spiritual educators, gardeners nurturing spirituality rather than architects designing and building our children's faith.

## THE "OBJECT" OF OUR DESIRE

C. S. Lewis, author of the children's books about the mythical land of Narnia and the Christ-figure Aslan, described "a particular recurrent experience" which dominated his childhood and adolescence, and which he felt was frequently shared, though misunderstood, by many other children and adults. "The experience is one of intense longing. It is distinguished from other longings by two things. In the first place, though the sense of want is acute and even painful, yet the mere wanting is felt to be somehow a delight... In the second place, there is a special mystery about the *object* of this Desire." People often mistake what they are focusing on at the time, for the object of desire. The true object of this longing is God.

Scientific researchers are currently exploring the question, "Are we hard-wired for God?" Has God put that longing within us to keep "our hearts restless until we find our rest" in the divine?

## WHAT DO WE DO ABOUT EGO?

One of the foundations for developing our discernment muscle is self-awareness. Knowing ourselves makes it easier to discriminate between the voice of Spirit and our ego.

Ego has been given a bad rap in some of the spiritual literature. It is often called the "false self." "Egocentric" is a pejorative term.

Yet psychological research shows the importance of a strong ego for healthy development. Without a developed ego, it is difficult to set appropriate limits and boundaries. Many adults experience low self-esteem, because they were discouraged from being "self-centered" as children. "A good Christian thinks about others rather than themselves," they were told repeatedly.

Jesus showed great care and concern for the welfare of others. He tells us to "love one another as ourselves." I wouldn't like to be loved the way many people love themselves! Obviously, Jesus was presuming that those he spoke to *did* love themselves, otherwise the commandment makes no sense.

In psychological literature, our ego is what we know as our conscious self. It continually sends us messages, both subliminal and conscious. Its mission is to help us by keeping us safe and by suggesting how to meet our needs. Unfortunately, it doesn't discriminate well. It tends to believe without question the messages of those who have power and authority in our life. The six-year-old hears, "You'll never amount to much," and takes it as truth. Even when reality shows a different picture, the child, and later the adult, is unable to see themselves as competent in life.

Our ego tends to extremes, either denigrating or putting the self on a pedestal. By doing this, the ego thinks it is protecting the self from threatening challenges by others.

## GOD DOESN'T CARE

Some people tell me that they would not think of "bothering" God for guidance when the choices they face are all good. It may be true that God doesn't care which of the good paths we finally choose. I do believe, however, that anything we do or say can be an opportunity for deepening our relationship with the Holy One. Cultivating a constant attitude of discernment will help us to be more aware of the delightful "God-incidences" that occur in our lives.

Also, it may be that one of the "good" choices is better for us and our world. Since we are often largely unaware of these factors, it is by being receptive to God's guidance that we will be nudged to that particular path.

## GOD CALLS US TO METHOD

A woman approached me at coffee time. "Usually I discern divine will by immersing myself in nature or by reading inspirational texts. A word seems to jump out of the book or be planted in my mind while I walk in the woods. Today, I was guided in a very different way. I was on the way to my usual church when I felt an extremely strong urge to come to this one, which is on the other side of the city from where I usually attend. I've never felt anything like that before. I've been to this church once or twice in the past ten years for concerts, but I don't know anyone here. Also, it added 25 minutes to my trip. I was intrigued by the strange urge, so I came. I walked in late and heard you being introduced. My daughter is going through a really rough time with her chronic illness and I was trying to find a book to help and inspire her. You told some stories that I think she could really relate to. So now I know why I was guided here."

I believe God invites us to the way of discernment that will be best for us at any one moment. We may have a chosen or preferred method, yet it was the Holy Spirit that put the idea in our heart and mind in the first place. Since our ego can get in the way, it is always helpful to ask about the method of discernment as well as the decision itself.

## TRANSFIGURATION

Jesus went up the mountain with Peter, James, and John, and he was transfigured (Matthew 17:1–2). I love watching transfiguration! For example, I saw a couple transfigured the other day in Beacon Hill Park, in Victoria, British Columbia. The two were staring into the stroller, eye to eye with their young baby. And they glowed. Then there was the older couple snuggling and holding hands as they sat on a park bench. They glowed too. As I left the park, I saw a couple in full wedding regalia having photographs taken by the rose gardens. We talk about the "radiant bride." Well, both the bride and the groom were radiant.

Most of us have had at least one experience of transfiguration in our lives. Any time we give our hearts totally, we glow. It is a wonderful experience; we feel we are walking in a bubble of love. We are not just enraptured by the object of our love, everything and everyone around us seems precious as well.

I believe God calls us to transfiguration with the first commandment. Loving God with our whole being is a surefire glow producer. And God, who is Love, often guides us *through* love. Many people, when faced with two possible paths, ask, "Which decision will release the most love into the world? Which path helps me grow in love?"

And yet many folks just dip their toes in the ocean of love. Teresa of Avila says we ask God for too little. Why don't we have these transfiguration experiences more often? I believe we hang back because of fear. Although we feel so good when we're in the middle of it, we also feel more vulnerable. Our heart "is on our sleeve." Maybe we worry others will think we are religious fanatics. Or, just like we do with a human lover, we worry about how God will respond. Will the Holy reject our love? Will we be asked to jump through hoops to demonstrate our commitment? Although Christianity says God's love is a free, unending gift, when we are not loving ourselves unconditionally, it can seem that God could not love us unconditionally either.

To experience more transfiguration in our lives, we need inclusive hearts – hearts that love ourselves, other people, all of creation, and God. As the prophet says, we need God's help to transform the stony parts of our hearts into hearts of flesh: hearts more vulnerable and therefore more able to receive and give the love God longs for us to experience. Because God is exquisitely respectful of our free will, we need to say "yes" to the call of transfiguration.

## Was It a Sign from God?

Some folks on an intentional Christian path roll their eyes when I talk about cultivating an attitude of discernment. "You probably think everything is a sign from God!" they say. "Not in the least," I reply. "It's so easy to decide something is a divine sign if it seems to align with our own wishes." As we become more familiar with the issues, concepts, and methods of spiritual discernment, we will be able to determine more effectively when God is sending us a sign.

I believe divine guidance is often about "nudges." Thirty people may be watching a sunset at a beach, marveling at the gorgeous colors. Wonder and awe can be two of the most effective faith developers, so it is possible that everyone will leave the experience with deepened faith. A few, however, may be nudged by God to take a specific meaning from their experience, a meaning that will help them with a decision. As they make their decision, they may or may not realize that God was playing an active role.

## Who Is the "Guide"?

In the stories Jesus told, he used numerous symbols to describe the kingdom or realm of God. He also referred to himself using many images. Having a multifaceted relationship with God means viewing the divine in a variety of ways. We may view the divine in terms of attributes, such as love, compassion, or faithfulness; in terms of roles, such as creator, healer, shepherd, or guiding power; or in terms of relationships, such as Father/Mother, holy friend, or brother Jesus. Some of the stories of divine guidance I hear demonstrate how the *manner* in which God comes to us may help our discernment.

Jamie came to see me for psychotherapy some years back. "I want to leave the company I work for and buy a franchise. It's a company that will really help people; the market research I've done says it will succeed; and every time I pray, I get a strong sense of rightness. It's like God is urging me on. Yet I can't seem to bring myself to sign the contract and send in the check. What's stopping me?"

We explored every psychological dynamic I could think of. Nothing seemed to be a reason for Jamie's "stuckness." So we turned to his spirituality. Responding to my question, "Are there any issues in your faith journey that could be getting in the way?" Jamie replied, "Actually, my faith has really deepened in the last six months. One day in church, the scripture reading was about 'stiff-necked people.' Wow, that's me I thought! So I asked God for help and the 23rd Psalm came into my mind. Now I think of God as my shepherd and I follow like a sheep. I have grown much more sensitive to God and am learning the joys of surrendering in prayer. So there's no problem there."

We sat looking at each other. "What could be blocking him?" I thought. Then an awareness floated into my mind. "Jamie, I'm not trying to make fun of your image of God as shepherd, and of yourself as a sheep, but what came to me was a question. If you consider animals as potential franchise purchasers, where on the continuum would a sheep be?"

Jamie looked startled for a moment and then began to laugh. "Actually, sheep would be terrible at running franchises. Probably just above a slug. Sheep follow well, but aren't known for their initiative and entrepreneurial skills."

"Although that image of your relationship with God has been very helpful to you in the past," I continued, "I wonder if you need a different image now."

"Makes sense," Jamie replied. "What image would be more helpful?"

"Nope, don't ask me. Ask God. That's who suggested the first image. Take it to prayer and be receptive."

A week later I saw Jamie again. "I began my prayer, 'How do you want me to see you God? How shall we be together?' Then I would sit receptively, keeping my mind and heart as open as possible. Sometimes no image would come. Three times, though, in the past week, I saw myself walking along a beach with Jesus. Just two buddies hanging out together. Jesus said to me, 'Are you going to buy that franchise?'

"'I'm thinking of it, Lord' I answered.

"'Well, I'm with you, Jamie. I know you can do it.'

"Then the image faded and I was left with the awareness that God has given me many gifts and, as an adult man, I can do well at this franchise. So, after the third time, I went to my desk, signed the contract and mailed it. Now I'm so excited about my career future."

## JIGSAW PIECES

Every decision we make has an impact on another person, or on our environment. Being aware of some of those potential impacts can help us to discern more clearly. In the section on group decision making in *I'd Say Yes God, If I Knew What You Wanted*, I say, "No one is given complete information about divine will for themselves or for others. By giving us partial information, God invites us into deeper awareness of our core need to be in relationship."

As I hear discernment story after discernment story, I believe even more strongly in this statement. If we imagine the decision that concerns us as a jigsaw puzzle, God gives each of us a few pieces. It is only by sharing our pieces with others and encouraging them to share with us that the puzzle will be completed. I have heard of decisions that finally came together when the six-year-old daughter, or the grandfather with dementia, was brought into the discussion. Sometimes, the few choices that seemed to be open to the "primary discerners," such as parents or the paid staff at a church, were expanded in delightful ways when others were invited to listen to God's guidance around the particular question or concern.

## CONCLUSION

Of course, God is always present, so it's not possible to do *anything* without God. Yet our free will allows us to ignore divine nudges and leadings. By intentionally growing our spiritual discernment muscle, by developing a constant attitude of discernment, each of our decisions will draw on the infinite well of love and grace that is our God. Our Christianity will be transformed. Each action will help build the City of God.

## ABOUT THE AUTHOR

**Nancy Reeves**, Ph.D., is a registered clinical psychologist who has specialized in the area of trauma, grief, and loss with adults and children since 1989. She is internationally respected as a workshop facilitator, psychotherapist, author, and poet. In her clinical practice she works with individuals, families, groups, and in trauma recovery sessions after community disasters. Nancy also conducts workshops and retreats in spiritual discernment. She is the author of several books, including *I'd Say Yes, God, If I Knew What You Wanted*; *A Path Through Loss*; and *Found Through Loss*.

# conclusion

# Inclusion in the Midst of Evolution

## Michael Schwartzentruber

These are exciting times for those who call mainline Christianity "home." It is also an exciting time for those who have "left home" – perhaps because of frustration, or boredom, or doubt – but are wondering if they might yet find a reason to return.

For many of us, the ideas expressed in this book inspire a sense of relief and of gratitude. It is a relief to discover that we are not alone, that there are other people out there who want a credible faith to embrace; and we are grateful that they have managed to articulate this faith so well. Quite naturally, our relief and gratitude lead to excitement. We imagine the possibilities. We imagine the transformation in ourselves, our ability to feel more at home with God, more at home in our congregations, more at peace in our souls, more "right" with the world. Yes, the world; for we imagine not just ourselves and our churches transformed, but the whole world, too. We feel in our bones the power of this imagining, "for what we make in our minds is only a step away from real," as Susan Burt reminds us.

These are also "exciting" times because the truth is that not all who call the mainline Christianity home feel this way. This is a good and sometimes difficult thing to remember. It's all too easy to assume that most people believe as we do, especially if we have believed something for a long time. Similarly, it's tempting to focus on those things we have in common, especially in the church where, so often, we strive to avoid conflict. Yet in most congregations, you don't have to scratch very far beneath the surface to discover real differences, and real *passion* around those differences.

I was reminded of this sometimes painful reality at a recent choir practice. Having done my own wrestling with the issue of inclusive language more than 20 years ago, and having begun to move beyond a literal understanding of the Bible a few years even before that, I was caught by surprise and found myself becoming more defensive and confrontational than I would have liked when another member of the choir expressed outrage and dismay at the use of feminine imagery for God in one of the anthems we were preparing.

The differences and divisions among us are real – so real, Marcus Borg tells us, that "it virtually produces two different religions, both using the same Bible and the same language."

Ideally, when we are confronted by those who hold a different faith perspective or worldview than we do, we will have the courage to speak our truth *and* be committed to honoring and respecting the truth of the other.

Of course, it's not just with people who hold a different faith perspective that we will discover differences. A careful reading of the preceding chapters will be enough to show that just because we may agree on general principles doesn't necessarily mean we will agree when it comes to specific applications. Not all who call themselves emerging Christians will agree on all points, or hold all points as equally important. We all bring our own perspectives, interests, and passions to the table.

The "exciting" part of all of this – in case you're wondering – is that this diversity and the tension it creates are part of a natural, *evolutionary* process that will inevitably take us to someplace new. In other words, they are an expression of life – the creative embodiment of God. Diversity and evolving complexity are present everywhere in nature. We can receive this as divine gift, if, as Sallie McFague encourages, we learn to *pay attention*, and are *respectful*. More than that, Matthew Fox and Bruce Sanguin remind us that honoring diversity – not just Christian diversity, but the diversity of other faiths and of creation – is part of our *calling*, as seen from within "the cosmology of the postmodern era."

If this is true, then the truly *radical* place to be in the church is not at the edges, which tend towards exclusion, but at the heart, at the center, at the place of *inclusion* in the midst of *evolution*. How different can we be and still recognize the face of the Christ in the one we meet? Can we see within creation, teeming with life in all its manifold forms – or within the earth itself – an incarnation of God?

In many instances, a concern for radical inclusion will lead us to issues of justice and to a desire to work to bring it about – not just for the sake of human life, but for the sake of *all* life, and for the planet itself.

Ultimately, it comes down to "walking the talk," to allowing our experience to transform our hearts and lives. This is, after all, the core, the very nature of the faith we proclaim.

---

## ABOUT THE AUTHOR

**Michael Schwartzentruber** is editorial director for the WoodLake, Northstone, and CopperHouse imprints of Wood Lake Books.

# Endnotes

## Chapter 3: New Creeds – Tom Harpur

[1] This is a slightly adapted version of Chapter 11, "Prologue and Creeds," from Tom Harpur, *Finding the Still Point: A Spirituality of Balance* (Kelowna, BC: Northstone Publishing, 2005).

[2] Martin Buber, *The Way of Man* (New York: Citadel Press, 1995).

[3] Alfred Lord Tennyson, "The Two Voices," stanza 69.

[4] Tom Harpur, *For Christ's Sake* (Toronto: Oxford University Press, 1986), 123.

## Chapter 4: The Great Work – Thomas Berry

[1] This chapter is a reprint of "Chapter 1" from Thomas Berry, *The Great Work: Our Way into the Future* (New York: Bell Tower, 1999).

## Chapter 5: Consider the Lilies of the Field – Sallie McFague

[1] This chapter is a reprint of "Chapter 2" from Sallie McFague, *Super, Natural Christians: How We Should Love Nature* (Minneapolis: Fortress Press, 1997).

[2] *The Confessions of St. Augustine*, bks. 1–10, trans. F. J. Sheed (New York: Sheed and Ward, 1942), 10.6.

[3] Letter to Mrs. Joseph Sweetser, 1884, *Letters of Emily Dickinson*, ed. Mabel Loomis Todd (New York: World Publishing Co., 1951), 349.

[4] Iris Murdoch, *The Sovereignty of the Good* (London: Routledge and Kegan Paul, 1970), 91, 52.

[5] Ibid., 84.

[6] Ibid., 85.

[7] *Lift Every Voice: Constructing Christian Theologies from the Underside*, ed. Susan Brooks Thistlethwaite and Mary Potter Engel (San Francisco: Harper & Row, 1990), 51.

[8] Frederick Buechner, *Listening to Your Life* (San Francisco: Harper & Row, 1992), 53.

[9] As quoted in Douglas Burton-Christie, "'A Feeling for the Natural World': Spirituality and Contemporary Nature Writing," *Continuum* 2 (2 & 3, n.d.): 176.

[10] May Sarton, *Endgame: A Journal of the Seventy-ninth Year* (New York: W. W. Norton, 1992), 336–37.

[11] Alice Walker, *The Color Purple* (New York: Washington Square Press, 1978), 178.

[12] The reverse, however, is also true: loving another motivates knowing.

[13] As quoted by Burton-Christie, "A Feeling for the Natural World," 175–176.

[14] Iris Murdoch, "The Sublime and the Good," *Chicago Review* 13 (Autumn, 1959), 52.

[15] Annie Dillard, *Pilgrim at Tinker Creek: A Mystical Excursion into the Natural World* (New York: Bantam Books, 1975), 126.

[16] Yaakov Jerome Garb, "Perspective or Escape? Ecofeminist Musings on Contemporary Earth Imagery," in *Reweaving the World: The Emergence of Ecofeminism*, ed. Irene Diamond and Gloria Feman Orenstein (San Francisco: Sierra Club Books, 1990), 267–268. I am indebted to Garb for the analysis in the following paragraph.

[17] Yaakov Jerome Garb, "The Use and Misuse of the Whole Earth Image," *Whole Earth Review* 45 (March 1985), 20.

[18] Marilyn Frye, "In and Out of Harm's Way: Arrogance and Love," *The Politics of Reality: Essays in Feminist Theory* (Trumansburg, N.Y: Crossing Press, 1983), 53–83.

[19] Ibid., 67.

[20] Ibid., 75, 76.

[21] Lorraine Code, *What Can She Know? Feminist Theory and the Construction of Knowledge* (Ithaca: Cornell University Press, 1991), 165.

[22] The following analysis is indebted to Evelyn Fox Keller and Christine R. Grontkowski, "The Mind's Eye," in *Discovering Reality: Feminist Perspectives on Epistemology, Metaphysics, Methodology, and Philosophy of Science*, ed. Sandra Harding and Merrill B. Hintikka (Dordrecht, Holland: D. Reidel Publishing Co., 1983), 207–224.

[23] Garb, "Perspective or Escape," 276.

[24] Murdoch, "The Sublime and the Good," 51.

[25] As quoted in Keller and Grontkowski, "The Mind's Eye," 219.

[26] For one such analysis, see Ruth Berman, "From Aristotle's Dualism to Materialist Dialectics: Feminist Transformation of Science and Society" in *Gender/Body/Knowledge: Feminist Reconstruction of Being and Knowing* (New Brunswick, N.J.: Rutgers University Press, 1989), 244–255.

[27] Jim Cheney, "Eco-Feminism and Deep Ecology," *Environmental Ethics* 9 (Summer, 1987), 124.

[28] Code, *What Can She Know?*, 273.

[29] See, for instance, Maria Lugones, "Playfulness, 'World-Travelling,' and Loving Perception," *Hypatia* 2 (Summer, 1987), 3–19; and Maria C. Lugones and Elizabeth V. Spelman, "Have We Got a Theory for You! Feminist Theory, Cultural Imperialism, and the Demand for 'The Woman's Voice,'" *Women's Studies International Forum* 6 (1983), 573–581; Elizabeth V. Spelman, *The Inessential Woman: Problems of Exclusion in Feminist Thought* (Boston: Beacon Press, 1988), 181–182.

[30] Anne Sellar, "Should the Feminist Philosopher Stay at Home?" in *Knowing the Difference: Feminist Perspectives in Epistemology*, ed. Kathleen Lennon and Margaret Whitford (New York: Routledge, 1994).

[31] This phrase is used by Evelyn Fox Keller, *Reflections on Gender and Science* (New Haven: Yale University Press, 1985), 165.

[32] Dillard, *Pilgrim at Tinker Creek*, 269.

[33] Alice Walker, *The Temple of My Familiar* (New York: Pocket Books, 1989), 289.

[34] Quoted in *Earth Prayers from around the World*, ed. Elizabeth Roberts and Elias Amidon (San Francisco: Harper, 1991), 267.

[35] Ibid., 365.

## Chapter 6: On Being a Postdenominational Priest in a Postdenominational Era – Matthew Fox

[1] The following chapter is excerpted and adapted from Matthew Fox, *Confessions: The Making of a Postdenominational Priest* (San Francisco: HarperSanFrancisco, 1996). Chapter 12 is the primary source, with several paragraphs also taken from Chapters 9 and 11.

[2] David Bohm, "Postmodern Science and a Postmodern World," *The Post-Modern Reader*, ed. Charles Jencks (New York: St. Martin's Press, 1992), 390.

[3] Walter Truett Anderson, *Reality Isn't What It Used to Be* (San Francisco: HarperSanFrancisco, 1990), 257.

[4] Don Lattin, "Dalai Lama Tells Truth-Seekers to Beware," *San Francisco Chronicle*, April 21, 1994, A18.

[5] *The Bhagavad Gita*, trans. Juan Mascaro (Middlesex, England: Penguin Books, 1962), 119.

[6] Bohm, "Postmodern Science," 13.

[7] See Henry Kamen, *Inquisition and Society in Spain* (Bloomington: Indiana University Press, 1985); Jeremy Cohen, *The Friars and the Jews: The Evolution of Medieval Anti-Judaism* (Ithaca, NY: Cornell University Press, 1982).

[8] See Carl Bernstein, "The Holy Alliance," *Time* (February 24, 1992): 28–35; Martin A. Lee, "Their Will Be Done," *Mother Jones* (June 1983): 21–27; Penny Lernoux, *People of God: The Struggle for World Catholicism* (New York: Viking Press, 1989).

[9] See Michael Walsh, *Opus Dei: An Investigation into the Secret Society Struggling for Power within the Roman Catholic Church* (San Francisco: HarperSanFrancisco, 1992); Don Lattin, "Opus Dei's Roots in Francisco Franco's Spain," *San Francisco Examiner*, June 1, 1986, A16.

[10] See E. R. Chamberlain, *The Bad Popes* (New York: Signet, 1969).

[11] Bohm, "Postmodern Science," 13.

[12] Walt Whitman, cited in William Everson, "Introduction to Leaves of Grass," *American Bard* (Santa Cruz: Lime Kiln Press, 1981), 33.

[13] Abraham Joshua Heschel, *God in Search of Man* (New York: Harper Torchbooks, 1955), 419.

[14] Thomas Merton, *The Springs of Contemplation* (New York: Farrar, Straus & Giroux, 1992).

[15] Fox, *Sheer Joy: Conversations with Thomas Aquinas on Creation Spirituality* (San Francisco: HarperSanFrancisco, 1992), 351.

[16] John Henry Cardinal Newman, *Apologia Pro Vita Sua* (New York: Norton, 1968), 193, 194.

[17] Newman, *Apologia*, 194f.

[18] Newman, *Apologia*, 149.

[19] Bishop William Swing, "Let 'em Rave, for God's Sake," *Pacific Church News*, July 1994, 2.

[20] Heschel, *God in Search of Man*, 414.

## Chapter 7: Paying Homage: Being Christian in a World of Many Faiths – Bruce Sanguin

[1] This chapter is adapted from a sermon given by Bruce Sanguin at Canadian Memorial Church and Centre for Peace, in Vancouver, British Columbia, on January 4, 2004, and subsequently published in Bruce Sanguin, *Summoning the Whirlwind: Unconventional Sermons for a Relevant Christian Faith* (Vancouver: Canadian Memorial Press, 2005).

## Chapter 8: Radical Inclusion – Anne Squire

[1] Don Cupitt, *Reforming Christianity* (Santa Rosa, CA: Polebridge Press, 2001), 2.

[2] Marcus Borg, *The Heart of Christianity: Rediscovering a Life of Faith* (San Francisco: HarperSanFrancisco, 2003), 132.

[3] Robert Funk, *Honest to Jesus: Jesus for a New Millennium* (San Francisco: HarperSanFrancisco, 1996), 311.

[4] John Dominic Crossan, *Jesus: A Revolutionary Biography* (San Francisco: HarperSanFrancisco, 1994), 55.

[5] Robert Funk, *Honest to Jesus*, 311. Quoting John Dominic Crossan.

[6] Marcus J. Borg, in *The Once and Future Jesus* (Santa Rosa, CA: Polebridge Press, 2000), 62.

[7] Anne Primavesi, *Making God Laugh: Human Arrogance and Ecological Humility* (Santa Rosa, CA: Polebridge Press, 2004), vii.

[8] Ibid., 14.

[9] Walter Wink, in *The Once and Future Jesus*, 39.

[10] Primavesi, *Making God Laugh*, 148.

[11] Katie Sherrod, "Celebrating Works in Progress: A Lenten Reflection," *Witness Magazine* (28 June 2005), 23.

[12] Roy Hoover, *The Historical Jesus Goes to Church* (Santa Rosa, CA: Polebridge Press, 2004), 16.

[13] Ibid., 13.

[14] Funk, in *The Once and Future Jesus*, 10.

[15] Diarmuid O'Murchu, *Reclaiming Spirituality* (New York: Crossroad Classic, 1998), 114.

## Chapter 9: Social Justice and a Spirituality of Transformation – Bill Phipps

[1] Rebecca Solnit, *Hope in the Dark: Untold Histories, Wild Possibilities* (New York: Nation Books, 2004), 123.

[2] Ibid., 80.

[3] Ibid., 57.

[4] National Council of Churches of Christ in the USA, *Living Micah's Call: Doing Justice, Loving Kindness, Walking Humbly with God: A Guide for Congregations* (May 2002), 35.

## Chapter 11: To Sing or Not to Sing – Bruce Harding

[1] With apologies to William Shakespeare.

[2] See John Blacking's seminal book, *How Musical is Man* (London: Faber and Faber, 1976) for an anthropological view of how fundamental music is to us as a species.

[3] Nicolò Paganini and Franz Liszt were famous for their virtuosity throughout Europe and North America.

[4] Joachim Neander, 1680, in the hymn *Meine Hoffnung stehet feste*, translated by Fred Pratt Green, 1986, as the hymn "All my hope is firmly grounded."

[5] The power of music was recognized by Greek philosophers, and carried over into the early church. Augustine, Bishop of Hippo, was hesitant regarding the use of music in worship because of its power to move the listener (see his *Confessions* 10:33).

[6] Colin Gibson, 1972, from the hymn "He came singing love."

[7] Strong vocal leadership can keep a congregation from dropping too far in pitch if the instruments are to come back in for further verses.

[8] A simple drum such as a West African djembe provides enough range of high and low tones to accompany singing on its own.

[9] Charles Wesley, 1747, from the hymn "Love divine, all loves excelling."

[10] The success of Compline services in many parishes, late evening services that lift up ancient chant and songs of the church, dispels the myth that "youth only like upbeat songs."

[11] Small language changes, such as the fairly recent shift from "thou" to "you," are nothing new. Hymn book compilers have always sought to make the language of hymnody accessible to singers of their day. But if the theology of a hymn really has become problematic, as in militant and triumphal songs like "Mine eyes have seen the glory," then we must be unafraid to name it as being no longer appropriate and move on.

[12] *Scottish Psalter*, 1650, plus many other hymns and psalms…

[13] See Linnea Good's song, "Roots and Wings," available from www.linneagood.com.

[14] John Bell, *The Singing Thing* (GIA, 2000), 83.

[15] Sydney Carter, 1963, from the song "Lord of the Dance."

[16] The use of *rubato*, of accelerating or slowing down the tempo as an expressive device, has a long history in the Western art music tradition (for example, in the interpretation of the music of Frédéric Chopin).

[17] The Iona Community, 1985, from the hymn "Praise with joy the world's Creator."

[18] A quick search on the Internet, looking at reviews of *The New Century Hymnal* on www.amazon.com for example, reveals the controversy.

[19] Africa and the Indian subcontinent are two regions in which dialogical forms of song are common.

[20] Carolyn McDade, from the song "This Ancient Love."

## Chapter 12: Christian Education and the Imaginative Spirit – Susan Burt

[1] Rev. Sean Gilbert, Christ Church Uniting Church in Australia, Wayville, South Australia, sermon, March 13, 2005.

[2] Edward Robinson, *The Language of Mystery* (Philadelphia: Trinity Press International, SCM Press, 1989), 24–25.

[3] Alan Jones, *Reimagining Christianity: Reconnect Your Spirit without Disconnecting Your Mind* (John Wiley & Sons, Inc. 2005), 155.

[4] David Heller, "A conversation with a nine-year-old," from *The Children's God* (Chicago: University of Chicago Press, 1988), 74.

[5] Carol Lakey Hess, "Education as an Art of Getting Dirty with Dignity" in *The Arts of Ministry: Feminist-Womanist Appraoches,* ed. Christie Cozad Neuger (Louisville, KY: Westminster John Knox Press, 1996), 71.

[6] Mary Ellen Ashcroft, *Spirited Women: Encountering the First Women Believers* (Minneapolis, MN: Augsburg Fortress, 2000), xii.

[7] Ibid.

[8] Carol Wehrheim, "Engaging the Imagination," *Seasons of the Spirit*, 2003–04 edition. First introduced in 2002, *Seasons of the Spirit* cites imagination as a vital component of the program. In its Theological and Educational Foundations Paper, the first affirmation is an invitation "to explore the meaning and mystery in the Bible through the lectionary." Further, these resources will "encourage children, youth, and adults to enter imaginatively into scripture, experiencing the message that transcends the printed words." Later in the same document, the fourth affirmation encourages us to nurture faith "by engaging the imagination through the Bible, tradition, science, technology, and the arts."

[9] "Theological and Educational Foundations Paper," *Seasons of the Spirit*, 8–9.

[10] "When the Bible is taken as metaphor and sacrament, it is liberated to be a powerful companion in our quest for an ever-deepening relationship with God. As metaphor, the Bible is a way of seeing God and our life with God. As sacrament, it is a way that God speaks to us and comes to us. To be Christian is to live within the biblical traditional and to let it do its transforming work on us." Educator Tim Scorer, educator and author of *Experiencing the Heart of Christianity* (Kelowna, BC: Wood Lake Books, 2005).

[11] Miriam Therese Winter in an interview with Julie Polter and Anne Wayne in "From the inside out," *Sojourners* (July/August, 1997).

[12] Scott Douglas, "David's Rule," in *Strange Angels & Other Plays* (Kelowna, BC: Wood Lake Books Inc., 2004), 90.

[13] Margaret Ackland, "Last Supper, No. 1," in *A Place at the Table: Women at the Last Supper,* eds. Judi Fisher and Janet Wood, Joint Board of Christian Education, 49.

[14] Examples and ideas taken from an exercise that will appear in the adult component of the *Seasons of the Spirit* worship and Christian educational resource March 18, 2007.

[15] John Dykstra Eusden and John H. Westerhoff III, *Sensing Beauty: Aesthetics, the Human Spirit, and the Church,* (Cleveland: The Pilgrim Press, 1998), 31.

[16] Heather Murray Elkins, *Worshipping Women: Re-forming God's People for Praise* (Nashville: Abingdon Press, 1994), 13–14. "Altar-ing": "to lift up the commonplace of human life to holy use."

[17] Jones, *Reimagining Christianity*, 56.

[18] Ibid.

[19] Rebecca Chopp, *Saving Work: Feminist Practices of Theological Education* (Louisville, KY: Westminster John Knox Press, 1995), 46.

[20] Kathleen D. Billman, "Pastoral Care as an Art of Community" in *The Arts of Ministry*, 23.

[21] Chopp, *Saving Work*, 197.

[22] Danny E. Morris and Charles M. Olsen, *Discerning God's Will Together: A Spiritual Practice for the Church* (Bethesda, MD: Alban Publications, 1997), 66.

[23] Carol Wehrheim, "Engaging the Imagination," *Seasons of the Spirit,* 2003–04 edition.

[24] Ibid.

[25] Peter A. Pitzele, *Scripture Windows: Toward a Practice of Bibliodrama* (Los Angeles: Torah Aura Productions, 1998), 13.

[26] Wehrheim, "Engaging the Imagination," (adapted).

[27] Douglas, "David's Rule," 90.

[28] Ibid., 40.